Engaging Employers in Apprenticeship Opportunities

This work is published under the responsibility of the Secretary-General of the OECD. The opinions expressed and arguments employed herein do not necessarily reflect the official views of OECD member countries, or those of the members of the ILO.

This document and any map included herein are without prejudice to the status of or sovereignty over any territory, to the delimitation of international frontiers and boundaries and to the name of any territory, city or area.

Please cite this publication as:
OECD/ILO (2017), *Engaging Employers in Apprenticeship Opportunities*, OECD Publishing, Paris.
http://dx.doi.org/10.1787/9789264266681-en

ISBN 978-92-64-26658-2 (print)
ISBN 978-92-64-26668-1 (PDF)
ISBN 978-92-64-27400-6 (epub)

ILO:
ISBN 978-92-2-130534-7 (print)
ISBN 978-92-2-130535-4 (pdf)

The statistical data for Israel are supplied by and under the responsibility of the relevant Israeli authorities. The use of such data by the OECD is without prejudice to the status of the Golan Heights, East Jerusalem and Israeli settlements in the West Bank under the terms of international law.

Photo credits: © Monkey Business Images/Shutterstock.com.

Corrigenda to OECD publications may be found on line at: *www.oecd.org/about/publishing/corrigenda.htm.*

Preface

While the jobs recovery is underway in many countries, persistently high rates of youth unemployment remain a significant labour market challenge. In response, there has been increasing interest in apprenticeships both as a route into employment and also in raising the skill levels of the workforce. Apprenticeships and other work-based training opportunities are valuable training pathways for improving the transition from school to work. At the local level, apprenticeship programmes can contribute to regional development objectives and provide local employers with the skilled workforce they require to remain competitive and create jobs.

G20 Employment and Labour Ministers have highlighted the importance of developing quality apprenticeship programmes, which can provide businesses with the skilled workers they need to succeed in a rapid changing global marketplace. Broadening the availability of apprenticeship programmes requires collaboration and co-ordination between a range of stakeholders at the local level, including the private sector, civil society, the third sector, as well as young people themselves.

Many OECD countries have a long tradition of apprenticeship programmes, which actively engage employers in their design, development and delivery, and many non-OECD countries are looking to replicate such schemes. However, these countries face a number of implementation issues, including poor perceptions of vocational education and training, a fragmented training landscape, and few incentives to encourage participation.

This joint publication by the OECD LEED programme and the ILO explores implementation examples of employer engagement in apprenticeship programmes through nine case studies. It draws from local experiences, including interviews with local employment offices, training institutions, economic development organisations as well as chambers of commerce and trade unions. We hope that this publication will provide policy makers and social partners with specific learnings to remove barriers to engaging employers in apprenticeship programmes, broaden access to training opportunities and improve the economic development and labour market performance of local areas.

Lamia Kamal-Chaoui
Director, Centre for Entrepreneurship,
SMEs, Local Development and Tourism
Organisation for Economic Co-operation
and Development

Azita Berar-Awad
Director, Employment Policy Department

International Labour Organization

Acknowledgements

This report was prepared within the framework of a policy innovation project on *Engaging Employers in Skills Development and Utilisation* by the Local Economic and Employment Development (LEED) Programme of the Organisation for Economic Co-operation and Development (OECD) undertaken in co-operation with the United Kingdom Commission for Employment and Skills (UKCES), the Australia Department of Education and Training, and the International Labour Organisation (ILO). This project is coordinated by Jonathan Barr as part of the OECD LEED programme of work under the supervision of Sylvain Giguère, Head of the LEED Division, and Lamia Kamal-Chaoui, Director of the Centre for Entrepreneurship, SMEs, Local Development and Tourism, who provided useful comments on this report.

The report was edited by Angela Attrey (OECD LEED Programme), Jonathan Barr (OECD LEED Programme), Anna Rubin (OECD LEED Programme), and Paul Comyn (ILO). Useful comments and inputs were also provided by Dr. Ewart Keep (Oxford University) as well as colleagues within the Directorate of Employment, Labour and Social Affairs (ELS) and the Directorate of Education (EDU). Thanks also go to François Iglesias for production assistance and Janine Treves who provided editorial support.

Chapter 1 was written by Angela Attrey (OECD LEED Programme), Jonathan Barr (OECD LEED Programme), and Paul Comyn (ILO). The case studies were drafted by Francesca Froy (University College London, United Kingdom); Andrew Dean (University of Exeter, United Kingdom); Werner Eichorst, Güliz Lali Azari and Florian Wozny (Institute for the Study of Labour (IZA), Germany); Naysa Brasil Teodoro, Robert Allen and Barbara Macnish (Miles Morgan Australia, Australia); Teresa Stevenson (Independent Consultant, New Zealand); Faith Goldstein (University of Pennsylvania, United States); Özlem Ünlühisarcıklı (Boğaziçi University, Turkey); T I M Nurunnabi Khan (International Labour Organization); and Erica Smith (Federation University, Australia).

This report also benefited from insights and information that were gathered at an OECD-Commonwealth of Australia workshop on engaging employers in skills development for the 21st Century in Adelaide, Australia from 2-3 June 2016.

Table of contents

Tables

Figures

Follow OECD Publications on:

 http://twitter.com/OECD_Pubs

 http://www.facebook.com/OECDPublications

. http://www.linkedin.com/groups/OECD-Publications-4645871

 http://www.youtube.com/oecdilibrary

 http://www.oecd.org/oecddirect/

Abbreviations and acronyms

BA	Bundesagentur für Arbeit
BIBB	Bundesinstitut für Berufsbildung
BMBF	Bundesministerium für Bildung und Forschung
BMFSFJ	Bundesministerium für Familie, Senioren, Frauen und Jugend
BMWi	Bundesministerium für Wirtschaft und Energie
CEDEFOP	European Centre for the Development of Vocational Training
COEL	Centre of Excellence for Leather Skills, Bangladesh
EC	European Commission
EU	European Union
EAFA	European Alliance for Apprenticeships
GAN	Global Apprenticeship Network
GDP	Gross Domestic Product
GVA	Gross Value Added
HIBB	Hamburger Institut für Berufliche Bildung
IES	Institut für Entwicklungsplanung und Strukturforschung
ILO	International Labor Organization
LEED	Local Economic and Employment Development programme
NEET	Not in Employment, Education and/or Training
OECD	Organisation for Economic Co-operation and Development
PV	Customised placement of Trainees in Enterprises programme
R&D	Research and Development
SME	Small and medium-sized enterprises
TESK	Public Employment Agency of Turkey
VET	Vocational Education and Training
WISE	Work Integration and Social Enterprises

Executive summary

Youth unemployment remains a significant labour market challenge across a number of OECD countries. Across the OECD, 13.9% of the youth labour force is unemployed. In several European countries, such as Belgium, France, Finland, Greece, Ireland, Italy, Poland, Portugal, the Slovak Republic, and Spain, the unemployment rate for youth sits above 20%. Many countries are looking at apprenticeships as a key programme response to improve the transition for youth from school to the world of work.

An apprenticeship is a vocational education pathway that combines both workplace and classroom-based learning. Vocational education and training systems vary significantly across the OECD in terms of what level of government (e.g. national or regional) manages the overall legislative and regulatory framework. Countries with well-developed apprenticeship systems, such as Germany, Austria, Norway, Denmark and Switzerland have formalised engagement with employers and other stakeholders through a dual-education system, which provides clear pathways for youth into training. Other countries have less formalised relationships with employers but are looking at ways to better meet their needs through targeted apprenticeship programmes and policies.

In emerging economies, apprenticeship programmes play an important role in tackling informality. Increasing attention is being taken to improve the quality and relevance of apprenticeship programmes, including a focus on formalising traditionally informal training arrangements. Small business associations at the local level can play a primary role in networking small and medium sized enterprises (SMEs) and providing incentives for people to participate.

The success of apprenticeship programmes depends on robust implementation at the local level. Local governments can play a critical role in developing a community wide vision for training and skills. Apprenticeship programmes can be used as an economic development tool to improve the skills of the workforce and labour market outcomes. Mayors and other local leaders (such as Vocational Education and Training Presidents) can act as "champions" of apprenticeship programmes and lead efforts to reach out to youth and employers to raise awareness of the benefits of participation and completion in a training programme, which is well linked to a quality job.

This joint OECD-ILO report examines best practices in employer engagement in apprenticeship programmes at the local level across nine countries. The case studies provide insights into how national policies are being designed in a manner, which leverages local leadership in fostering business-education partnerships. Issues of system reform, participation from small and medium-sized enterprises (SMEs), specific challenges associated with rural areas and meeting the diverse needs of young people and places are examined. The following key lessons and recommendations emerge from this report:

Key lessons and recommendations

Local leadership can facilitate connections between employers, training providers, and other stakeholders

Local leaders can be "champions" forging connections between employers, young people and training providers to encourage participation and completion in apprenticeship programmes. Mayors, regional development organisations, and other local level government representatives are important actors in reaching out to employers to promote awareness on the benefits of investments in apprenticeship and assist employers (especially SMEs) in navigating the administrative processes to participate as well as the government supports available.

Time, effort and resources are necessary in order to facilitate local leadership. Intermediaries, such as the local chambers of commerce, youth groups and trade unions, can also help to promote 'buy-in' from local stakeholders.

Mechanisms that facilitate collaboration between local stakeholders can enable the alignment of incentives

Building "spaces" or networks for employers to provide advice is central. Collaboration is often formalised in countries with a long tradition of apprenticeship training. For example, as noted in the case study from Germany, representatives from groups of employers, including the German Chambers of Industry and Commerce, actively collaborate with trade unions and government actors in the process of developing national training regulations that enable apprentices to move between federal states.

However, collaboration can also arise organically through local efforts to promote skills development. For example, the case studies from New Zealand and the United States highlight the role of local leaders, including those from civil society, in building organic and community-driven skills development mechanisms. In these cases, informal partnerships were developed into broader efforts to promote apprenticeship with both local employers and young people.

SMEs will often require specialised assistance to provide apprenticeship places

By virtue of their size, SMEs will require more assistance to provide apprenticeship placements. Specialised incentive mechanisms, including tax exemptions, subsidies, the provision of networks or custom placement assistance, can help to improve SME participation in apprenticeship programmes.

Local organisations can particularly helpful throughout this process by bringing together employers and articulating the benefits of hiring apprentices. For example, local apprenticeship hubs described in the case study from the United Kingdom are quite effective in providing tailored advice to SMEs and helping them access the assistance and services that they need in order to participate.

Apprenticeships must be flexible in their design and delivery to accommodate changing labour markets

At the local level, successful apprenticeship programmes will involve the participation of a number of stakeholders, including young people, employers, civil society and actors from all tiers of government. Apprenticeship programmes should be flexible to meet the diverse and shifting needs of these groups to remain an attractive skills development mechanism.

Flexibility can be incorporated into vocational education and training systems in a variety of ways. For example, incorporating modular components into programmes can take into account past work experience and can enable movement between conventional academic and vocational pathways for young people. This can address perceptions of "lock-in" and path dependency, where young people choose not to pursue vocational pathways because of a lack of transferability to other learning pathways.

Providing options for apprentices, such as intensive courses or part-time arrangements, can provide flexibility for young people and can also better fulfil the demand for employers with more variable or seasonal demand. For remote and rural places, like those illustrated from the case studies from New Zealand and Norway, flexibility in the delivery of vocational training can encourage participation. For example, using e-learning platforms can be useful in helping apprentices complete their course requirements.

Young people who do not traditionally participate in apprenticeship schemes should be targeted

Young people are among the core beneficiaries of apprenticeship programmes and they face specific barriers to participation in the apprenticeship system and thus require customised support and counselling.

Apprenticeship programmes can be targeted to young people living in disadvantage communities to provide them with work experience opportunities that can lead to a quality job. Public employment services can work with the training sector to develop pre-apprenticeship programmes, which provide a basic skills foundation and smooth their passage into the vocational education and training system.

Perceptions of apprenticeship and vocational education should be improved

Apprenticeship pathways suffer from a lack of "parity of esteem" in many countries, particularly those without a strong or well-developed history of vocational education and training. Perceptions can be improved by enhancing career information and engaging employers in the marketing and dissemination process.

Often, young people and their parents are under-informed about the opportunities that apprenticeship programmes can offer for a stable and long-term career. Local leaders can play a particular role in helping to articulate these benefits through a well-rounded career and information system that presents local apprenticeship opportunities to young people alongside more conventional academic routes.

Emerging economies should continue to support apprenticeship systems as an effective skills development mechanism

Emerging economies often face specific skills development challenges with weak institutions delivering vocational education and training. Informal apprenticeship is the often the core mechanism used to provide young people in emerging economies the ability to learn a trade and enter the world of work.

Apprenticeship programmes can be used to formalise aspects of the existing informal apprenticeship structure by including formal assessment and certification systems, strengthening community involvement and developing standardised contractual arrangements and codes of practice. Actively engaging the private sector in local apprenticeship schemes is particularly important in order for formal mechanisms to become relatively more attractive than informal channels.

Chapter 1

Boosting employer engagement in apprenticeships: Synthesis findings

Apprenticeships have been identified as an effective mechanism for smoothing the transition for young people between school and the world of work. While apprenticeships and work-based learning opportunities have demonstrable benefits for young people and employers, many countries face a number of barriers to broadening their availability. This chapter synthesises findings across nine case studies on best practices to increase the engagement of employers in the design, development and delivery of apprenticeship programmes at the local level.

Apprenticeship programmes can better connect young people to jobs

Relatively high youth unemployment and falling youth participation in education and training opportunities have been a persistent trend across a number of OECD countries since the global financial crisis. About 73.3 million people aged 15-29 and one in five (20.4%) of all young people in the European Union are unemployed and seeking work (OECD, 2016). This trend has a strong regional dimension, with youth unemployment rates over 40% in southern European countries such as Greece, Spain and Italy.

There are also worrying trends of declining participation rates in the labour market and increased numbers of young people not in employment, education and training (NEETs). The global youth labour force participation rate declined by 11.6% between 1991 and 2014, while the adult labour force participation rate declined by 1% over the same period. The youth labour force fell by 29.9 million despite an overall increase in the total youth population of 185 million over this period, indicating that increasing numbers of young people are no longer employed nor seeking work. Similarly, although global NEET rates have declined slightly from their peak of 13.1% during the financial crisis, they remain stubbornly high at 12.4% (ILO, 2015).

These trends are typically magnified for young people with disabilities or social disadvantages, who have more limited access to education and training opportunities. Youth disengagement from the labour market is a particularly worrying issue because early labour market experiences can affect the nature and duration of employment throughout the entire working life. Young people who disengage with the labour market early in their careers tend to find it harder to find stable, long-term and good quality employment in the future (OECD, 2010).

Figure 1.1. **Youth unemployment, 2007, 2015**

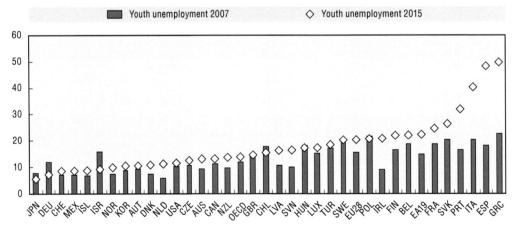

Source: OECD (2016) Youth unemployment rate (indicator).

The limited integration of young people in the labour market is occurring at the same time as employers report an inability to find suitable labour with the appropriate skills and experience. Globally, 34% of employers were unable to fill positions due to a lack of available talent (Aring, 2012). Over a third of European employers report having difficulty filling vacant positions due to a shortage of applicants with the right skills and abilities (CEDEFOP, 2015a). This remains despite consistent increases in the number of young people who complete compulsory secondary education (Eurostat, 2014). This points to mismatch between the skills developed through the education system and the skills expected by employers.

In this context, apprenticeships and work-based training opportunities are increasingly recognised as a useful mechanism to better connect the education system with the labour market. Apprenticeships are programmes provided to young people that involve work-based training, often linked to off-the-job vocational education, in order to impart both job-specific and general skills to aspiring workers.

Box 1.1. **What do we mean by the term "apprenticeships"?**

The International Labor Organization (ILO) defines apprenticeships as a form of "systematic long-term training for a recognised occupation that takes place substantially within an undertaking or under an independent craftsman and should be governed by a written contract… and be subject to established standards". (ILO, 2012a).

Given growing interest in apprenticeship programmes and broader work-based learning as a key success factor in school-to-work transitions, it is worth noting that the term "apprenticeship" is increasingly used to describe a range of programmes that might be alternatively referred to as "traineeships", "internships", "learnerships" and "work placements", depending on the country context. As noted by the G20, "apprenticeships are a combination of on-the-job training and school-based education. In the G20 countries, there is not a single standardised model of apprenticeships, but rather multiple and varied approaches to offer young people a combination of training and work experience" (G20, 2012). The common feature of all programmes is a focus on work-based training, but they may differ in terms of their specific legal nature and requirements.

Apprenticeships in modern industrialised economies typically combine work-based training with off-the-job training through a standardised written contract that is regulated by government actors. These programmes usually result in a formal certification or qualification. The nature of apprenticeships necessarily differ based on the institutional and structural features of the local, regional, national and supra-national vocational education and training system.

Throughout this report, we will refer to apprenticeships that occur both during and following compulsory secondary education. The case studies depict employment programmes that are regulated by law and based on an oral or written apprenticeship contract, where apprentices were provided with compensatory payment and standard social protection coverage.

Source: G20 (2012), *Key elements of quality apprenticeships*, G20 Task Force on Employment; ILO (2012a), "Overview of apprenticeship systems and issues".

A diverse body of research indicates that completing an apprenticeship can improve overall labour market outcomes for young people. Young people with apprenticeship experience tend to have higher average rates of employment than the national average (ILO, 2014). They also tend to have below average repeated periods of unemployment than students who have graduated from a more school-based system. The successful completion of apprenticeship can ease the path into employment for young people, even if they do not find employment with the firm that provided the training place (Quintini and Manfredi, 2009). Apprenticeship graduates can earn up to 15-20% more than graduates from compulsory education (CEDEFOP, 2011). Those who complete work-based training are also more likely to find adequate employment in comparison to those who completed full-time vocational education (Bertschy et al., 2009; Parey, 2009).

More broadly, the work-based training component of apprenticeships provides young people with the chance to develop job-ready "soft" or generic skills that are as relevant as technical vocational competences. Skills like problem solving, conflict management and entrepreneurship are more effectively developed in workplaces than in off-the-job situations like classrooms or simulated work environments (OECD, 2010; Brewer, 2013).

Apprenticeships also have broader benefits for the larger economy. Figures from the British National Audit Office (2012) suggest that the net present value to the economy for every GBP 1 of government spending invested in apprenticeships was estimated to be between GBP 16 and GBP 21. Other research has found that increased incidence of apprenticeships is negatively correlated with youth unemployment and rates of NEETs (ILO, 2014). Cross-country evidence show that countries with high relative shares of young people in vocational education, including Germany, Denmark and Australia, tend to have among the lowest rates of youth unemployment across OECD countries (ILO, 2014; OECD, 2016). Similarly, countries with higher shares of apprentices had better performance among youth in the labour market during the financial crisis of 2008-2009 (European Commission, 2013). In Italy, young people on an apprenticeship scheme enjoy greater employment stability than fixed term contract holders, with a 5% lower probability of unemployment and 16% higher chance of having a permanent contract (European Commission, 2013).

Apprenticeship programmes can help to improve the general level of skills in the local economy and can boost overall economic growth and productivity (Cappellari et al., 2012). While no national data is available in the United States, state-level analysis shows the return on investment in vocational training, including apprenticeships, can range from 8.4% in Wyoming to 48.3% in Massachusetts (Courtright and Fry, 2007). The institutional set-up of some apprenticeship systems has also enabled small businesses to better manage fluctuations in business cycles. Group training companies and other intermediaries who employ apprentices and then hire them out to different subcontractors in a sector can continue the training of apprentices during downturns and then make them available again as business activity increases.

Engaging in the apprenticeship system by providing training places to aspiring apprentices can also pose significant rewards for employers. Embedding young people within an existing business is an effective way to train future workers to the specific requirements, values and expectations of a particular workforce. While some time must be devoted to training young and inexperienced people, many employers recoup the cost of training before the completion of the apprenticeship and others within a time frame as short as 1-2 years, depending on the extent to which apprentices are engaged in productive activities (Mohrenzweiser and Zwick, 2009; Hasluck and Hogarth, 2012; ILO, 2014; Jansen et al., 2012). Investing in apprenticeship training has other diffused benefits for the business, including increased skills development for other employees as a result of interaction with training organisations, increased entrepreneurship and increased exposure to new technologies in the workplace (London Economics, 2011; Lerman, 2013; and Molenaar, 2012).

The connection between apprenticeships and organisational productivity also provides a rationale for employer investment in apprenticeships (Mieschbuehler and Hooley, 2015). Employers often cite the benefits of training apprentices as a method of ensuring skilled workers in the future, thus reducing skills and occupational mismatch. Research on larger firms that become registered as training organisations in their national system has shown a range of benefits. These include the ability to deliver qualifications through apprenticeships and other forms of work-based learning to large groups of workers quickly and in a manner that is customised to the enterprise's own needs and requirements; the ability, through increased knowledge of the national vocational education and training (VET) system, to seek available government funding for training and to use this funding to develop their own training infrastructure; and the ability to gain supply chain benefits by training workers from other organisations such as subcontractors or suppliers to ensure the quality of work performed by these organisations (Smith and Smith, 2009a).

They have an ability to shape their approach to human resource management around the awarding of national qualifications, creating more innovative ways of managing and developing people (Smith and Smith, 2007). Firms that invest heavily in apprenticeships have reported reduced rates of staff turnover in entry-level positions and see apprentices and trainees as a stream of workers ready to move onto higher – level training and promotional positions (Smith et al., 2009). Firms that invest in apprenticeship programmes also report other benefits, including reduced recruitment costs, enhanced job satisfaction among workplace supervisors and achievement of corporate social responsibility outcomes (University of Warwick Institute for Employment Research, 2008).

Why is this publication important?

This publication aims to summarise the international literature on the role of employers and other actors in apprenticeship programmes. It provides a summary of the barriers to engaging employers and then draws on case study work to highlight key lessons for policy makers and practitioners on how to increase the overall engagement of employers in apprenticeship programmes. Table 1.1 provides an overview of the case studies that are summarised in this chapter, the key reform or programme, as well as the key actors involved in the programme.

Table 1.1. **Case studies on employer engagement in apprenticeship programmes**

Country	Key reform/programme	Key actors
United Kingdom	Apprenticeship Hubs at the city region level	City regions; local employers
Norway	Apprenticeship design and delivery in hyper-rural spaces	City Council; local employers; Group Training Organisations
Germany	Youth-focussed active labour market policies and school to work transition	Federal Employment Agencies; Federal ministries; Federal State actors
Australia	Enterprise-embedded model of apprenticeship delivery	ABN Group
New Zealand	Promoting apprenticeship retention and completion rates at the local level	Local leaders in Otorohanga; local employers; local training providers
United States of America	Promoting apprenticeships to build information technology skills among disadvantaged urban youth	Not-for-profits; Philadelphia school system; local Philadelphia IT sector
Turkey	Work-based training programmes for unemployed young people	Federal employment agency; GAN National Network; local employers
Bangladesh	Apprenticeship programme design and delivery in the informal and formal sectors	Leatherworking industry; SMEs; not-for-profit organisations; national employment agency
India	Legislative reform to improve employer engagement	National ministries and employer organisations

Building a better apprenticeship system: The role of employers

The use of apprenticeships varies across OECD countries (See Figure 1.2). To increase overall participation, policy makers need to strengthen the involvement of employers in vocational education and training systems. Employers can take a leadership role in steering apprenticeship programmes at the local level. As noted by Kramer et al. (2015), a new wave of companies is taking a far more active role by partnering with schools, non-profits and governments to directly improve educational outcomes. Bridging the gap between education and the world of work is fundamental to creating shared value, growing revenue and increasing productivity by raising the skills levels of youth and the overall workforce.

Figure 1.2. **Apprentices per 1000 employed persons, 2011 or most recent year**

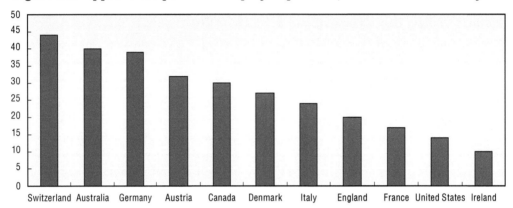

Source: ILO (2012a), "Overview of apprenticeship systems and issues", *ILO Contribution to the G20 Taskforce on Employment,* Skills and Employability Branch, International Labour Organisation, Geneva.

Engaging employers in the apprenticeship system can also improve the alignment between the supply and demand of skills. In particular, employers can ensure that curricula and competences remain up to date with the needs of the labour market, which can in turn improve the value and employment prospects associated with apprenticeship programmes (Steedman, 2005). Improving the match between education and work is particularly important at the local level, where globalisation and technological changes are creating a polarised labour market of high and low paid jobs.

Where apprenticeship systems are dictated by centralised policy priorities developed at the national level, employers can play an important role in translating these broader objectives into local reality. The success of national apprenticeship priorities hinges upon their acceptance and integration into the practical day to day reality of local business. For example, although the German apprenticeship system is based on a series of occupational skills profiles that are determined at the national level, the engagement of employers in this process helps to ensure that the system remains relevant and practical at the local level (Hoeckel and Schwartz, 2010). Engaging employers through the entire apprenticeship life cycle can help to ensure that the system meets the needs of the employers and apprentices alike. As noted by Smith et al. (2009), the apprenticeship life-cycle includes the period during recruitment, sign-up and induction of apprentices; training delivery and assessment; support during the apprenticeship; and completion.

The importance of developing genuine collaboration between employers and other stakeholders in the apprenticeship system is increasingly being recognised by policymakers at the national and local level (Skills Development Scotland, nd; Van Horn et al., 2015). Successful apprenticeship systems are underpinned by a strong tradition of collaboration between stakeholders, including employers, training providers, unions and government partners. These include the systems of Australia, Germany and Norway, who also have dual systems of vocational education where there is an integrated programme of on- and off-the-job training. These systems tend to be "industry-led" and driven by the demands of employers.

Employers in these countries tend to view engagement in the system as a fundamental social responsibility. Institutional knowledge and strong public opinion about the value of apprenticeship not only increases the number of training places provided by employers but also their willingness to engage in the entire lifecycle of the design and delivery of apprenticeship programmes. For example, Norwegian employers and a wide variety of social partners are represented in advisory bodies for upper-secondary and post-secondary VET programme development at both the national and county level and are actively engaged in the development of curriculum content, competence requirements and assessment. This is important to ensure that local labour market actors are able to communicate their training needs and requirements to policymakers.

The depth of employer engagement in industry-led countries reflects the breadth and quality of access to apprenticeships. Completing an apprenticeship in countries like Germany, Australia and Norway acts as a pathway to employment in a wide variety of industries and occupations, ranging from the traditional trades sector to white collar work. This helps to meet the diverse needs of young people and improves perceptions of apprenticeship pathways in comparison to tertiary or other vocational education pathways.

In contrast, other systems have less formal linkages between the worlds of work and education. For example, the apprenticeship system in the United States features less formal governance relationships with employers, because each relationship is developed on an ad-hoc basis at the local level with the relevant stakeholders and there is no systematic and long-term tradition of close co-operation between actors federally.

Barriers to employer engagement in the apprenticeship system

There is considerable variation across national systems with respect to the degree that employers choose to become engaged in the provision of apprenticeship and training places, varying from estimates below 1% in the United States, 8% of employers in England to 30% in Australia (Steedman, 2010). While employer participation is affected by many variables, the design of apprenticeship systems has a major influence on the level of employer participation (Kuczera, 2017). Employers within national frameworks also differ in their engagement with the apprenticeship system – typically enterprises in the trades sector are more likely to offer training places than public sector organisations or enterprises in other sectors. Broadening the range of apprenticeship pathways available across a greater number of occupations and industry sectors opens more opportunities for employers to participate in an apprenticeship system.

VET systems are diverse and can be administered by governments at the local, regional, or national level. OECD and ILO work has found variation across countries in terms of the duration, qualifications, requirements, employer and union involvement, level, occupation and gender balance of modern work-based training programmes (OECD, 2014b; Quintini and Martin, 2014; ILO, 2013). These variations have an impact on the structure of financial and non-financial incentives that are available to employers for providing apprenticeship training places.

Financial incentives and the distribution of training costs can also boost engagement in the apprenticeship system. Costs are usually shared between the government, the employer and the apprentice, but the distribution of these costs can vary. Many countries have used subsidies and vouchers to increase the number of training places, but these may not necessarily be effective in expanding demand for apprentices in firms that already train them (Mühlemann et al., 2007). Some governments also target subsidies, vouchers and other financial incentives towards key industries – for example, the Australian government contributes to funding towards training costs for workers in the aged care, childcare, nursing and disability care sectors. However, care should be taken in the design of these mechanisms to ensure that they do not displace existing workers.

Apprenticeship systems are often very complex in terms of their governance and legislative structure. Apprenticeships and vocational education can often fall into the jurisdictions of national governments, regional governments or some combination of the two. In Germany, the jurisdiction for apprenticeships is shared between the thirteen federal states and the national ministry for employment, while the legislative regulation and operation of Australian apprenticeships is driven by the eight states and territories. Similarly, while there may be national standards of vocational competences, these can be implemented or enforced in different ways within regions or local areas. This poses difficulties for engagement from employers who operate beyond regional boundaries in terms of ensuring that they meet the relevant legislative requirements.

Similarly, the degree of institutional fragmentation can dis-incentivise participation from employers. The English and Australian case studies in this publication (see Chapters 2 and 5) highlight the difficulties of navigating a complex structure of institutions and incentives when attempting to access government assistance for training costs. This sentiment has been recognised by policy makers in both countries who are now attempting to streamline the system (Australian Government, 2013; HM Government, 2015). This challenge can be minimised by improving support services for employers. Employers often value receiving local advice for their institutional and legislative questions – the English case study found that local employers preferred being able to "get hold of someone" rather than interacting with an impersonal national website. Similarly, employers could be more likely to engage with the apprenticeship system that is streamlined across and between government institutions.

The English system also featured a fragmented training landscape, which further discouraged employers from engaging with the apprenticeship system. The apprenticeship system was characterised by a large degree of public support for training providers where 63-67% of all apprenticeships between 2005 and 2012 were government funded (HM Government, 2013). This resulted in a proliferation of training providers with "perverse incentives" to provide many short-term training places with high transaction costs (Chankseliani and Relly, 2015). This was discouraging for employers in Leeds, United Kingdom who reported discouragement with a local training environment that featured over 600 individual trainers and lacked streamlined support and information services. This indicates that government incentive mechanisms should be carefully considered to both ensure that training remains of a high standard and encourage employer engagement.

Some OECD countries "compel" employers to contribute to broader vocational education and training schemes through mandatory contributions to training funds

(Hoeckel, 2008). While not all national training funds operate on the same basis, many provide financial support for apprenticeship schemes. This is the case in the UK, which announced a levy on large businesses to fund the expansion of the apprenticeship system in 2016. Other countries such as Denmark and Korea also operate such systems. Industries in some places, such as Belgium and some Australian states, have implemented sectoral training funds. The funds raised by these levies are usually redistributed to firms who provide training places or are used to fund institution-based training in that sector.

While these measures may be poorly received by some employers, they can increase employer and employee awareness of training and VET measures and have been generally found to increase the extent of training provision (Smith, 2005; ILO, 2016 forthcoming). However, smaller firms may not have the capacity or the resources to provide training places and thus may be unfairly penalised, unless specific measures are taken to encourage the participation of small businesses, as is the case in Malaysia and Singapore. These compulsory levy-based systems contrast starkly with the systems of New Zealand, the Netherlands and other countries, where enterprises have no legal obligation to fund training. Most countries do not use compulsory employer levies to fund apprenticeships, relying instead on a mix of incentives to encourage employer participation. In those countries with more established systems, such as Germany, employers voluntarily take significant financial responsibility for training apprentices on the basis of both a long tradition of vocational education and well-documented evidence that illustrate the return on investment from providing training opportunities.

Another barrier to employer engagement can include fears of other firms "poaching" newly trained apprentices. This fear is particularly significant for SMEs, who tend to experience more labour turnover and also may have fewer opportunities for career progression (McIntosh et al., 2011). However, an analysis of German firms that engage in the apprenticeship system found that fewer than 3% of firms that offer apprenticeship places had been affected by poaching, smaller firms actually tended to retain apprentices more than larger companies, and that it had negligible effects on expected returns to apprenticeship training for firms (Mohrenweiser et al., 2013). Kitching and Blackburn (2002) found that only 2% of employers reported the risk of trained employers being "poached" or leaving the company as a main argument against offering training. This suggests that the fear of poaching may be somewhat misplaced for firms.

In addition to incentives, one way to improve the engagement of employers in apprenticeships is to support intermediaries that can help employers navigate the apprenticeship system. Bridging institutions such as industry organisations, employer groups, trade unions, chambers of commerce and skills bodies can mobilise businesses, find appropriate training places and negotiate with governments. Additionally, specific "apprenticeship centres" have also been established to provide customised brokerage services, which are bundled with broader business advisory services in some cases.

However, intermediary bodies need deep knowledge of the training system to be able to advise on such issues, and this knowledge is sometimes lacking (Schofield, 2000). They can also act as sources of local knowledge and can help to translate national or regional schemes into practice. The German case study in this publication (Chapter 4) highlights how chambers of commerce and chambers of craft are particularly important actors in the German VET system because they maintain records of potential training places available among their members. They also help to customise the placement of apprentices with particular skillsets.

SMEs require targeted programmes and services to enable them to provide apprenticeship opportunities

Small to medium-sized enterprises (SMEs) are significant sources of employment and job creation. SMEs employ on average 65% of the workforce and comprise over 75% of total enterprises across OECD countries (Criscuolo et al., 2014). The significance of the SME sector is even larger in emerging countries, which tend to have higher degrees of informal employment (World Bank, 2015). However, SMEs tend to engage less in the apprenticeship system than might be otherwise expected by their share of the industrial sector – for example, SMEs in the UK comprise 99.9% of all enterprises but less than 25% provide apprenticeship places (Department for Business Innovation and Skills, 2015; Holt, 2012).

Ensuring that SMEs are able to reap the greatest net benefits from apprenticeships should be a priority of VET systems in order to increase competitiveness, productivity and skills development for the wider economy. SMEs have also been found to benefit in terms of improved access to the latest technological innovation gained through apprentices who regularly attend local technical colleges (ILO, 2012a). However, SMEs are often unable to provide apprenticeship opportunities due to reasons of scale, variable demand, perceived lack of utility, geographical remoteness or issues with skills matching (Steedman, 2015). They consequently require more specialised assistance to become engaged in apprenticeship schemes.

In areas with little penetration from large or international employers, SMEs play the principal role in supporting local employment and promoting a thriving economy. It is therefore crucial that SMEs are able to both contribute to skills development and also reap the benefits of apprenticeships in terms of improved productivity and production in order to sustain the local economy. This is particularly significant for SMEs in emerging countries, where apprenticeship is often the only method of learning a particular trade or skill (Walther, 2007). For example, the case study from India (Chapter 10) highlights how specific measures that target SMEs can be integrated in policy reforms. Specific changes to the legislation and regulations governing apprenticeships allowed SMEs previously excluded due to their small size (as defined by the number of employees) to engage apprentices for the first time. This was supported by new financial incentives targeting employers in the form of public funding of apprentice wages.

The needs of SMEs will differ across local areas. For example, rural sectors tend to have higher concentrations of SMEs in their industrial structures and may have specific challenges associated with the provision of training opportunities, such as transportation and remote access to education and support facilities. In contrast, SMEs based in areas with clusters may need more support with building training networks with other local businesses to meet training regulations. This highlights the need for flexibility at the local level to ensure that specific local challenges can be met and addressed, flexibility not only in programme design and regulation, but also from training organisations prepared to offer flexible delivery options. Similarly, a supportive local training infrastructure is important to help SMEs deliver and ensure the quality of their apprenticeships (CEDEFOP, 2015b). In some cases, focussing on SMEs in a particular industry can help to enable rapid engagement from energised and relevant local actors, as was observed in the case of the mechanical trades sector in the New Zealand case study (see Chapter 6 of this publication).

Apprenticeships require financial, organisational and time investments from employers because they necessitate the sharing of responsibilities between the worlds of work and education. However, SMEs are less likely to have well-developed human resource and support functions that can find, train, support and protect apprentices. Lacking these capacities can be particularly difficult for SMEs operating in a fragmented or very complex VET environment. The case studies from the UK (Chapter 2), Norway (Chapter 3) and Australia (Chapter 4) highlight the success in the use of collective training offices that can provide training services and act as an intermediary between groups of SMEs and the government. These intermediaries can remove administrative or bureaucratic boundaries that may deter SMEs from providing training places to aspiring apprentices, while also performing some of the functions of a specific apprenticeship support manager. In some cases, they also act as the employer, removing the burden of full-time employment from smaller enterprises.

Box 1.2. **Group training organisations and SMEs: The cases of Australia and Norway**

Collective training offices are organisations that act as a mediator between employers, apprentices and the government. The structure of the organisation differs between apprenticeship systems but their common feature is that they serve as method of shifting the bureaucratic and administrative burden of engaging with the apprenticeship system away from employers. This enables more employers to engage with the apprenticeship system.

In Australia, group training organisations are not-for-profit organisations that receive government funding to directly employ apprentices, manage their training and support needs and hire them out to employers. The advantage of this model is that training offices boast institutional knowledge about navigating the apprenticeship system and supporting apprentices. In the Australian case study, the group training organisation ABN Training featured a dedicated training manager who was able to support apprentices through the programme by providing pastoral care and practical assistance with off-the-job training and theory requirements. This organisation has been successful in improving apprenticeship completion rates in the ABN Group above the state and national average.

In Norway, collective training offices sign apprenticeship contracts with the government on behalf of groups of small firms who offer training places. This shifts the legal obligation of off-the-job training to the collective organisations, who are then able to use economies of scale to provide a full range of training services to apprentices. This is particularly useful for SMEs, who would not otherwise be able to meet the national minimum standards for training apprentices and uphold the quality of apprenticeship programme.

SMEs also tend to have more specialised operations and may thus require more specific skillsets from apprentices. Similarly, the narrow focus of SMEs, particularly micro-enterprises, can leave them unable to provide the full range of general training often required by apprenticeship training regulations (Schweri and Müller, 2008). A potential solution to this problem could be to rotate apprentices among groups of SMEs or training networks, which would allow apprenticeships to have the benefit of experiencing a range of different production technologies. Similarly, local flexibility in the provision of training options could ensure that the packages available are able to be customised for the specific skills needs and requirements in local areas. Occupational and skills mismatches can be lessened by developing customised placement services for SMEs, such as the German PV placement programme (see Box 1.3). This can improve SME engagement in vocational education while strengthening the sector in the medium- to long-term.

Box 1.3. **Meeting the needs of SMEs: Customising the placement of apprentices**

The SME sector is a key driver for growth in the Germany economy. They cumulatively employ over 15 million staff, have higher turnover than the top 30 listed German companies and are among the most innovative and resilient enterprises in Europe.

However, despite their economic importance and Germany's long tradition of vocational education, German SMEs were less likely to engage with the apprenticeship system than their larger counterparts. This was in part due to the customised nature of some SME craft businesses, which resulted in a need for firm- or occupation-specific skillsets required from aspiring apprentices.

In 2007, the German federal Ministry for Economic Affairs and Energy developed a programme to customise the placement of apprentices and trainees in the SME sector in order to lessen occupational mismatch, improve productivity and competitiveness and strengthen the SME sector over the medium- to long-term. Intermediaries interviewed both SMEs and apprentices with respect to their needs and desired skills and then matched suitable candidates with appropriate businesses.

The programme helped to improve the attractiveness of apprenticeships for SMEs. The majority of targeted SMEs found that they received accurate and appropriate apprentices for the apprenticeship vacancies available and the programme allowed them to save 40-50% of apprenticeship recruitment costs. Similarly, around 90% of apprenticeship applicants found the mediation services "largely helpful".

Another barrier associated with SME engagement with apprenticeship systems is retaining and engaging youth in potential training opportunities. SMEs, and micro-enterprises in particular, often do not enjoy the reputation and network benefits associated with firms of larger sizes and may struggle to recruit an apprentice. For small companies who form part of a larger supply chain, this can be addressed by sharing applications among other suppliers (Lewis, 2013).

Some research has suggested that SMEs that provide training places to apprentices tend to be motivated by the desire to substitute full-time workers. An Italian study on the impacts of a recent reform of apprenticeship contracts found that there was an increase in overall apprenticeship-employment but that this came at the expense of full-time staff (Cappellari et al., 2012). While the meaning of "apprenticeship" in this case might differ from that generally applied in other training regulations, the displacement effect may be due to the smaller scale of SMEs, which results in increased marginal benefits of savings on payroll and wages.

Consequently, rigour and care must be taken to ensure that minimum standards are upheld such that apprenticeships undertaken in SMEs are of comparable quality and utility as those undertaken in larger firms. To a large extent, this responsibility falls to training organisations as much as regulators, as the interaction between individual employers and the training organisation responsible for the off-the-job training component of an apprenticeship provides a valuable channel to ensure the quality of on-the-job training while providing support to apprentices and employers alike. Management systems should have the capacity to identify employers who "churn" large numbers of apprentices or whose apprentices consistently fail to meet assessment standards.

Increasing employer participation involves aligning the needs and clarifying the roles of all stakeholders

VET systems are comprised of a diverse network of actors, including employers, aspiring apprentices, intermediaries including training providers, social partners and employer groups, and a range of policymakers and leaders at the local, regional, and national levels. Each actor in the VET system has a range of financial and non-financial incentives that will impact their engagement in the provision of apprenticeships. Aligning these desires and needs is central to ensuring that access to apprenticeships remains broad and of high quality.

Care must be taken in the design of vocational education and training systems to ensure that the standard and quality of apprenticeships remains high and that young people are not exploited. There may be a trade-off between ensuring that the costs of firm investment and training in apprenticeships are low enough to promote engagement but remain high enough to ensure a quality placement for aspiring apprentices (OECD, 2012).

Box 1.4. **Building apprenticeships of higher quality**

At the G20 meeting in Mexico in 2012, ministers committed to "promote, and where necessary, strengthen quality apprenticeship systems that ensure high level of instruction and adequate remuneration, and avoid taking advantage of lower salaries".

Apprenticeships must be of high quality in order to attract young people and be recognised as valuable by employers. High quality apprenticeships have a number of features, including:

● Relevant and rigourous training both on and off the job.

● Adequate remuneration that reflects the skills and productive input of apprentices, while costs are shared among employers, governments and the apprentice.

● Adherence to minimum standards of workplace and occupational health and safety standards.

● Flexible and integrated pathways with the formal education and tertiary education system.

● Broad and equitable access, particularly for people of all stages of life, women, people with social, mental or physical handicaps and those with an immigration background.

Strong governance mechanisms are necessary to ensure that employers adhere to minimum standards and to ensure that apprenticeships are not exploited as a form of cheap labour. Similarly, a robust governance system should be developed to ensure that apprenticeships remain valuable to both apprentices and employers during periods of economic recession or social, institutional or demographic pressures.

Source: G20 (2012), *Key elements of quality apprenticeships*, G20 Task Force on Employment, 27 September 2012.

For many countries with established apprenticeship systems, the solution to this trade-off has been through a focus on mandatory assessment and certification to ensure that apprenticeship programmes have the same status and credential outcome as non-apprenticeship pathways. With the expansion of national qualification frameworks across the globe, apprenticeships that once resulted in a certificate of completion are increasingly leading to nationally recognised qualifications that create pathways for learners and give greater certainty to employers that off-the-job training meets occupational competences set by employers (ILO, 2012a). This allows apprenticeships to successfully meet minimum standards that can then be certified, while also ensuring that employers are able to focus on building competences on-the-job rather than solely through external training provision. Other measures can also be introduced to safeguard the quality of apprenticeships in micro, small- and medium-sized enterprises (SMEs), such as fixed ratios of skilled workers to apprentices and minimum training qualifications for supervisors of apprentices (ILO, 2013).

The case studies from Australia (Chapter 5) and the United States (Chapter 7) highlight the movement towards competence-based training models and away from time-based models as a positive method of improving practical, on-the-job skills development while meeting the needs of employers. When coupled with modular and flexible VET systems that recognise past experiences, competence based training models can also hasten the attainment of other certifications and qualifications. Recent research from Australia indicates that there are growing numbers of individuals across all ages completing their apprenticeship in a shorter timeframe through a range of options, including early sign-off, competency-based progression or recognition of prior learning and gap training (Hargraves and Blomberg, 2015). This has resulted in well over half of adult apprentices completing their apprenticeship in under two years. However, some of the barriers to competence progression include a lack of flexibility in training providers and employer attitudes to allowing apprentices to complete early (Clayton et al., 2015).

While the engagement of employers is clearly fundamental to the operation of apprenticeship systems, the involvement of unions in the design, development and implementation of apprenticeships is also a key success factor. As apprenticeships are employment-based training arrangements, issues such as the employment status, wages and other legal entitlements of apprentices need to be negotiated by the main actors in the labour market, and thus requires the active involvement of unions. If apprenticeships are included in collective bargaining agreements at the sectoral or enterprise levels, there is increased potential for apprenticeships to be taken up across a range of occupations and enterprises. As evident from the case studies on Germany and Australia, unions are active partners in apprenticeship systems and are key contributors to the success of the broader technical and vocational education and training systems in those countries.

However, the balance between the alignment of the different priorities and needs of stakeholders will vary between countries and within national systems, namely at the local level. Variation in local development necessitates the development of robust systems that can be varied to meet specific skills supply and demand requirements. Balancing both the employment and training imperatives of apprenticeships and other work-based learning programmes requires effective institutional arrangements between social partners at the local level.

Local and regional stakeholders can make or break the success of apprenticeship programmes

At the local level, effective apprenticeships programmes can help to achieve key economic development objectives. They provide a mechanism to boost the competitiveness of strategic local sectors. Apprenticeship programmes can stimulate quality employment opportunities in service-based occupations by providing skills development opportunities that are tied to the workplace. They can thus be targeted beyond the traditional trades to new and emerging sectors which can provide new economic growth opportunities.

A precondition for a high quality apprenticeship system is effective implementation at the local level. The potential role for local governments, public agencies and social partners to enhance apprenticeships can often be overlooked at the national level and even by local actors themselves when they do not have the ability to shape local actions. The design of national schemes should include specific measures to encourage engagement of stakeholders at the local level to incentivise their engagement with the apprenticeship system.

Leadership from key stakeholders is particularly important in ensuring that national schemes are effectively implemented at the local level. In the New Zealand town of Otorohanga, (see Chapter 4) employers and young people were targeted by a group of concerned local leaders, including the mayor, church leaders and major employers. The activism and leadership from these actors resulted in custom initiatives to improve apprenticeship participation and completion rates, including personalised assistance, increased access to off-the-job vocational training and personal pastoral care. The mayor, a former apprentice himself, prioritised the development of a network of local stakeholders to improve the outcomes of the apprenticeship system and to reach out to local employers. Similarly, the presence of a hands-on tutor to help apprentices liaise with employers and complete their academic training requirements was critical to improving apprentice retention and completion rates.

While the initial collaboration was largely informal, the outgoing leaders developed formal governance and implementation mechanisms for the stakeholders through the creation of a District Development Board for Economic Development. Since the initiation of the project, local youth increasingly engage in the apprenticeship system and Otorohanga now has one of the lowest percentages of youth unemployment in New Zealand (Sustainable Business Council, 2013).

Similarly, the active leadership of key stakeholders in the leather industry in Bangladesh (see Chapter 9) was a major factor in stimulating an effective and supportive response from government and the donor community. This leadership was more easily harnessed because of the concentration of major enterprises in a geographical cluster, and the ability of the industry-owned Centre of Excellence to support a network of firms in the implementation of apprenticeships in that area.

There are a number of methods of developing a supportive, stakeholder-led infrastructure of local actors in the apprenticeship system. In Western Australia (see Chapter 5), a core employer identified skills shortages in the local building and construction industry as a result of the attraction of labour to the booming mining industry. The employer then specifically approached the regional government to develop a discussion committee that included representatives of the state government, industry councils and associations and unions. As a result, the regional apprenticeship system was reformed to allow the recognition of previous qualifications from apprentices and the development of enterprise specific competence-based learning frameworks. In this case, direct engagement from employers was necessary to build a strategic partnership to align the goals and needs of the relevant stakeholders.

Granting concrete powers to regional and local governments to develop the priorities for apprenticeships can also be effective. For example, the devolution of national powers to local regions in England has allowed city areas to independently develop and implement apprenticeship and skills policies. In the case of Manchester and the Greater Leeds city regions (see Chapter 2), new local powers enabled the development of grant schemes to employers that supported the economic priorities of each local area. They were also able to emphasise high-quality apprenticeships by prioritising advanced or higher apprenticeships or those with career progression opportunities. They also enabled the local regions to specifically target core social groups, including young people with ethnic minority origins. However, while locally developed apprenticeship frameworks are more able to suit individual enterprises and local needs, they may do so at the expense of greater occupational and labour market mobility facilitated by wider sector/occupational-based frameworks.

Figure 1.3. **Key components of successful local employer engagement strategies**

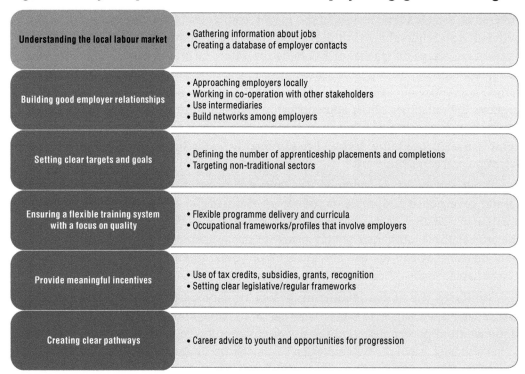

Understanding the local labour market	• Gathering information about jobs • Creating a database of employer contacts
Building good employer relationships	• Approaching employers locally • Working in co-operation with other stakeholders • Use intermediaries • Build networks among employers
Setting clear targets and goals	• Defining the number of apprenticeship placements and completions • Targeting non-traditional sectors
Ensuring a flexible training system with a focus on quality	• Flexible programme delivery and curricula • Occupational frameworks/profiles that involve employers
Provide meaningful incentives	• Use of tax credits, subsidies, grants, recognition • Setting clear legislative/regular frameworks
Creating clear pathways	• Career advice to youth and opportunities for progression

Flexibility in programme delivery is essential to ensure that apprenticeship programmes can respond to local demand

Employers and young people in local areas have different needs depending on local regulations, industrial structure, geography, labour markets and education systems. National and regional schemes must have enough flexibility to respond to local variation in the supply and demand of skills. Building flexibility into local apprenticeship programmes can involve adapting delivery and assessment arrangements, administrative and bureaucratic procedures and methods of programme delivery.

Many OECD countries have incorporated flexibility into apprenticeship programmes through increased modularisation of off-the-job training. This allows the programme offering to be tailored to the custom needs of the apprentice as well as the specific skills requirements of the local region. This trend can be observed in Denmark, Italy, the Netherlands and Poland where local VET provision increasingly varies according to region and local education providers (CEDEFOP, 2015c).

Another feature of programme design that can improve local engagement is improving access to flexible options for training for employers with seasonal or variable operations. The case study from Germany in this publication (Chapter 4) shows how employers with seasonal or variable demand offer more training places to aspiring apprentices when they were able to do on a part-time basis, which also allowed the apprentice to pursue other activities alongside work-based training. This feature is of particular interest to employers in rural areas that may experience more variable demand, as noted in the case studies from Norway and New Zealand (Chapters 3 and 6).

The German dual system also allows some apprentices the option of flexibly completing work-based training through intensive blocs if they so choose. This method of building flexibility into these systems can also help to tailor modules and curricula to local skills needs. This may also suit the desire for flexibility among young people, who may prefer to combine apprenticeships with work or other education opportunities. Other flexible delivery options include apprenticeship programmes for part-time employees, and RPL/accelerated completion options for mature age apprentices and apprenticeships offered to existing workers who wish to expand their skillsets.

Apprenticeship programmes can be tailored to local needs by adapting the method of local programme delivery. For Norwegian apprentices in rural settings, apprentices have had success in completing programme requirements through e-learning platforms. This can reduce the logistical barriers to inclusion faced by apprentices completing work-based training in remote regions (see Box 1.6). The use of ICT by training organisations can also enable the provision of more flexible delivery and assessment platforms for students and employers.

The use of video-enabled devices (tablets, smartphones) and new technologies to capture evidence of skilled performance in the workplace, and the use of SMS and text-based chat systems are improving the level of pastoral care and instructional support available to apprentices. The Government of Canada is also testing the use of these and other

---

Box 1.5. **Flexible programme delivery in Norway**

In Norway, apprentices are now able to complete training requirements, provide documents and access government assistance through specialised e-platforms. One popular system known as OLKWEB has been optimised for use by training offices, who are able to follow up on their apprentices and generate reports that document the apprentice's activities and outputs. Training providers are able to perform a number of key functions, including:

- Access the contacts and details of member companies.
- Analyse and monitor the apprentice's progress through curriculum goals provided through traditional means or through the use of films, images and mobile apps.
- Access details of grants and general accounting.

Apprentices are also able to interact with each other through the system, and can use the interface to record meetings and receive information. The employer is also able to monitor the apprentice's progress in off-the-job training.

In the hyper-rural Norwegian area of Nordland, the customised apprentice interface allows apprentices to fulfill their training requirements without travelling vast distances. E-platforms also remove administrative burdens and allows young people to flexibly complete their apprenticeship requirements.

---

innovations, including increased use of videoconferencing, in-class simulators and flexible in-class training delivery approaches, in order to determine whether they can be used to tailor apprenticeship programmes to local requirements (Government of Canada, 2015).

Flexibility in apprenticeship programme delivery is also necessary in order to address the changing policy environments in local areas. In the case of the local apprenticeship initiatives spearheaded by English city regions, the objectives, mechanisms and targets of the apprenticeship programme were shifted to accommodate the changing demand for skills in the local area. In both the Greater Manchester region and the Greater Leeds City region, the newly developed Apprenticeship hubs were able to pivot towards engaging young people after successful efforts to engage employers resulted in a surplus of apprenticeship vacancies.

Successful apprenticeship programmes must target the specific needs of young people

In order to ensure that apprenticeships and work-based training programmes are as successful as possible, more effort should be made to ensure that they are targeted towards the needs of young people. Young people are a key source of labour supply and programmes that are intended for more mature jobseekers may not be effective in reaching young aspiring apprentices, who may prefer more flexibility or vocational opportunities outside of traditional apprenticeship sectors. Young people also increasingly prefer to pursue and combine a number of activities following compulsory education, (OECD/EC, 2013).

In this context, increasing the amount of modular or unitised apprenticeships and education programmes, wherein the training and competence requirements of programmes are met through flexible combinations of units and modules, could be an effective method of meeting the needs of young people. A broad assessment of trends towards modularisation and unitisation in apprenticeship programmes across Europe found that the new structures have resulted in increased flexibility to the perceived needs and demands young people, particularly with respect to programme duration and multiple entry and exit points (CEDEFOP, 2015c). In many cases, modularised VET was initially targeted towards young people with disadvantages to help them engage with apprenticeships in a method customised to their needs.

Modularised and competency-based apprenticeship programmes also provide the opportunity for early completion based on the achievement of competence rather than the completion of a programme of fixed duration. While the needs of employers must be considered when reducing the period of apprenticeship, the potential for early completion can be an attractive option for young people. Increasing the range of occupations through which apprenticeships are offered is also a way to increase the attractiveness of apprenticeships to young people. New and emerging sectors, particularly in the service sector, are a rich source of potential growth for apprenticeships and provide the opportunity to rebrand through social marketing.

Additional attention should also be paid to flexible delivery arrangements which provide different options for apprentices to undertake their off-the-job training. Evening and weekend classes, mobile and on-site training facilities coupled with part-time apprenticeship options provide greater choice for young people and employers to participate in programmes designed to suit their needs.

In broad terms, young people with social or physical disabilities, low educational attainment, non-native background or low socio-economic education tend to face greater challenges in engaging with the post-secondary education system. These challenges can be magnified when engaging in apprenticeships, which typically involve structured participation in both vocational education and embedded on-the-job training. Some barriers to engagement in apprenticeship for disadvantaged young people can include (Buzzeo et al., 2016):

- Financial issues;
- Prohibitive entry requirements;
- Lack of basic skills;
- Attitudes and behaviours towards work;
- Lack of awareness of the value of apprenticeship;
- Lack of pastoral care or support.

While vocational education pathways tend to have higher percentages of students of low socio-economic background and low educational attainment, these groups also have lower participation and completion rates (Ainley, 2010). This indicates a need to improve the quality of vocational education pathways such that young people with disadvantage have support to successfully complete apprenticeship programmes and transition into employment. The use of "pre-apprenticeship" programmes that address basic skills deficits and sensitise apprentices to the occupation and sector that they are about to enter have also been found to increase completion rates.

Non-completion of apprenticeships is also an issue for employers who lose the opportunity to recoup their investment when an apprentice fails to complete the programme. Enhanced completion rates have been achieved for apprentices who have undertaken some form of pre-apprenticeship programme that introduces apprentices to the sector and provides guidance on practice-based learning prior to employment in a workplace (Cannon, 2015).

Young people with social disadvantages or disability, including those who have failed to complete secondary education or those with a migrant or low socioeconomic background, may need more specialised assistance to complete apprenticeships. Young people, particularly those who are disenfranchised, often require pastoral guidance and support throughout the transition from school to work. Examples from New Zealand, the United States and Australia found that embedding mentorship and guidance into the apprenticeship programme helped to increase participation and completion rates. The New Zealand case study found that support from trusted local figures of authority is also perceived to be more effective than services provided from regional centres.

The German federal state of Hamburg has had some success with addressing the needs of young people who are not in employment, education or training (NEETs) by developing custom youth employment services. The federal government has partnered with a vast coalition of social partners, employer groups and government agencies to streamline programme delivery through a "one-stop- shop" of employment services for young people. Young people can choose to have their data shared between agencies to access integrated employment assistance as well as custom supervision and advisory services.

Young people with social or physical disadvantages tend to exist on the margins of mainstream institutions and apprenticeship opportunities may not be visible to them. Conventional information dissemination mediums, including schools or government institutions, may not necessarily reach them. As a result, successful programmes should

---

Box 1.6. Apprenticeships in rural areas: Broadening access for young people

Young people in rural areas face a number of specific barriers to engagement in the apprenticeship system, including:

- Limited access to off-the-job vocational education providers.
- Logistical difficulties associated with traversing long distances to reach training commitments.
- Limited access to career guidance and information.
- Limited access to public employment services or youth services.
- Fewer employment, higher education and training opportunities.

Young people in rural areas are also more likely to be in low-paid or insecure employment or employed within SMEs than urban youth, indicating a need to improve access to quality jobs and employment within rural areas.

Rural areas have differed in their approach to assist local youth to successfully complete apprenticeships. In the New Zealand town of Otorohanga, these challenges were addressed by providing local training support and assistance to aspiring apprentices. The town established a local satellite campus of the vocational education provider while also providing mentorship and guidance to aspiring apprentices. In contrast, the Norwegian region of Nordland pursued a flexible model to allow apprentices to complete programme requirements through e-learning platforms. Public transport and home sharing services also serve to overcome some of the logistical barriers associated with rural areas.

Source: Commission for Rural Communities (2012).

---

partner with intermediaries such as youth organisations, who may also have specialised local knowledge regarding the needs and desires of disadvantaged young people.

A method increasingly pursued across European countries to include young people with disadvantage into apprenticeship programmes are work integration social enterprises (WISE). WISE are programmes that aim to provide work-based training opportunities for people with disadvantages, including young people with social and physical disabilities or lacking a secondary leaving certificate. WISE programmes operate on a not-for-profit basis in the private training market and aim to integrate disadvantaged persons into the world of work by providing them with opportunities that are tailored to their needs and skills. The focus on job-ready skills acquired through active employment is central to ensure that disadvantaged youth remain engaged with employment during the initial apprenticeship period (European Commission, 2015).

Apprenticeship programmes are a key skills development mechanism to tackle informality

Apprenticeship structures and systems vary among and between developed and emerging economies. While formal apprenticeship systems do exist in some emerging economies, in many cases they only cater for small numbers and are outside of the formal VET system. In such cases, apprenticeships in the informal economy typically offer many more young people an opportunity to learn a trade and enter the world of work. In many emerging economies, these informal or traditional apprenticeships are the largest provider of skills for the mostly informal labour market (ILO 2011a).

Practices in informal apprenticeship vary according to local context. In some African countries, apprentices are trained in specific skills for a shorter period of time rather than in all skills relevant for an occupation over a longer period of time. In many cases, the apprentices pay a fee. In West Africa, more structured systems of informal apprenticeships exist, which culminate in graduation ceremonies that involve other members of the community. Given the lack of official records on informal apprentices, most countries where this system exists have only rough estimates of the number of apprentices in the informal economy. Within the informal economy, apprenticeships are not unorganised but social rules and local traditions provide a conducive framework for training to take place. However, informal apprenticeship systems are typically characterised by low quality training and various decent work deficits that can lead to exploitation (ILO, 2012b).

The case studies of apprenticeships programmes in Bangladesh (Chapter 8) and India (Chapter 9) in this publication highlight the specific challenges faced when trying to develop an apprenticeship system in developing countries. These challenges include the limited tradition of employer engagement in skills development, poor governance and co-ordination, and limited integration of apprenticeship training into the formal vocational education and training system. These constraints are compounded by high levels of informality, weak links between training organisations and employers and relatively low levels of basic and foundation skills among jobseekers. In developing countries, limited access to training places, low quality and limited programme relevance have led employers, students and parents to see formal VET as an unattractive choice.

However, as increasing attention is paid to improving the quality and relevance of vocational training and reducing informality in developing countries, the reform of skills systems is increasingly including a focus on formalising informal apprenticeships so they can be upgraded to more legitimate pathways for learning and school-to-work transition (Comyn, 2015). In South Asia for example, while countries such as India, Pakistan, Bangladesh and Sri Lanka have formal apprenticeship systems, they are based on archaic regulations and severe penalties for non-compliance as well as limited enterprise eligibility and participation, thus contributing to the on-going participation in the informal apprenticeship systems outside of those governed by formal apprenticeship legislation (ILO, 2013).

In this context, and as outlined in the Bangladesh case study in this publication, efforts are needed to improve and expand informal apprenticeship systems so a greater number of quality training and employment places are available for more young people. ILO experience in strengthening informal apprenticeships has found that steps can be taken to:

- Complement learning at the workplace with more structured institutional learning;
- Upgrade the skills of master craftspersons, e.g. by introducing them to modern technology and on-the-job training techniques;
- Introduce formal assessment and certification systems;
- Introduce standardised contracts of employment and codes of practice to address deficits of decent work;
- Strengthen community involvement, especially with a view to increasing opportunities for young women;
- Include literacy/numeracy training and livelihoods skills; and
- Involve business associations and labour organisations, especially those representing the informal economy (ILO 2012b).

A key strategy for upgrading informal apprenticeship systems is to foster improvements from within the existing system. If small business associations exist, they need to play the primary role in upgrading informal apprenticeships. Any outside intervention in informal apprenticeship systems must be based on a sound understanding of local practices and of the incentives to participation for both master craftspersons and apprentices in order to avoid the risk of destabilising what is in many cases the most significant skills development system in that industry, sector and country (ILO, 2013a).

In emerging economies, there is also potential for third-party actors to develop sustainable apprenticeship programmes alongside the conventional employment and skills system. This can occur in both the formal and informal economy. In emerging economies that do not have a well-developed formal vocational education and training system, apprenticeship programmes administered through intermediaries have proven to be an attractive option. Egypt, for example, has a well-established alternative apprenticeship system that is managed by the Egyptian Federation of Building and Construction Contractors.

Whether part of a formal system or not, the importance of active engagement of business and labour organisations is a well-established success factor in apprenticeship systems in both developed and emerging countries (ILO 2012b). In the case study on Turkey (Chapter 7), the establishment of the GAN national network as part of the Global Apprenticeships Network (GAN) highlights the potential benefits of integrating both formal and informal apprenticeship systems. It also highlights the important role that employer associations can play in facilitating and supporting member companies to participate in apprenticeship schemes. However, the existence of formal employer apprenticeship networks are not necessarily a guarantee of success.

Earlier ILO research in Indonesia noted that while Apprenticeship Forums were supposed to operate in all of Indonesia's 33 provinces, they were weak and barely functioning in many areas due in part to the lack of a clear national policy framework and the absence of clearly defined roles in the system for social partners (ILO 2013). As noted in ILO (2015a) the success of the regional forums has depended entirely on the dedication of the people appointed as co-ordinators in the provinces. While OECD countries are exploring ways to deepen the level of collaboration in local areas, limited local institutional capacity in some emerging economies coupled with weak labour market information can dampen the potential for local collaboration on apprenticeships.

However, as detailed in the case study on Bangladesh in this publication, revitalisation of apprenticeships in the leather industry occurred as a result of leadership from key industry associations and enterprises in the sector with support from development partners, and was subsequently integrated into the formal apprenticeship system with support of the government and the national skills regulatory body. The industry associations were instrumental in establishing an industry-led training centre which acted as a broker for the new apprenticeship scheme. The centre took an active role in working with individual firms in the cluster to identify training places and establish a network for apprenticeships in the sector. Participating firms have reported reduced labour turnover and reduced skills mismatch as a result of participating in this new industry-led apprenticeship scheme. A key success factor that influences employer engagement in apprenticeship systems is thus the extent of their role in delivery, assessment and certification arrangements.

Box 1.7. **Global Apprenticeship Network**

The Global Apprenticeships Network (GAN) was founded with the aim of promoting work-based training and improving the status of apprenticeship programmes. It also aims to provide a method of sharing best practices among countries at the local, regional, national and international levels. The GAN is co-ordinated by the International Organisation of Employers (IOE) with the support of the International Labour Organisation (ILO). Major corporations involved with the GAN include Adecco Group, Astra International, Ericsson, GI Group, Hilton Worldwide, Huawei, IBM, Mastercard Foundation, Nestlé, Randstad Holding, Samsung, Telefónica and UBS.

At the national level, the GAN acts through national networks, which helps them to act quickly and agilely to disseminate new ideas and best practices. It also enables advice and assistance to be tailored to the national regulatory framework.

The first three national networks were:

● Turkey with 25 member companies.

● Indonesia with 19 member companies.

● Spain with 29 member companies.

Other national networks have been established in Colombia, Argentina and Mexico, with preparatory work underway to establish national networks in Malawi, Tanzania, Nigeria and Namibia.

Source: www.gan-global.org.

In the cases of Turkey and Bangladesh, the respective roles of TESK and COEL (Centre of Excellence for Leather Skills Bangladesh) in conducting assessments of apprentices across the sector ensured strong engagement with the system and parallel promotion and marketing of apprenticeships throughout their industry networks. The importance of this assessment role has also been highlighted in earlier ILO work in Africa, Asia and Latin America (for example, see: ILO, 2015) which has supported the active engagement of industry bodies, including in the informal sector, to lead the development of improved delivery, assessment and certification arrangements for apprenticeships. As noted in ILO research (2015b), assessment at the end of an apprenticeship should involve tripartite actors and certification of successful completion of apprenticeships should be recognised nationally, an ideal which is not always achieved in either developed or developing countries.

In emerging economies, the eligibility of enterprises and employers to take on apprentices is also a key factor influencing the extent of industry engagement. The case study on India (Chapter 10) shows that requirements surrounding supervision ratios, enterprise size, workplace training facilities and occupational coverage were key barriers to employer engagement in the system. In many developing countries, the legislative and other responsibilities of employers in apprenticeships are set out in a complex array of industrial laws (ILO, 2013). While the case studies on both Bangladesh and India in this publication found that it was obligatory for eligible employers to take on apprentices under the legislation, compliance was weak, and apprenticeship numbers are low relative to the size of the labour force.

Despite this, reforms have been introduced which increase the number of apprenticeships and participating enterprises, illustrating that even in developing countries there exists considerable potential to utilise the apprenticeship model to improve access to quality training relevant to employers. In both these countries and Turkey, the need to revise and update existing legal frameworks for apprenticeships have been central to efforts to revitalise the apprenticeship systems, for as noted by Steedman (2015), removing regulatory uncertainty lowers the transaction costs of apprenticeships both for employers and for apprentices.

The perception of low quality employment and "lock-in" associated with apprenticeship schemes is also a feature in some emerging economies. Challenging these perceptions can increase employer engagement in this sector. The revitalisation and promotion of the apprenticeship brand by governments and social partners is an important social marketing strategy particularly in developing countries where the status of apprenticeships is low. Initiatives such as the Global Apprenticeship Network (GAN), which has established national networks in Turkey, Indonesia, Spain and Argentina, the European Alliance for Apprenticeships (EAfA) and targeted marketing by sector bodies such as SENAI in Brazil, NAMB in South Africa and industry skills councils in the UK, NZ, Canada and Australia have highlighted the importance of branding and promotion to employers, family and students. In emerging economies, where the introduction of NQFs continues at pace, new opportunities to integrate apprenticeships into recognised learning pathways have emerged. In India, Bangladesh, South Africa and the UK, new apprenticeship credentials are now leading to NQF based qualifications.

Central to effective marketing to employers is the value proposition that apprenticeships present. However, firm level data on the return on investment from apprenticeships is not widely available despite its potential to promote employer take-up of apprenticeships (see for example ILO 2014a). In developing countries however, structured recruitment systems in many firms are absent, thus limiting the immediate potential of apprenticeships to form part of strategic human resource management practices in enterprises. However, despite this, the case studies of India and Turkey demonstrate that through the targeted use of financial incentives and support from intermediaries, steps can be taken to link apprenticeships with the immediate skill needs of enterprises, especially in the formal economy.

In developed and emerging countries, multinational corporations have a particular role in modelling good practice apprenticeship arrangements. The ILO (2014) has highlighted the role of German companies in promoting innovative apprenticeship programmes through active co-operation with community colleges and municipalities in the United States, a similar situation to the Skillsonic initiative in India which involved Swiss firms partnering with Industrial Training Institutes (ITI) and Swiss training organisations with financial assistance from the Swiss government in India. In both cases, well-established enterprise HRM systems and experience with formal apprenticeships in the countries of origin provided multinational corporations with a foundation for introducing formal apprenticeship arrangements through local partnerships in their different countries of operation.

The reform of TVET and skills systems in emerging economies typically focuses on engaging with employers and industry to improve current arrangements. However, in developing countries, the tradition of social dialogue involving employer and worker organisations does not have a strong tradition. As such, the limited capacity of social partners often acts as a barrier to improved engagement of enterprises in the skills system and calls for increased attention to the capacity building of unions and employer organisations so they can more effectively promote the introduction and uptake of apprenticeships. However, as apprenticeships are an option to respond directly to skills needs in enterprises, they can be a more effective vehicle to promote social dialogue on skills development than is possible through other mechanisms (ILO, 2016).

Increasing the participation of employers and individuals involves changing perceptions of apprenticeships

Countries with long histories of vocational education tend to view vocational education as an equivalent, or in some cases preferred, pathway from school to work in comparison to tertiary education. However, in other countries apprenticeship programmes are stigmatised as less worthy educational choices (Brophy et al., 2009; European Commission, 2015b). The UK case study in the publication (see Chapter 2) highlights the impacts of a lack of "parity of esteem" between vocational education and tertiary education pathways which is also a major issue in developing countries. Increasing the engagement of employers and individuals with the apprenticeship system demands that apprenticeships are considered a good method of entering high quality and desirable employment as well as an option for employers to address skills shortages.

Cultural attitudes towards apprenticeships can influence the attractiveness of apprenticeship for young people. In countries with a strong tradition of vocational education where apprenticeships are viewed as desirable and respectable pathways, apprentice candidates tend to have higher secondary education scores (ILO/World Bank, 2013). In contrast, employers and young people can be discouraged from engaging with the apprenticeship system where that training and the employment it leads to is viewed as of low quality. Perceptions can also vary among sectors, businesses and geographical areas – smaller companies in less attractive industries or in declining local areas can struggle to attract suitable apprentices. In England, apprenticeships in industries with a strong history of craft instruction tend to be viewed as more desirable than those in more traditional trades sectors (ILO/World Bank, 2013).

Some of the misinformation surrounding apprenticeships is due to the historical association between vocational education and careers in the trades or secondary sector. As noted in the United States case study (see Chapter 7), the apprenticeships are broadly perceived within OECD countries as typically within blue-collar and male-dominated sectors. Broadening training opportunities to other sectors and occupations may help to improve engagement from both employers and apprentices. The case study from the United States found that training opportunities can boost later career prospects despite an unconventional employer, namely the public secondary education system, and what has been traditionally an unconventional focus, namely information technology. Mohrenweizer and Zwick (2009) found that the net benefits for German employers are actually higher in commercial, trade, craft and construction occupations than for manufacturing occupations, indicating that there might be increased incentive for tertiary industry occupations to pursue apprenticeships if these benefits were made more widely known.

The association between the trades and apprenticeships is further linked to the historical association of apprenticeships with particularly demographic sectors, namely young white men. As noted in the American case study, this perception can discourage inclusion from more diverse aspiring apprentices. This is particularly significant because occupational and sectoral segregation has been found to reduce the economic benefits of work-based training for women (Ryan, 2001). Of the surveyed countries, only the German apprenticeship system has similar entry rates and pay benefits for women (European

Commission, 2013), but there are still stark differences in the choice of apprenticeship occupations. This suggests that more needs to be done to broaden access to apprenticeships to equitable and inclusive economic benefits for the full spectrum of young people, including women, who are typically underrepresented in apprenticeship schemes (ILO, 2013).

The German and British case studies in this publication highlight potential negative perception among students and parents that apprenticeships can be inflexible and result in path dependence. Thus, improving perceptions of apprenticeships may require improving the ability of vocational students to transition to other educational or occupational paths to avoid 'lock-in'. This may involve developing more modular and integrated education systems such that students and apprentices are able to freely move between programmes and between the vocational and tertiary education systems. As noted earlier, developing robust qualification recognition systems and credit transfer arrangements is particularly relevant to ensuring that VET systems have flexible entry and exit points and that apprenticeship programmes provide opportunities for higher level study, as is the case in the UK following recent reforms. To address this, the German VET system has enabled higher vocational attainment and successful as an alternative to secondary leaving certificates as a means of gaining acceptance into university, but this has not been widely adopted. Improving the flexibility of the apprenticeship system can help to improve its responsiveness to shifts in skills supply and demand at the local level.

Adequate support and guidance for young people is necessary to ensure that they have the broadest range of information of future education and career paths following compulsory education. The negative impression of apprenticeships may be partially due to the underdevelopment of career guidance and information. Current career guidance systems at the secondary level across the OECD pay little attention to vocational pathways in comparison to tertiary education (Watts, 2009), indicating that young people may be uninformed about the potential benefits of pursuing work-based career options. The British case study also noted that improving misperceptions regarding the wages and conditions of apprenticeships among both students and parents helped to improve the pool of aspiring apprentices.

As noted by Sweet (2013), countries with large or medium-sized apprenticeship systems tend to have a stronger emphasis on external support, experiential learning and labour market relevance. In Germany, local secondary schools have found success with incorporating skills assessments within career guidance two years before the final compulsory year of education. A focus on assessing hard and soft skills and relating those skills to potential career paths was found to be helpful in directing students towards the most appropriate vocational or general educational pathways. Careers guidance should be embedded throughout the secondary education system to provide coherent and labour market relevant information to enable young people to make the best careers choices (OECD, 2014a). As career and vocational guidance is also provided by public employment services and training organisations in the TVET sector, it is important that they also be included in any systematic approach to providing young people with high quality advice and guidance related to apprenticeship programmes and the career pathways they support. As noted in the British case study, the governance responsibility for career guidance and information should be clear in order to ensure stable and streamlined services to the local community.

Local community leaders and "success stories" can also play an important role in building the "parity of esteem" between apprenticeships and other vocational educational pathways and tertiary pathways following compulsory secondary education. In the New Zealand town of Otorohanga, the former mayor was a key driver of the initiative to improve the participation and completion rates for local apprentices. As a former apprentice himself, he prioritised the celebration of the successful completion of apprenticeships through a formal graduation ceremony. By personally honouring trades apprentices, the mayor played an important role in helping to elevate the status of work-based training paths.

Employers can also play a role in boosting awareness about work-based training opportunities to students at the secondary level. Developing integrated partnerships between workplaces and compulsory secondary education can help to inform students about the world of work and future career opportunities (OECD, 2010). The New Zealand and Australian case studies highlight the utility of using local employers to highlight the apprenticeship opportunities available in the local community. In particular, the Otorohanga community had great success with a careers fair that highlighted a range of work-based training opportunities in a variety of sectors from the local sector, ranging from accounting to the dairy industry. This stimulated engagement from both aspiring apprentices and local businesses and allowed both actors to develop an immediate and close relationship. Alongside other initiatives, the careers fair was credited with improving both the participation and completion rates for apprenticeships in the area.

Career guidance and information should also be incorporated into apprenticeship programmes to inform apprentices about the future applications of their acquired skills and importance. Career advice throughout the process is particularly important in inflexible education systems, where VET pathways can "tighten" career prospects (Watts, 2009). Alongside a robust and flexible apprenticeship system, the provision of career guidance to apprentices can increase retention rates by allowing them to shift to different paths instead of dropping out altogether. The provision of additional support to highlight the self-employment potential of graduate apprentices is also an important strategy to increase completion rates and deliver successful employment outcomes from apprenticeship programmes.

References

Acil Allen Consulting (2014), *Review of the Joint Group Training Program And the Role of Group Training*, Australian Department of Industry, Canberra.

Ainley, J. (2010), *Apprenticeships and Traineeships: Participation, Progress and Completion*, Australian Council for Educational Research.

Aring (2012), *Report on Skills Gaps*, Background paper prepared for the Education for All Global Monitoring Report 2012, Youth and skills: Putting education to work, *www.unesdoc.unesco.org/ images/0021/002178/217874e.pdf*.

Australian Government (2013), "Skills Connect: Reforming support services for the Australian apprenticeships system", *Discussion Paper*.

Bertschy, K., M.A. Cattaneo and S.C. Wolter (2009), "PISA and the transition into the labour market", *Labour: Review of Labour Economics and Industrial Relations*, 23, 111-137.

Brewer, L. (2013), *Enhancing Youth Employability: What? Why? and How? Guide to Core Work Skills*, International Labour Organisation, Geneva.

Brophy, M., B. McNeil and A. Shandro (2009), *Thinking about apprenticeships: Perceptions and expectations of employers, parents and young people*, the Young Foundation, London.

Buzzeo, J., R. Marvell, C. Everett and B. Newton (2016), *Tackling unemployment among disadvantaged young people*, Institute for Employment Studies.

Cannon, J. (2015) "Pre-apprenticeships towards apprenticeships using practice focused learning" in Smith, E., P. Gonon and A. Foley (eds.), *Architectures for Apprenticeship: Achieving Economic and Social Goals*, pp. 21-25, Federation University, Ballarat.

Cappellari, L., C. Dell'Aringa and M. Leonardi (2012), "Temporary employment, job flows and productivity: a tale of two reforms", *The Economic Journal*, 122 (August), pp. 188-215.

Cedefop (2015a), "Skill shortages and gaps in European enterprises: Striking a balance between VET and the labour market", *Cedefop reference series*, No. 102, *www.cedefop.europa.eu/en/publications-and-resources/publications/3071*.

Cedefop (2015b), "Outcomes of Cedefop's 2nd European Apprenticeship conference: Engaging SMEs in Apprenticeships" 2015, *www.cedefop.europa.eu%2Ffiles%2Facvt_181215_cedefop_apprenticeship_conference_91115.pdf*.

Cedefop (2015c), "The role of modularisation and unitisation in vocational education and training", *Working Paper*, No. 26, Luxembourg: Publications Office of the European Union, 2015.

Cedefop (2011), "The benefits of vocational education and training", *Research Paper*, No. 10, Luxembourg: Publications Office of the European Union, 2011, *Journal of Vocational Education and Training*, Vol. 67, No. 4, pp. 515-528, *http://dx.doi.org/10.1080/13636820.2015.1076499*.

Chankseliani, M. and S.J. Relly (2015), "From the provider-led to an employer-led system: Implications of apprenticeship reform on the private training market", *Journal of Vocational Education and Training*, 2015, Vol. 67, No. 4, pp. 515-528, *http://dx.doi.org/10.1080/13636820.2015.1076499*.

Clayton, B., H. Guthrie, P. Every and R. Harding (2015), *Competency progression and completion: How is the policy being enacted in three trades*, National Centre for Vocational Education Research, Adelaide.

Courtright, S.H. and C.G. Fry (2007), *Public Rates of Return by State On Government Investments in Higher Education*, College Teaching, 4 (8), 13-26.

Criscuolo, C., P.N. Gal and C. Menon (2014), "The Dynamics of Employment Growth: New Evidence from 18 Countries", *OECD Science, Technology and Industry Policy Papers*, No. 14, OECD Publishing, Paris, *http://dx.doi.org/10.1787/5jz417hj6hg6-en*.

Department of Business Innovation and Skills (2015), *Business Population Estimates for the UK and Regions*, 2015, Statistical Release.

European Commission (2015a), *A map of social enterprises and their eco-systems in Europe: A Synthesis Report*, Directorate-General for Employment, Social Affairs and Inclusion, European Commission, Luxembourg: Publications Office of the European Union.

European Commission (2015b), *Good for Youth, Good for Business*, European Alliance for Apprenticeships, Luxembourg: Publications Office of the European Union.

European Commission (2013), *The Effectiveness and Cost Benefit of Apprenticeships: Results of the Quantitative Analysis*, Luxembourg: Publications Office of the European Union.

Eurostat (2014), Europe 2020 indicators – Education. Persons with upper secondary or tertiary education attainment by age and sex, EU-28, 2013 (% of population).

Frazer, G. (2006), "Learning the master's trade: Apprenticeship and human capital in Ghana", *Journal of Development Economics* 81 (2006), pp. 259-298.

G20 (2012), *Key Elements of Quality Apprenticeships*, G20 Task Force on Employment, 2012, *www.ilo.org/wcmsp5/groups/public/---ed_emp/---ifp.../wcms_218209.pdf*.

Government of Canada (2015), *Flexibility and innovation in apprenticeship technical training*, *www.esdc.gc.ca/en/support_apprentices/fiatt.page*.

Green, A. and L.E. Martinez-Solano (2011), "Leveraging Training Skills Development in SMEs: An Analysis of the West Midlands, England, UK", *OECD Local Economic and Employment Development (LEED) Working Papers*, No. 2011/15, OECD Publishing, Paris, *http://dx.doi.org/10.1787/5kg0vststzr5-en*.

Hargraves, J. and D. Blomberg (2015), *Adult trade apprentices: Exploring the significance of recognition of prior learning and skill sets for earlier completion*, National Centre for Vocational Education Research, Australia.

HM Government (2015) "Apprenticeship Reforms – progress so far", *Policy Report*, *www.gov.uk/government/uploads/system/uploads/attachment_data/file/411827/bis-15-179-Apprenticeship-reforms-progress-so-far.pdf*.

HM Government (2013) "Apprenticeship by Provider Type: Starts and Achievements 2005/06 to 2011/12", www.gov.uk/government/uploads/system/uploads/attachment_data/file/298288/January2013_Apprenticeship_Provider_Type.xls.

Hoeckel, K. and R. Schwartz (2010), "OECD Reviews of Vocational Education and Training: A Learning for Jobs Review of Germany 2010", OECD Reviews of Vocational Education and Training, OECD Publishing, Paris, http://dx.doi.org/10.1787/9789264113800-en.

Hoeckel (2008), "OECD Costs and Benefits in Vocational Education and Training", OECD Education Working Papers, EDU/EDPC/CERI (2008)3, OECD Publishing, Paris.

Holt (2012), "Making apprenticeships more accessible to small and medium-sized enterprises", Department of Business, Innovation and Skills, UK Government, www.gov.uk/government/uploads/system/uploads/attachment_data/file/34731/12-891-making-apprenticeships-more-accessible-to-smes-holt-review.pdf.

ILO (2016 forthcoming), "National Training Funds: A Review of International Experience and Global Best Practice".

ILO (2016), "The Involvement of Trade Unions in TVET and Skills Development Systems", International Labour Office, Geneva.

ILO (2015), "Global Employment Trends 2014: Risk of a jobless recovery?", International Labour Office.

ILO (2013), "Towards a Model Apprenticeship Framework: A Comparative Analysis of National Apprenticeship Systems", International Labour Organisation and the World Bank, New Delhi.

ILO (2012a), "Overview of apprenticeship systems and issues", ILO Contribution to the G20 Taskforce on Employment, Skills and Employability Branch, International Labour Organisation, Geneva.

ILO (2012b), "Upgrading informal apprenticeship: A resource guide for Africa" (Geneva), www.ilo.org/skills/pubs/WCMS_171393/lang--en/index.htm.

Kitching, J. and R. Blackburn (2002), "The Nature of Training and Motivation to Train in Small Firms", (DfES Research Report 330), Nottingham: DfES.

Kramer, M., G. Hills and K. Tallant (2015), "The New Role of Business in Global Education", FSG, Boston.

Kuczera, M. (2017), "Incentives for apprenticeship", OECD Education Working Papers, No. 152, OECD Publishing, Paris, http://dx.doi.org/10.1787/55bb556d-en.

Lewis, P. (2013), "The Over-Training of Apprentices by Large Employers in Advanced Manufacturing in the UK", Gatsby Foundation.

McIntosh, S., J. Wenchao and A. Vignoles (2011), "Firms' Engagement with the Apprenticeship Programme", Research Report DFE-RR180, Sheffield: CAYT, www.researchonline.org.uk/sds/search/download.do;jsessionid=713FD6DB22BB69A1A9C43FDCFD102F46?ref=B23579.

Mieschbuehler, R. and T. Hooley (2015), "World-Class Apprenticeship Standards: Report and Recommendations", International Centre for Guidance Studies, University of Derby and Pearson Education.

Mohrenweiser, J., T. Zwick and U. Backes-Gellner (2013), "Poaching and Firm Sponsored Training: First Clean Evidence", in ZEW discussion Paper, 13-037.

Mohrenweiser, J. and T. Zwick (2009), "Why do firms train apprentices? The net cost puzzle reconsidered", Labor Economics, 16 (5), pp. 631-637.

Mühlemann, S., J. Schweri, R. Winkelmann and S.C. Wolter (2007), "An empirical analysis of the decision to train apprentices", Labour: Review of Labour Economics and Industrial Relations, 21 (3), pp. 419-441.

OECD (2016), Youth unemployment rate (indicator), http://dx.doi.org/10.1787/c3634df7-en (accessed on 20 June 2016).

OECD (2014a), "Skills beyond School: Synthesis Report", OECD Reviews of Vocational Education and Training, OECD Publishing, Paris, http://dx.doi.org/10.1787/9789264214682-en.

OECD (2014b), Background Paper for the G20-OECD-EC Conference on Quality Apprenticeships for Giving Youth a Better Start in the Labour Market.

OECD/European Commission (2013), "Policy Brief on Social Entrepreneurship", OECD Publishing, Paris.

OECD (2012), "OECD Note on 'Quality Apprenticeships' for the G20 Task Force on Employment", www.oecd.org/els/emp/OECD%20Apprenticeship%20Note%2026%20Sept.pdf.

OECD (2010), "Learning for Jobs", *OECD Reviews of Vocational Education and Training*, OECD Publishing, Paris, *http://dx.doi.org/10.1787/9789264087460-en*.

Quintini, G. and T. Manfredi (2009), "Going Separate Ways? School-to-Work Transitions in the United States and Europe", *OECD Social, Employment and Migration Working Papers*, No. 90, OECD Publishing, Paris, *http://dx.doi.org/10.1787/221717700447*.

Parey, M. (2009), "Vocational Schooling versus Apprenticeship Training. Evidence from Vacancy Data", mimeo.

Rothboeck, S. (2014), "Using Benefit Cost Calculations to Assess Returns from Apprenticeship Investment in India: Selected SME Case Studies", International Labour Organisation, New Delhi.

Ryan, P. (2001), "The school-to-work transition: A cross-national perspective" *Journal of Economic Literature*, 39 (1), 34-92.

Schofield, K. (2000), "Delivering Quality: Report of the Independent Review of the Quality of Training in Victoria Is Apprenticeship and Traineeship System", Office of Post-Compulsory Education and Training, Melbourne.

Schweri J. and B. Mueller (2008), "Die Ausbildungsbereitschaft der Betriebe: Entwicklungen 1995 bis 2005", Bundesamt fur Statistik BFS.

Skills Development Scotland (nd), "Key issues in employer engagement in education: Why it makes a difference and how to deliver at scale", The Edge Foundation.

Smith, A. and E. Smith (2007), "The role of training in the development of human resource management in Australian organisations", Human Resource Development International, 10:3, pp. 263-279, *http://dx.doi.org/10.1080/13678860701515208*.

Smith, E. (2015), "Enterprise training providers in Australia and England. Researching Vocational Education and Training", *Journal of Vocational Education and Training 11th international Conference*, Worcester College, Oxford, 3-5 July.

Smith, E., P. Comyn, R. Brennan Kemmis and A. Smith (2009), "High-quality traineeships: Identifying what works", Adelaide: NCVER.

Steedman, H. (2015), "Promoting safe work and quality apprenticeships in small and medium-sized enterprises: Challenges for developed and developing economies", International Labour Office, Geneva.

Steedman, H. (2010), "The State of Apprenticeship in 2010: International Comparisons", a report for the Apprenticeship Ambassadors Network.

Steedman, H. (2005), "Apprenticeship in Europe: Fading or Flourishing?", *Centre for Economic Performance Discussion Paper*, No. 710, International, 10 (3):263-279.

Sustainable Business Council (2013), "All In: A New Zealand Inc. approach to solve youth unemployment".

Sweet, R. (2013), "Apprenticeship, pathways and career guidance: A cautionary tale" in Deitmer, L., U. Hauschildt, F. Rauner and H. Zelloth (Eds.), *The Architecture of Innovative Apprenticeship*, Dordrecht: Springer Netherlands.

University of Warwick (2008), "The Net Benefits to Employer Investment in Apprenticeship Training", a report for the Apprenticeship Ambassadors Network.

Watts (2009), "The Relationship of Career Guidance to VET", National Institute for Careers Education and Counselling.

Walther, R. (2007), "La formation professionnelle en secteur informel : les conclusions d'une enquête terrain dans sept pays africains", Agence Française de Développement Département de la Recherche.

World Bank (2015), *Small and Medium Enterprises (SMEs) Finance Brief*, *www.worldbank.org/en/topic/financialsector/brief/smes-finance*.

Chapter 2

Local initiatives to promote apprenticeships in the United Kingdom

This chapter reviews two local Apprenticeship Hubs that have been developed in the Greater Manchester and Leeds City Region as part of the current devolution process of new powers to English cities. The case study explores the effectiveness and efficiency of the Apprenticeship Hubs in a context of high youth unemployment and structural change in the United Kingdom, and provides an opportunity to compare and contrast differing approaches to implementation and governance changes.

Key findings

- The Leeds and Greater Manchester city regions of the United Kingdom have recently assumed new responsibilities to manage apprenticeship programme through local apprenticeship hubs. This has occurred in a broader context of high youth unemployment, and historically negative perceptions towards apprenticeship and vocational pathways in comparison to traditional academic routes.

- Each city region has pursued different governance and administrative structures for apprenticeship programme delivery and adopted separate objectives and processes in accordance with their specific local circumstances.

- Capacity building among local training providers and a focus on engaging both employers and prospective apprentices are common features to the Apprenticeship Hubs in both city regions. The jurisdictions also both aim to deliver improved career guidance and improved accessibility mechanisms for apprentices. Similarly, both city regions aim to build flexibility into local apprenticeship management in order to remain agile to shifts in local growth sectors.

Introduction

Vocational training provision in the United Kingdom has been a historically devolved jurisdiction that is managed differently in England, Scotland, Wales and Northern Ireland. In the English system, responsibility for the management of apprenticeships have been recently further devolved to a number of specific city regions as part of a series of "City Deals". Consequently, the Leeds and Greater Manchester city regions have recently assumed the capacity to manage apprenticeship provision in accordance with local requirements and needs.

Each city region has taken a separate approach to building employer engagement and streamlining training provision in their local areas. The strategies pursued by each city region differ in a variety of core ways, including the degree of further decentralisation and the focus of apprenticeship provision. The role of careers guidance and the landscape of training providers are also examined in this chapter.

Policy context

Apprenticeship hubs were developed at a time of recovering growth in the United Kingdom after the global financial crisis, but of high youth unemployment, which rose to 21.2% in 2012 (OECD, 2016). Since the start of 2013, the economy has grown in every quarter, with GDP growth being at 3% in 2014. Overall unemployment has fallen from 7.9% in 2012 to 6.1% in 2014 with youth unemployment at 16.3% in 2014 and still falling.

Vocational training provision in England[1] counts for a relatively small proportion of the overall education and training system, which is dominated by academic studies. Fewer than 10% of English youth participate in vocational training, in comparison to a third or more in many European countries. Vocational training is however more likely to be undertaken in the fields of education, health, social work, financial services and public administration (CEDEFOP, 2013). Much of the vocational training undertaken by adults is relatively low level, with many courses at the National Vocational Qualification (NVQ) level 2, which is equivalent to lower secondary education usually undertaken up to age 16 (ISCED level 2).

England is relatively unique in the OECD in that both upper secondary and post-secondary qualifications are designed and accredited by independent awarding bodies as opposed to central government. This has resulted in a plethora of different qualifications available for study (Musset and Field, 2013). The government is currently attempting to rationalise the number of qualifications and increase their rigour, while at the same time move learners towards Level 3 or upper secondary level. There is also a plethora of training organisations across the country, with nearly 3 000 training providers operating in England (UK Government, 2014).

Recent reforms have included the introduction of an employer-endorsed "technical level" at NVQ level 3. The government is also seeking to boost employer engagement more generally in training design and delivery. Throughout this process, England is moving from a centralised VET system to a system that is decentralised and market driven. This is intended to improve the ability of employers and local colleges to design courses, compete for funding and respond to enterprise skill needs.

A national push towards apprenticeships

There has also been a recent push to increase the number of apprenticeships in the UK at both the upper secondary and post-secondary levels. Apprenticeships have received significant policy attention and increased funding under the last two British governments, which has coincided with an almost 100% increase in apprentices in England between 2010 and 2015. However, there are still fewer apprentices as a share of the workforce in England (11 per 1 000 employees) in comparison to other OECD countries (39/1 000 in Australia, 40/1 000 in Germany and 43/1 000 in Switzerland) (What Works Centre for Local Economic Growth, 2015). There is now an aim to increase the number of apprenticeship starts in the UK from 2.3 million in the last parliament to 3 million within the current parliament (HM Treasury, 2015).

Apprenticeships can be offered at a number of different levels, including intermediate (NVQ level 2), advanced (NVQ level 3) and higher (NVQ level 4 and above) – with degree level apprenticeships currently being introduced. Despite this diversity, 58% of apprenticeships were at the intermediate level (NVQ level 2) from 2013-14.

While many have welcomed the government focus on increasing apprenticeships, there have been concerns that the rise in absolute numbers has led to a sacrifice in quality. It has been argued that many employers, particularly in retail, have adapted existing short-term employer training into an apprenticeship structure to secure government funding, which has the potential to undermine the perceived quality of the "apprenticeship" brand. Further, because training providers are only paid the full "outcome related" payment for delivering apprenticeships on completion, there have been concerns that providers are prioritising getting people into "easier" apprenticeships, while also working with those people who would find apprenticeships easier to complete, resulting in a "drive to the bottom" (Wolf, 2015).

The largest share of apprenticeships in England is in the area of business, administration and law (which together represent a quarter of all apprenticeship starts), followed by retail and commercial enterprise, and then health, public services and care. Apprenticeships rates have not increased to the same extent in sectors that have the highest skills shortages, such as engineering, manufacturing and construction (UKCES, 2013). There have been further concerns that small to medium enterprises (SMEs) are less likely to take apprentices than larger firms.

Until recently, there had been additional concerns about a rise in adult apprentices at the expense of younger people. For example, only 24% of surveyed employers had recruited any 16-18 year old apprentices throughout 2012, while 53% had recruited 19-24 year olds (IFF Research, 2012).

There have been a set of national reforms to boost the reach of apprenticeships to ensure that they reach the young and are undertaken in smaller employers (Mirza-Davies, 2015). These include:

- Each apprenticeship must have a minimum duration of 12 months (the majority last 1 or 2 years).
- Apprenticeships need to include 30 hours of employment a week (including off-site learning) and 280 guided learning hours in the first year, of which 30% are on the job.
- A series of apprenticeship grants have been developed for SMEs (in particular micro-enterprises).
- For those aged under 19, apprenticeships are free and 50% of costs are reimbursed to 19-24 year olds. Adults over the age of 25 are now obliged to take government loans, which must be repaid to the state.

The shift towards non-funded apprenticeships for workers above the age of 25 has had a significant impact on adult apprenticeship numbers in recent years.

Following the 2012 Richard Review, the system for developing and awarding apprenticeships has also been simplified from the former situation of over 250 different apprenticeship frameworks (What Works Centre for Local Economic Growth, 2015). The existing apprenticeship frameworks (which were based on national occupational standards) are being replaced by new employer-designed apprenticeship standards. A set of apprenticeship "trailblazers"– groups of 10 or more industry employers – have been established to develop new occupational standards. By 2017, it is expected that all apprenticeships will be based on such standards. The standards involve a relatively simple description of the skills, knowledge and behaviour required to do a job competently and meet professional requirements where they exist (HM Government, 2015). They are therefore thought to make training less bureaucratic and accessible to small- and medium-sized enterprises (SMEs). 140 trailblazers have developed 169 occupational standards to date (Mirza-Davies, 2015). However the numbers of starts on trailblazer-designed apprenticeships have so far been small – just 300 in 2013-14 (BIS and Skills Funding Agency, 2015). Graduate-level apprenticeships have also been introduced that are designed to offer a formal alternative to a full-time degree.

Future policy commitments include an Apprenticeship Levy that will cover all larger employers by April 2017, bringing the UK system more in line with the systems in Germany, France and Denmark. The apprenticeship levy will represent 0.5% of an employer's total wage expenses, which can then be accessed by the employer to fund apprenticeship training and assessment. A GBP15 000 allowance for employers will mean that the levy will only be paid on employers' pay bills over GBP 3 million. This means that less than 2% of UK employers will pay the levy, which is mainly targeted towards larger employers. A new Institute of Apprenticeships will also be established in April 2017 to carry out quality assurance.

Local variation in apprenticeships: Quality and quantity

The take-up, nature and quality of apprenticeships varies across cities in England (see Box 2.1). It might be expected that cities that have the highest job density should also have the highest take-up of apprenticeships per working-age population, as employers are more willing to take on extra staff. However, Centre for Cities find that this is not reflected in their data. There actually appears to be an inverse relationship between job density and apprenticeship take-ups (Centre for Cities, 2016). Cities in the north of England are broadly more likely to offer apprenticeships than in the south. However several southern cities, such as Reading and Portsmouth have been particularly likely to offer advanced apprenticeships, and apprenticeships in engineering, construction, maths and science. Success rates have also been particularly high in Plymouth and Portsmouth on the south coast (ibid):

Box 2.1. **Local variation across English cities in apprenticeships delivery and take-up**

There are variations across England in terms of a number of dimensions of apprenticeship delivery:

- **Number** – In 2013/14, the top three cities for apprenticeship starts per thousand of working-age population were Sunderland, Barnsley and Middlesbrough. Oxford, Cambridge and London were the bottom three cities.

- **Age group** – Across all cities, 38 per cent of apprenticeships were undertaken by those aged 25 and over, 35 per cent by 19 to 24 years old and 27 per cent by 19 and under. In some cities the apprentices tended to be younger. Those aged 19 and under accounted for 33 per cent of all apprenticeship starts in Barnsley, Derby and Sheffield.

- **Level** – The majority of apprenticeships across all cities were intermediate – across all cities one in three starts were in advanced apprenticeships and just 2% were higher apprenticeships. At 4 per cent, the share of higher apprenticeships was highest in Blackpool, while these apprenticeships were less than 1 per cent of all starts in Swindon.

- **Occupation** – In 40 out of 56 English cities most apprenticeship starts were in business, administration and law (on average 31 per cent of all starts). In Blackburn 43 per cent of all apprentices trained in these subjects. But fewer than one in five apprentices trained in engineering, construction, maths and science. These subject areas were the most common choice of apprentices in Reading (42 per cent), Portsmouth and Chatham (30 per cent), and Plymouth (27 per cent).

- **Success rates** – In 2013/14, across all cities 68 per cent of apprentices successfully completed their training. But chances of completion varied between cities. The success rate was highest in Barnsley (77 per cent) and lowest in Milton Keynes (59 per cent). Success rates were also high in Blackburn (76 per cent).

Source: Centre for Cities (2016).

Figure 2.1 shows variation in apprenticeship starts and job density across English cities.

Figure 2.1. **Apprenticeship starts and job density in cities, 2013**

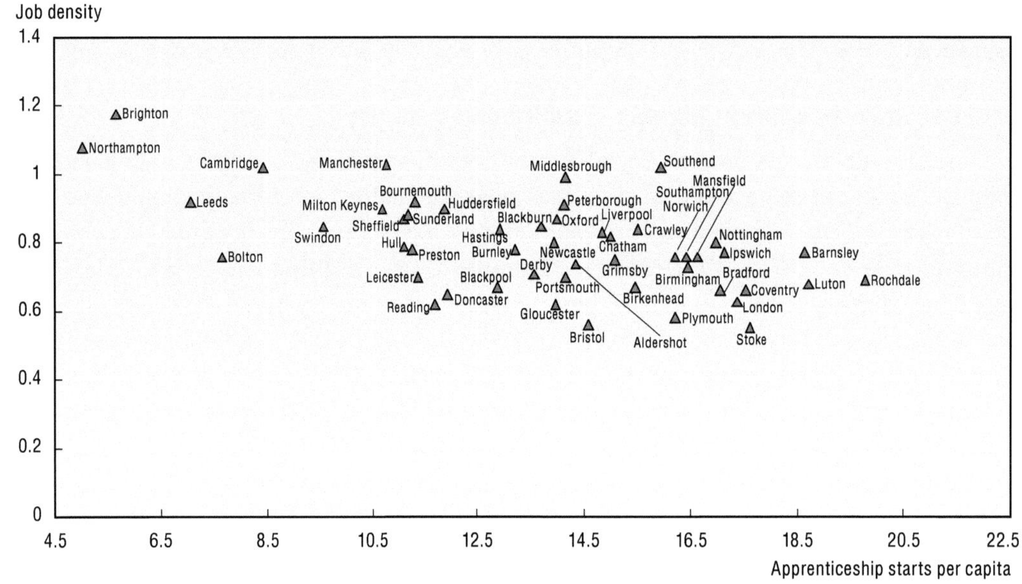

Source: Centre for Cities (2016).

Administrative and governance reform in the United Kingdom

The recent establishment of new local institutional structures (e.g. Combined Authorities) and the devolution of funding and greater responsibility to local areas to support economic growth (e.g. via City Deals/Local Growth Deals) is providing new opportunities for UK cities to lead, shape and implement skills strategies.

As part of the City Deal process, the city of Manchester and Leeds City Region both decided to invest in skills, with a priority focus on apprenticeships. A new Apprenticeship and Skills Hub was set up in Manchester in 2012-13 with a budget of GBP 6 million to increase the number of people taking apprenticeships at level 3 and above, and to support apprenticeships within SMEs. The initial aim was to increase the number of 16-24 year olds starting apprenticeships by 10% a year every year until 2017-18, but this target was later abandoned. The key partners include Manchester New Economy, the National Apprenticeship Service, the Skills Funding Agency, Greater Manchester Chamber of Commerce, Greater Manchester Learning Provider Network, Greater Manchester Colleges Group and the Greater Manchester Local Authorities.

The Leeds City Region received GBP 4.6 million within its City Deal to establish eight new apprenticeship hubs and two apprenticeship training agencies (ATAs), with the objective of creating a "NEET-free" city region (i.e. a region free of young people not in education, employment or training). Key partners include the Leeds City Region Enterprise Partnership (LEP), the National Apprenticeship Service, the Skills Funding Agency, ten local authority areas that make up the Leeds City Region, further education colleges and training providers and others.

This case study will summarise each local apprenticeship hub strategy in detail, assessing the problem that the initiative sought to address, the key objectives, the governance arrangements, the activities, the impacts to date and their strengths and weaknesses.

The apprenticeship initiatives: Activities and governance frameworks

The population of Greater Manchester is 2.73 million people. There are 105 000 businesses which generate 56 billion of gross value added (GVA) annually, accounting for nearly 40% of the GVA of the North West of England. The unemployment rate in Greater Manchester was 6.8% in 2015 – a decrease compared to 2014 but above the UK average. Manchester performs slightly below average when it comes to skills levels, with 31.9% of the working age population having a NVQ level 4 or above (this is equivalent to a bachelor's degree) compared to 36% for the UK as a whole. A further 10.6% of the working age population has no qualifications, as opposed to 8.8% for the UK as a whole (ibid.). Greater Manchester is the third most deprived Local Enterprise Partnership in the country according to the 2015 Indices of Multiple Deprivation (Department for Communities and Local Government, 2015).

The Leeds City Region has a population of 3 million people and a GVA of GBP 60.5 billion, the largest in England after London and the South East. There were 119 000 businesses in the region in 2015. The sub-region is composed on ten local authority districts located in West, North and South Yorkshire. The city of Leeds is an important legal and financial centre. The unemployment rate was 6.2% in 2015. Skills levels are slightly below the UK average, as 30.6% of the population had NVQ 4 and above in 2015, while 9.9% of the population had no qualifications (NOMIS, 2015). The Leeds City Region is ranked 9th in terms of the most deprived Local Enterprise Partnerships in the country (Department for Communities and Local Government, 2015).

The apprenticeship hubs that were established in Manchester and Leeds sought to tackle broadly similar issues. Both city regions aimed to address the low level of engagement of SMEs in apprenticeships and increase the engagement of young people. Leeds had an additional specific objective to reduce the number of NEETs in the city (those young people not engaging in education, employment or training). In Manchester there was a further focus on increasing the number of higher and advanced apprenticeships, and on building training provider capacities to target key employment growth sectors.

The Greater Manchester Apprenticeship Hub

The Greater Manchester Apprenticeships and Skills Hub is managed, co-ordinated and facilitated by New Economy on behalf of Greater Manchester Combined Authority and the Greater Manchester Local Enterprise Partnership.

The process of developing the **Apprenticeship Hub Delivery Plan** highlighted a number of significant and critical issues in previous apprenticeship delivery, including:

- Low volumes of NVQ level 3 and above apprenticeships available;
- Low recruitment into apprenticeships of young unemployed people;
- Limited availability of impartial information, advice and guidance for young people that was restricting demand among learners;
- SMEs were not fully engaged in the skills system, which they often perceive as complex and disjointed.

The main objectives and activities of the Manchester apprenticeships hub can be seen in Figure 2.2:

A primary aim of the Apprenticeships Hub was to maximise demand for apprenticeships from employers, through carrying out marketing exercises, encouraging the public sector

Figure 2.2. **The main aims of the Manchester Apprenticeship Hubs**

Maximise employer take-up of apprenticeships in GM's key sectors by:	Improve information, advice and guidance (IAG) services for young people by:	Develop the capacity of providers, ensuring that supply is matched to demand, by:
•Delivering city-wide collaborative activities to stimulate demand for apprenticeships and increase the number of vacancies and traineeship work placements. •Delivering targeted marketing and communication activities. •Supporting the public sector to provide civic leadership on apprenticeship recruitment in Greater Manchester. •Build and support the capacity of employers to recruit and employ apprentices including those progressing from traineeships.	• Increasing the proportion of 16-18 year olds that participate in learning through apprenticeships and traineeships with a focus on delivering better IAG. • Increasing the number of NEET and unemployed young people starting apprenticeships and traineeships. • Tackling wider barriers to the take-up of apprenticeships and traineeships in Greater Manchester with a specific focus on transport.	•Developing market intelligence to influence provider activity. •Developing provider capacity to deliver apprenticeships at level 3+ in key sectors. •Improving the quality of apprenticeship provision across Greater Manchester. •Building the capacity of the provider base to present an integrated offer to employers and young people across Greater Manchester e.g. workforce development, employer engagement and progressing young people into apprenticeships.

Source: Hutchins (2015).

to provide civic leadership by taking on apprentices, and building capacities among smaller employers to recruit and manage apprentices. At the same time, there has been a campaign to increase the take-up of apprenticeships among young people by investing in careers advice and guidance in schools. A third aim has been to boost the capacity of local training providers to develop higher-level apprenticeships in growth sectors within the Manchester economy.

Key priorities and activities of the Greater Manchester Apprenticeship Hub

To date most of the work of the Apprenticeship Hub has focused on the following elements, namely:

- Providing information, advice and guidance to young people;
- Building capacity among training providers;
- Engaging employers.

Providing information, advice and guidance to young people

The emphasis given in Greater Manchester to the promotion of information, advice and guidance for young people has reflected broader concerns about careers advice in schools and colleges, and the extent to which vocational training and apprenticeships were being promoted. A recent study by the quality standards agency Ofsted found that three quarters of schools in England were not implementing their duty to provide impartial careers advice effectively. The report also found that vocational training and apprenticeships were rarely promoted well, especially in schools providing education up until the age of 18 (Ofsted, 2012). This may be because schools have only recently been given the main responsibility for delivering careers advice, after national funding ceased for the careers advice agency Connexions in 2010. At the same time, stakeholders in Greater Manchester noted that a significant barrier to apprenticeship take-up by 16-18 year olds is a lack of understanding about the labour market and future earnings potential associated with apprenticeships among both young people and their parents. This contrasted with 19-24 year olds, where stakeholders noted greater concerns about apprenticeship quality, the breadth of opportunities available and pay (Cambridge Policy Consultants, 2014).

Each local authority in the Greater Manchester city region received 24 000 pounds in 2013 to deliver a set of initiatives relating to careers information, advice and guidance in schools. The local authorities were asked to develop various activities in order to:

- Increase the proportion of 16-18 year olds in apprenticeships;
- Raise awareness;
- Encourage take-up of work experience, employer engagement activities and pre-apprenticeship offers;
- Target groups that are currently underrepresented, including unemployed young people.

The approach has generally been to embed information about apprenticeships in the context of other forms of career advice. Each local authority was required to produce materials and electronic resources to be used in careers events and tutorials, both locally and across the Greater Manchester area. The collective aim was to engage at least 50 compulsory and post-compulsory secondary schools across Greater Manchester in project activities (at least five per local authority area). The team also aimed to create encourage at least 3 000 young people aged 15-18 to register to the National Apprenticeship Service website (300 per local authority area). New Economy envisaged that the local authorities would work together and pool resources while specialising in different areas.

Examples of projects undertaken include an initiative by the Sharp Project focused on the Creative and Digital Media Sector. This project has involved engaging with five schools through taster sessions and mini projects. An initiative called "Engineering Futures" is also currently working with 47 schools to develop Engineering & Manufacturing Partnership Clusters that bring together young people, parents, schools and employers in order to stimulate demand for apprenticeships – particularly advanced apprenticeships – within engineering and advanced manufacturing. The project has included inviting inspirational speakers and ambassadors from the sector to speak to young people, organising site visits/ tours, and encouraging employers to engage in dialogue with training providers. Following positive feedback from the first phase of activity, this activity has been further expanded within Greater Manchester.

In Rochdale, a pop-up apprenticeship shop was opened to provide guidance on apprenticeships to interested parties and unemployed people referred to them by Job Centre Plus. Particularly successful schemes included the employment of "apprenticeship ambassadors" – for example, after apprenticeship ambassadors in Bury spoke to students about their experiences undertaking apprenticeships, the local area saw a dramatic increase in post-16 sign ups. Professional development courses for teachers and school staff in careers advice were also found to be particularly valuable.

The aim of these youth-focused activities has recently shifted towards targeting the hardest to reach, focusing on specific communities. This includes young people that have been living in care (i.e. those without families who are looked after by the state). This group has been targeted by Rochdale Metropolitan Borough Council through a project called Care to Work (C2W). Some of the approaches in this area have been shared across Greater Manchester.

The activities in each local authority area have been complemented by an apprenticeships marketing campaign across the city. There have also been negotiations with transport planners in the city to create a transport deal for apprentices, so that young people are not dissuaded from applying for apprenticeships due to accessibility and cost issues.

Building capacity among training providers

The second main area of activity in Greater Manchester to date has been building capacity in the training provider sector, particularly in the field of higher and advanced level apprenticeships. New Economy has carried out a series of stakeholder discussions regarding advanced and higher apprenticeship programmes geared towards the Greater Manchester labour market. Some stakeholders considered that young people had been put off apprenticeships by the limited range of opportunities available. For example data from the National Apprenticeships Service (April 2013 to February 2014) showed that almost half of all vacancies (45%) were in Business Administration and Law, while just 14% of total jobs were in this sector. Sectors with a possible under-supply of apprenticeships in comparison to employment include retail, health, public services and care, engineering, construction, education and science and mathematics (Cambridge Policy Consultants, 2014).

The work under this priority has consisted of engaging with 13 different providers on 22 higher apprenticeship frameworks. The focus has been on Greater Manchester priority growth areas, namely those sectors which are the most productive and which have skills gaps. This includes health/social care, advanced manufacturing, digital and creative, finance and professional and retail. More recently there has been a specific bid for providers to develop capacity in delivering science-based apprenticeships, given Manchester's growing scientific sector. Up to 50 000 pounds was available to contribute to 50% of start costs. New Economy has also brought training providers together to discuss progress and share good practice.

Engaging employers

As identified above, a key priority for Greater Manchester has been to engage more small to medium-sized enterprises or SMEs, of which there are 97 000 in Greater Manchester. The learning so far is that this process is partly about managing the expectations among these employers as to what makes somebody "job ready" at the age of 19. The direct engagement of employers has received less attention than the other two objectives thus far, although there have been specific pieces of work to engage the black and minority ethnic (BME) community, and to increase apprenticeships in the voluntary sector (identified as the "hidden sector" for apprenticeships). In the future, Greater Manchester is hoping to create a comprehensive Greater Manchester-wide support framework for employers in order to engage them in new standard setting exercises around apprenticeships, and ensure that employers feed further into apprenticeship curricula.

Governance

The Greater Manchester apprenticeships hub is overseen by a core partnership involving the ten Greater Manchester Local Authorities, the Chamber of Commerce, the Skills Funding Agency, the Learning Provider Network, the Colleges Group and the North West Business Leadership team. These organisations are involved in project commissioning, and steering. The core partners meet every four months, and there are sub-groups that involve business and apprenticeship representatives to focus on specific issues, such as

---

Box 2.2. **A training provider's perspective on engaging employers to deliver apprenticeships**

QA Apprenticeships is a training provider that delivers higher and advanced apprenticeships in information technology to both Greater Manchester and the Leeds City Region. They originally worked with employers to deliver customised training for their own staff and have since branched into apprenticeships. They have found that most employers, including SMEs, would like to host apprenticeships but find it difficult to effectively recruit young apprentices. QA Apprenticeships has therefore focused to a large extent on this aspect of their support to SMEs. They run advertising through social media; establish job boards; advertise positions on specialist websites; run an assessment centre; and develop short lists for employers. As they can do these activities at scale, they feel that it makes more sense for them to do this as opposed to an individual SME. They also provide on-going support for apprentices once in post, particularly over the first three months, which they identify as often the hardest. While QA Apprenticeships have welcomed employer involvement in the design of their programmes, they have found it difficult to fully engage in the "trailblazers" discussions with industry and associated stakeholders because there have been a number of hold ups in implementation.

Source: Interview with QA apprenticeships, 18 December 2015.

---

marketing. New Economy (an agency owned by the 10 local authorities in Greater Manchester) directly manages the Skills and Apprenticeships Hub. A Contract Manager and a Policy Officer are employed to manage the initiative. In addition, four people work within New Economy on strategy and policy around apprenticeships. The actual work of the Hub has been commissioned and tendered out on a project-by-project basis (except for the careers advice in schools where local authorities received direct grants).

Vertically, the hub reports to the Greater Manchester Skills and Employment Partnership which sits under the Local Enterprise Partnership and the Greater Manchester Combined Authority. Figure 2.3 shows the arrangements set in place to support vertical reporting,

Budget and financing

As identified above, Greater Manchester received GBP 6 million to run the apprenticeships hub. The budget for the Greater Manchester Apprenticeships Hub was due to be spent between 2012 and 2015 but spending will now continue until 2017.

The Leeds City Region Apprenticeship Hub

While the aims of the apprenticeships hubs in Greater Manchester and the Leeds City Region have been broadly similar, their management and administration styles differ. The apprenticeship hub in the Leeds city region has been decentralised to the eight local authorities that make up the region.

In Leeds, there has been a particular focus on NEETs (those 16-24 year olds not in education, employment or training). There were 28 000 young people in the NEET category at the start of the initiative three years ago, with the Leeds City Region Enterprise Partnership (LEP) aiming to make Leeds a "NEET-free city region". However, the initial focus of the Hub Programme was the engagement of SMEs, based on the understanding that there was a glut of young people waiting to take-up apprenticeship opportunities but the availability of vacancies was limited.

Figure 2.3. **Reporting arrangements for the Greater Manchester Apprenticeships Hub**

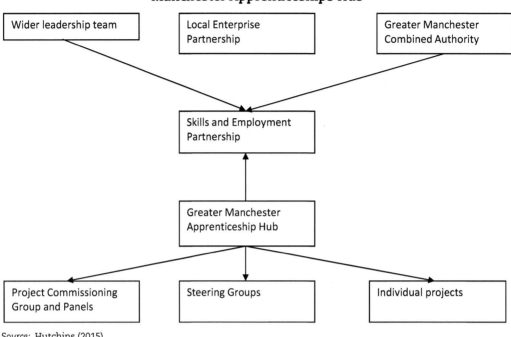

Source: Hutchins (2015).

SMEs make up 98% of local firms and constitute nearly 117 000 businesses. However, the Skills Funding Agency found that only 12% of SMEs were taking on apprentices before the hub activities began. Small businesses noted that they would like to provide apprenticeships but did not know where to turn – they were being marketed to by many different training providers but wanted free independent advice on what to do. This situation was made worse by the fact that training delivery in the city region is relatively fragmented, with over 600 training providers. Local SMEs also found that national advice and guidance on apprenticeships (available through a national phone line and website) was difficult to negotiate and they sought a degree of handholding from an impartial organisation that knew their local context well.

The specific goals of the Leeds City Region apprenticeship hubs were therefore to:

● Create 2 500 new apprenticeships among those aged 16-24;

● Engage 2 142 new businesses.

There is a central apprenticeship programme in the Leeds City Region with eight local apprenticeship hubs in Barnsley, Bradford, Calderdale, Kirklees, Leeds, North Yorkshire (covering Craven, Harrogate and Selby), York and Wakefield. Each local hub developed its own model for delivery depending on local circumstances. The employment and skills officers from the eight local authorities were involved in the bid for City Deal funding from the very beginning – each local authority developed their own business case, which were then combined into the application to the national government. When the City Deal funding was allocated, the eight local authorities were given the initial local lead, although this responsibility was outsourced in some cases, for example to a local college.

The City Deal has also supported the development of two Apprenticeship Training Agencies (or ATAs) in Leeds and Bradford – these are private agencies that help by taking on the administration associated with the employment of apprentices where companies are not able (for example because they could not offer the required length of contract). They act as "proxy-employers" that release the business from day to day employment of the apprentice. The ATAs can be particularly helpful in sectors that are based on more short-term project contracts, such as construction, where apprentices can be moved around according to the project's needs. For example, in Bradford, the ATA has enabled apprentices to be involved in the construction of a new shopping centre. They also help young apprentices with any personal problems that they experience so that the employer does not need to be engaged with this. The aim is for the ATAs to be commercially sustainable by 2016 and thereafter charge a management fee to employers.

Activities

Each local hub in the Leeds City Region has been free to develop its own set of activities according to local priorities and in line with local business support infrastructure. All hubs work towards the combined aims of the partnership programme and agreement of increasing young people's uptake of apprenticeships and the involvement of SMEs. Indeed although there was a broad aim for the programme to support the region's aspiration to be "NEET-free", NEET targets were not quantitatively specified to the local authorities. However, programme targets were based on and allocated to locations based on the number of NEETs as of 2012.

The local authorities have managed their hubs in various different ways. For example, Barnsley local authority outsourced their hub activities to the local college where an independent company was set up to deliver the programme. It started by focusing purely on employer engagement, cold calling employers, doing seasonal campaigns, and inviting referrals from the local development agency and Job Centre. They particularly targeted employers within the LEP priority sectors, while also developing innovative "seasonal" campaigns aimed at industries that are likely to recruit at certain times of year ahead of business peaks – for instance travel agents and estate agents in the months before New Year, and the hospitality industry before Christmas. After an initial period, the local apprenticeships hub realised that the pool of young people available to do apprentices was shrinking. They then broadened their focus, and started to better connect the hub to the wide range of Council services and agencies that connect with young people, such as schools and careers information, advice and guidance (IAG). Barnsley performed particularly well in comparison to other English cities in both apprenticeship starts and completions in 2013-14 (Centre for Cities, 2016), while starting from a relatively high base.

Calderdale local authority matched the grant from the Apprenticeship Hub with additional local funds to create a larger scale project with more intensive employer engagement. Their aim was to create 4 040 apprenticeships by 2020. The title of their campaign is "Grow your own future". They have employed three employer engagement officers, worked with employers proactively on job design, delivered pre-apprenticeship work placements to help young people to identify the most appropriate employer and role for them, made monthly visits to apprentice work places, and established broader education-business partnerships in schools. They offer bursaries to apprentices who not able to access other grants. They have recruited apprenticeship ambassadors to talk to young people in schools so that they have a better understanding of the value of apprenticeships. The hub has also focused on specific local sectors – manufacturing, creative, digital industries – and prioritised quality apprenticeships. The local authority has also insisted that apprentices were paid at least the standard minimum wage for all employers for their work (the minimum wage for apprentices is usually lower).

The other local authorities have also developed approaches to delivery that have been adapted to their local conditions. In the city of Leeds, there has been a strong focus on career progression and developing apprenticeships as "pathways of choice". In Wakefield, there has been a focus on longer-term job prospects – it was decided not to work with one particular local sector because they were consistently not retaining apprentices as employees after the apprenticeship training was over. In Bradford, it was decided to move from a focus on apprenticeship starts to apprenticeship completions, due to concerns over the number of people not finishing their apprenticeships.

Over time, across the programme, there has been a greater focus on engaging young people into apprenticeships, as opposed to carrying out employer engagement. This was due to the success of engaging businesses which created a wealth of vacancies. There has been a simultaneous fall in the pool of young people seeking apprentices due to reductions in youth unemployment and the new Raising Participation Age [RPA] requirement that young people remain in education until the age of 18 (which many have interpreted as remaining in school education). Once the hubs had helped SMEs to prepare for taking on an apprenticeship, there was a long lag time before the vacancy could be matched with somebody that was "apprenticeship ready". As part of activities to reach the remaining unemployed youth, the apprenticeship hub representatives regularly go into Jobcentre Plus team meetings to talk about the benefits of apprenticeships and explain further how they work. Young people are also being targeted by another city region scheme called Headstart, which is operated by each local authority with funding that the LEP secured from government. The programme has a budget of GBP 4.6 million to help 18-24 year olds into work, and has helped over 1 000 young people to date.

Unlike in Greater Manchester, the Leeds City Region has not featured any direct work to build capacities among local providers, or to help them to focus on higher or advanced apprenticeships. However, each Hub has strong relationships with providers who are part of the "partnership delivery model" at the local level as the providers play a key role in providing apprenticeship learning opportunities through their core funding.

However, like in Greater Manchester, there has been a focus on transport and accessibility in the Leeds city region, to make sure that young apprenticeships could reach their work place easily and economically. The apprenticeship hub has worked with the West Yorkshire Combined Authority, transport operators and political leaders to ensure that apprentices are treated like all young people attending more academic strands of education, and are able to access transport half price. There have also been smaller pilots to give apprentices a free "metro card" for free transport for apprenticeships in their first month and a free bike campaign to give apprentices easier and healthier access options to their place of employment. At the same time, the links with the Combined Authority has enabled promotional advertising about the apprenticeship hub to be disseminated as part of real time travel information at bus stops throughout the city region and posters embedded into bus timetables at bus stops and bus stations around West Yorkshire.

Governance

As identified above, the Leeds City Region has established a rather different way of managing its apprenticeship hub in comparison to Greater Manchester. The central apprenticeships hub has decentralised control over the activities of the eight local hubs to the individual local authorities. However, all the hubs are managed within the same overall contract to build transparency and achieve common goals. The overall programme outputs were set broadly to enable flexibility for the individual local authorities to allow complementarity to local business support infrastructures. The local authorities have discretion regarding the targeting of the programmes within the broad quantitative targets to raise numbers of young people taking apprenticeships and apprenticeship placement in SMEs. However, as part of the City Deal funding received from the Skills Funding Agency is results-based, this was felt to create a fairly rigorous performance culture.

The central hub carries out a number of co-ordination activities. Every six weeks there are network meetings of all the hubs. These function both as places for sharing best practices and "self-help groups" to report on overall performance. There are also six weekly one to one meetings between the hub manager and each local hub. Some specific hub activities are also taken forward centrally such as engaging with the National Health Service to establish apprenticeships in the health care sector. Marketing and communication have also been developed centrally under a central communications contract, with a common website that contains promotional material including films featuring success stories. However local hubs have also been encouraged to take forward different marketing campaigns and to develop their own form of branding to complement other local business targeted marketing activities.

In terms of the vertical management of the central hub itself, the Apprenticeship Hub Manager reports to the Head of Skills and Enterprise of the Leeds City Region Enterprise Partnership. Performance on the programme is monitored by and reported to the LEP's Employment and Skills Panel and its associated advisory groups and then upwards to the LEP Board. The manager is responsible for ensuring that the initiative remains aligned to the goals of the LEP and its Skills Plan.

Budget and financing

As in Greater Manchester, the apprenticeship hub activities in the Leeds city region are funded by the Department of Business, Innovation and Skills (BIS) via the Skills Funding Agency. Leeds City Council was identified as the central accountable body. The funding was then allocated down to the eight local hubs according to their numbers of NEETs (young people not in education, training or employment). Payments to the LEP were based on results.

Other similar schemes

In both Greater Manchester and the Leeds City Region, the apprenticeship hubs work alongside a number of related national programmes including:

- **Traineeships:** courses of up to 6 months that can prepare people for taking an apprenticeship. The core content of Traineeships is work preparation training, English and Maths and a work experience placement;

- A Jobcentre Plus sector-based **Work Academy** which offers young people preparatory work trials that can help them to prepare for apprenticeships;

- The **Apprenticeship Grant to Employers (AGE):** nationally this scheme is aimed at enterprises of 50 people or less with the grant covering the first five apprenticeships that an enterprise might offer. However, through devolution of an AGE allocation both the

Leeds City Region and Greater Manchester have designed grant schemes that support the economic priorities of each locality including adapting eligibility criteria to support companies with up to 250 employees, while also prioritising advanced/higher apprenticeships, and those apprenticeships showing progression.

● The **Employer Ownership** pilot – for example the Leeds City Region has won a GBP 17.5 million grant associated with the Employer Ownership pilot in the UK to set up a skills fund for SMEs from 2015-16.

Impacts of the Apprenticeship Hub initiatives

Both Leeds City Region and Greater Manchester are confident that they are on track to meet their overall aims and objectives for the apprenticeships hubs. However both city regions have had to adjust their expectations in terms of their quantitative impacts on apprenticeship numbers in the context of a plateau of apprenticeships in the UK as a whole – particularly for adult apprenticeships (see Figures 2.4 and 2.5). For example in Greater Manchester, the Hub has not reached its target of increasing the number of apprenticeships by 10% per year. This has been blamed in part on a nationwide drop in the number of adults taking apprenticeships following funding changes.

Figure 2.4. **Number of people participating in apprenticeship programmes since 2009**

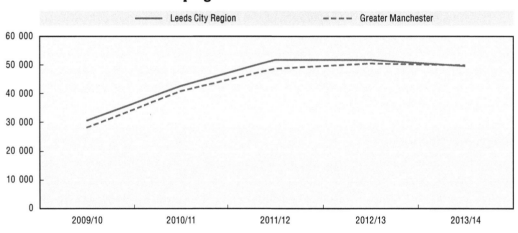

Source: Skills Funding Agency (2014).

Greater Manchester

As identified above, most of the work in Greater Manchester has so far has focused on their Objectives 2 and 3 – recruiting more young people to undertake apprenticeships through better information, advice and guidance; and building the capacities of training providers to deliver higher level and advance apprenticeships in key employment growth areas. The outcomes of the work to support Information Advice and Guidance in Manchester have exceeded expectations in terms of apprenticeship registrations, although there is recognition that this does not always translate into new apprenticeship starts. In addition, evaluators have found evidence to suggest that 16-18 year old starts have begun to improve from 2011-12 (Cambridge Policy Consultants, 2014).

In terms of the more specific impacts of the two programmes, the results appear relatively positive. Over time, it has been understood that it is not just important to spread information

Figure 2.5. **Numbers of people participating in apprenticeship programmes in 2009/10 and 2013/14 by Leeds local authority area**

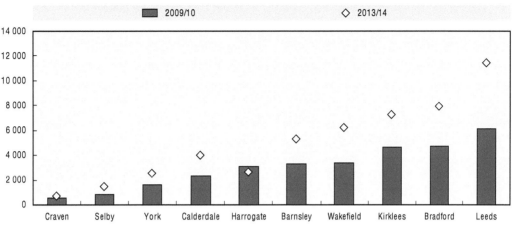

Source: Skills Funding Agency (2014).

on apprenticeships but also to reassure young people that apprenticeships are a path to quality employment with opportunities for progression. The Apprenticeship Hub is now aiming to create a "parity of esteem" between apprenticeships and more academic forms of training, while also setting out the different opportunities for apprenticeships more clearly. A report on apprenticeship progression in Greater Manchester found that the ability to progress up an apprenticeship level varied significantly by sector because of the varying supply of higher-level provision in each sector to facilitate progression. Progression was also found likely to be higher in sectors where there was professional body representation, sector regulation and the need to undertake higher levels of study to provide a license to practice (Regeneris Consulting, 2015). The recent development of "Apprenticeship degrees" (now being delivered by Manchester Metropolitan University) was found to be particularly helpful in illustrating the opportunities and possibilities for progression. In addition, it was found easier to market apprenticeships to young people where wages for apprentices were higher. For example progression through apprenticeships in the financial sector works well because the pay is relatively good.

An evaluation of work in Manchester to boost capacities among training providers to deliver higher-level apprenticeships in skills shortage areas has also been relatively positive. However it was felt that the funding intervention had brought forward course delivery that may have occurred anyway. It was also identified that training providers had found it difficult to bring in new employers, and had often worked to encourage their existing employer base to sign up to the new apprenticeships. Further, the degree of employer engagement in the actual design of apprenticeships has been limited to choosing modules and planning work-based training late in the apprenticeship development process. In terms of the chosen sectors, introducing higher apprenticeships in hospitality management and finance has been much more successful than in retail. In the future, the hub would like to do more to professionalise growing sectors such as retail and to move towards assuring quality in apprenticeships, for example by having a quality standard and ensuring that providers focus further on progression pathways.

Leeds

In terms of the original commitments made within the City Deal, the Leeds City Region Apprenticeship Hub is expecting to reach its initial goal of 2 500 new apprenticeships among

16-24 year olds by March 2016. In addition, the hubs have already exceeded their target of engaging 2 142 businesses. In terms of broader impacts, the number of NEETs in the Leeds City Region has fallen from 28 000 to 10 000 – however this has to be placed in the context of falling youth unemployment across the country. The overall conclusion of the mid-term evaluation of the programme was that, "it has made a major impact in a short period of time".

In the Leeds City Region, the balance between the two specific goals of the apprenticeship hub has shifted over time. To begin with the principal focus of the programme was to target SMEs to ensure that young people could get apprenticeship placements. Over time, it was noted that SMEs were receptive and that the main challenge was to engage young people who were "apprenticeship ready". Once the hubs had helped SMEs to prepare to take on an apprenticeship, there was a long lag time before the vacancy could be matched with somebody that was "apprenticeship ready". The apprenticeship hubs therefore 'turned the programme on its head' halfway through to focus more on encouraging young people to take-up apprenticeships.

Strengths of the Apprenticeship Hub initiatives

In both Greater Manchester and the Leeds City Region, there has been a certain amount of evolution in the aims and mechanisms of the apprenticeship hub activities, and the flexible delivery arrangements in both local areas has helped in this process. Flexibility in programme delivery allowed the objectives, mechanisms and targets to be adjusted along the way. For example, as the number of apprenticeship vacancies for young people were increased in Leeds City Region, the Apprenticeship Hub website shifted from principally targeting SMEs towards engaging young people. This coincides with the recognition that those still out of work or training and those seeking a change in learning direction were proving harder to reach. A good relationship with the Skills Funding Agency grant holder in each city region enabled some negotiation on funding and targets. In a similar fashion (and outside these particular city deals), flexibility has also been built into the National Apprenticeship Grant to Employers (see above), which has enabled both Leeds City Region and Greater Manchester to adjust the target group to larger SMEs while also prioritising local growth sectors and apprenticeships offering progression.

The decentralised approach taken in the Leeds City Region was also found to have benefitted from flexible performance management. In reality, some local authorities have over-performed while others underperformed. The flexibility in the management processes has allowed good performance to compensate for the poorer performance elsewhere. At the same time, it was felt that the national government's insistence that some payment should be on the basis of results had created a strong performance-orientated culture.

Local authorities were key players in the delivery of the apprenticeships hubs in both city regions. In the UK, local authorities generally have a strong overview of local economic development and tend to be responsible for promoting growth while also ensuring local social inclusion. In addition, in both cases, the local authorities were closely linked to the Local Enterprise Partnership (LEP) so that the initiative could be partially steered employers with a focus on broader regional strategic aims. In Greater Manchester it was felt that this vertical relationship could have been stronger – more support from the LEP, for example, could have raised the profile of the initiative.

Unlike the Leeds City Region, Greater Manchester has developed a model which is largely based on tendering out projects, and while the commissioning process was sometimes challenging to manage, New Economy felt that it helped the hub to become embedded within mainstream provision as opposed to being managed separately or in parallel to other agencies and services.

In terms of other strengths, the Apprenticeship Training Agencies (ATAs) in the Leeds city region have been seen as particularly useful by national government in facilitating apprenticeships for those employers that could not take on the employment responsibilities associated with this training. The view locally is that such agencies have a role to play in supporting the apprenticeship agenda and are particularly suitable where it is difficult for a business to guarantee longer-term employment for the apprentice due to seasonal demand. However, there is a limit to the degree that employers are willing to pay for externalising apprenticeship management, which could have an impact on the commercial opportunity for ATAs.

Weaknesses of the Apprenticeship Hub initiatives

Both Greater Manchester and the Leeds City Region have struggled somewhat to bring more young people into apprenticeships in their region, partly because of a difficulty in establishing a 'parity of esteem' between apprenticeships and other more academic learning routes. This is to some extent outside their control as apprenticeships are defined nationally and this is a broader national issue. However, even if this were outside the direct scope of the city deal programmes, more could have been done in both city regions to raise the quality and relevance of apprenticeships and ensure that they lead to further learning and good employment prospects.

In the Leeds City Region, it was felt that encouraging employers to pay above the apprenticeship minimum wage, from the outset or from progression points such as at three months, had helped to attract more and stronger candidates to apply for apprenticeships and to deliver better results for businesses. It was found by evaluators that such actions had helped to convince both pupils and parents of the merits of apprenticeships. These actions could thus be further expanded (Les Newby Associates, 2015).

Both Greater Manchester and the Leeds City Region have also had to deliver their programmes in a changing national context for apprenticeships. In addition to changing the funding structure for adult apprenticeships, the UK Government has also recently raised the participation age so that young people are required to stay in education until the age of 18. Many schools have used this as a lever to encourage young people to stay in their own institution. This has resulted in some difficulties for the Apprenticeship Hubs in the Leeds City Region in engaging with certain schools, as they were seen to be in competition for students.

In both Greater Manchester and the Leeds City Region, the City Deal programme came a few years after a widespread collapse of careers education and guidance at local level in the UK. Schools now have responsibility for providing careers education through independent advisors but this has resulted in fragmented and inconsistent provision. In both regions, the City Deal initiatives have been "picking up the pieces" to deliver effective careers advice, thereby filling a gap in national policy provision. This may explain the significant emphasis on providing information, advice and guidance for young people, as opposed to investing in apprenticeships themselves. While this was obviously a necessary activity (and formed part of the initial city deal contracts), it is not necessarily the best use of apprenticeship-specific funding streams.

In the Leeds City Region, it was felt that the plethora of different national initiatives launched to support young people and increase apprenticeships had not helped to boost the engagement of employers. As different national initiatives that share target groups and outcomes were launched with different timelines, it was difficult to design and co-ordinate a fully integrated delivery infrastructure at the local level.

In both the Greater Manchester and the Leeds City Regions, it was felt that the time that was needed to build SMEs and secondary school engagement should not be underestimated. Turning around perceptions of the value of apprenticeships and increasing "parity of esteem" was identified as a long-term task. Building relationships with training providers had also required some perseverance in the Leeds City Region, as the providers initially saw the hubs as competitors as opposed to a potential supporter and partner.

Further, the Leeds City Region Enterprise Partnership felt that they did not have enough power to properly influence training providers to focus on skills shortage areas such as engineering, software development and computer engineering. In 2009-2010, the city region Employment and Skills board had been on the cusp of being awarded statutory powers to manage local skills policy, before these plans were abandoned by the then new Coalition government in favour of a policy of local management by "persuasion". In reality, the City Region has found that colleges and training providers were more likely to be persuaded by demand from individual learners than the strategic recommendations of the LEP. Training providers are often particularly reluctant to develop and provide capital-intensive courses, such as engineering, without the necessary student demand. This was also a driver for the focus on influencing careers advice and IAG in schools, which was hoped to increase interest in the value of studying particular subjects of relevance to the broader city region economy, and thereby have a knock on impact on training providers. Upon review, Manchester's decision to use its funds to tender out support for capacity building in particular sectors of importance to the local economy could also have worked well in Leeds if they had been given similar funding.

The UK government is currently devolving new powers to the local level to shape provision under "area based reviews". The 16+ education area reviews will enable city regions to examine at their current FE and sixth form college base to determine the relationship with local skills needs and help to reshape delivery where necessary.

In both city regions, the work with employers focused on persuading and enabling employers to take on apprentices and instead of working with employers to design curricula. The administration felt that SMEs were more concerned about day-to-day issues and less invested in strategic engagement in training design. This may explain the limited progress made so far by the national Trailblazer initiative that enables groups of employers to get together and design new apprenticeship standards. In the Leeds region, the Trailblazer initiative is being facilitated by colleges instead of employers and has not yet resulted in substantive change.

There were also a number of lessons learnt in terms of the optimal governance arrangements for apprenticeship services. The Apprenticeships Hub in Greater Manchester, for example, regretted having initially started with a piecemeal approach instead of funding larger projects. However they felt that this was part of their growth and development process, and are now moving onto projects with higher critical mass.

The partnership between stakeholders in Manchester was felt to have worked well – while it has not always been possible to get the most senior level of management to meetings, everyone who is involved is very committed. However it was felt that this partnership could function sometimes as a relatively "closed network" of "usual suspects". Care had to be taken to separate roles (i.e. so the same organisation could both bid for projects, while at different points helping to advise during the tendering process). It was also felt that there had not been enough employer engagement in the operation of the hub. For future initiatives, it may be beneficial to allow employers to play a greater role within the steering partnership.

Conclusions: Transferable lessons and considerations for the successful adoption of similar initiatives in other OECD countries

This case study to some extent underlines the benefits of working locally to promote apprenticeships, particularly among small to medium-sized enterprises. The Greater Manchester hub manager notes that working at the local level can maximise the use of local partners while understanding local labour market needs. New Economy's actions in building capacities among training providers to deliver more apprenticeships in key local growth sectors is a good example of how to build on this potential. Further, working at the local level can bring the possibility of increasing resources at the local level to achieve critical mass (as can be seen in the case of Calderdale) and exploring synergies with other local and regional strategies. As an example, Greater Manchester has recently received more responsibility for strategically managing the health and care sectors and carrying out new commissioning. This has linked in well with campaigns to increase the number of apprenticeships in these sectors, which could enhance the role of the public sector as a 'civic leader' to then inspire other employers. In addition, as identified above, both apprenticeship hubs have been working to influence transport provision in order to reduce transport costs and increase accessibility for apprentices.

In the Leeds City Region, the value of delivering local support and activity to promote apprenticeships was also strongly underlined. In particular, it was felt that the decentralisation to local hubs had played an important part in the success of the initiative because the local authorities were able to integrate the funding into broader business support provisions, while harmonising the new programme with other local initiatives while contributing to the overall aspirations, ambitions and priorities of the LEP. At the same time, it was felt that SMEs and other employers strongly valued receiving advice from a local independent body who understood their locality. Being concretely able to "get hold of someone" as opposed to negotiating a national website was perceived as important.

At the same time, the case study highlights the challenges of working locally to promote the provision of essentially a national policy objective (boosting apprenticeships) when the 'rules of the game' keep shifting, such as changing funding arrangements and the arrival of new and sometimes competing programmes.

While the aims of the hubs are broadly similar, the governance arrangements have been quite different. Both models seem to have their advantages. Greater Manchester benefitted from its centralised tendering scheme to steer training to growing sectors, while in the Leeds City Region decentralising the activities to eight local hubs created a fertile field of experimentation which has led to some lessons (eg the need to focus on quality placements) which are now being mainstreamed to broader city region.

Both apprentice hubs have ultimately come to focus on two key issues in their work:

1. Improving careers advice so that apprenticeships were seen as a real option (to raise "parity of esteem");

2. Simultaneously ensuring that apprenticeships were indeed a high quality vocational training option with progression opportunities.

While these issues are perhaps particularly relevant to the current UK economy, and the nature of apprenticeships in this country, such aims and objectives may well be relevant elsewhere. In particular, it seems that employer engagement is less of a problem where there is a pool of willing and good quality candidates available to carry out apprenticeships. It also seems to have been particularly valuable to SMEs in both regions to have training providers or other agencies such as the ATAs who are willing to help with recruitment while also managing some of the day-to-day problems experienced by apprentices.

More broadly, the quality of apprenticeships, the salaries available and the possibilities for progression are particularly important in building a 'parity of esteem' for this vocational route. Centre for Cities (2016) argue that there is considerable variation in the quality of apprenticeship provision across English cities, and this may also be a problem in other countries. Because of this, an emphasis on quality, progression and the local relevance of apprenticeship sectors may be just as important as trying to boost apprenticeship numbers at the local level. In the UK, the current plethora of lower quality apprenticeships may be reduced by the new Institute of Apprenticeships to be developed in 2017. Indeed, there is evidence from elsewhere in the OECD that the decentralisation of vocational training provision should be accompanied by a strong national quality assurance framework. In Sweden, for example, the Higher Vocational Education (*Yrkeshögskolan*), system is highly decentralised and is based on groups of employers that commission and design training courses (OECD, 2015), which are then quality approved and monitored at the national level.

Finally, in terms of learning for other OECD cities and regions the following points would seem to be key:

- Taking a decentralised approach to apprenticeships programmes can be effective, particularly in bringing on board SMEs. It takes time to build employer engagement in apprenticeships and SMEs may in particular require some "handholding" which can be effectively achieved at the local level;

- There is little point in building employer engagement without a simultaneous investment in increasing the pools of "apprenticeship-ready" young people;

- Attracting new young people into apprenticeships requires more than just effective marketing campaigns – it is also important to convince people that apprenticeships are a quality training offer, with good salary prospects and promotion possibilities. This may require a greater focus on reforming apprenticeships themselves;

- It is important to invest in good quality careers guidance locally for young people so that they understand how apprenticeships can lead to quality careers in local growth sectors;

- It is useful to build flexibility into the management of vocational training and employer engagement projects so that they can be adapted to local employment growth sectors, while being agile in the face of a shifting economic and policy context;

- There is a need for central government to be co-ordinated in terms of the tendering out of different programmes and policies, while avoiding "drip by drip" policy reforms that can create a confusing policy landscape at the local level and reduce the possibilities for sensible long term planning.

References

BIS and Skills Funding Agency (2015), "Further education and skills: Statistical first release – learner participation, outcomes and level of highest qualification held", London, United Kingdom.

Cambridge Policy Consultants (2014), "Evaluation of Greater Manchester Apprenticeships Hub: Phase 1", Careers Education, Information, Advice and Guidance Newton, Cambridge.

CEDEFOP (2014), "United Kingdom: VET in Europe country report", *Refernet*.

Centre For Cities (2016), "Briefing: Apprenticeships in cities", London.

Department For Communiites And Local Government (2015), "The English Indices of Deprivation", *Statistical Release*, London.

HM Government (2015), "The future of apprenticeships in England: Guidance for trailblazers – from standards to starts", *BIS Guidance*, London, UK.

HM Treasury (2015), "Fixing the foundations: Creating a more prosperous nation", *White Paper*, London, UK.

Hutchins, N. (2015), "Greater Manchester Apprenticeships Hub – the Story So Far: Powerpoint Presentation", New Economy.

IFF Research (2012), "Employer Perspectives Survey 2012", *Evidence Report 64*, London: UKCES.

Les Newby Associates (2015), "Research and Reporting on the City Deal Apprenticeship Programme. Leeds: Leeds City Region Enterprise Partnership", *www.the-lep.com/LEP/media/New/Research%20and %20publications/LEP-City-Deal-Apprenticeship-Programme.pdf*.

Mirza-Davies, J. (2015), "Apprenticeships Policy, England", in: LIBRARY, H.O.C. (ed.) *Briefing Paper*.

NOMIS (2015), "Labour Market Profile: Leeds City Region", *Official Labour Market Statistics*, London: Nomis.

OECD (2016), *Youth unemployment rate (indicator)*, *http://dx.doi.org/10.1787/c3634df7-en* (accessed on 16 March 2016).

OECD (2015), *Employment and skills strategies in England, United Kingdom*, OECD Publishing, Paris.

OFSTED (2012), "Going in the right direction? Career guidance in schools from September 2012", Manchester: Office for Standards in Education, Children's Services and Skills.

Regeneris Consulting (2015), "Apprenticeship Progression in Greater Manchester", Manchester: New Economy.

UKCES (2013), *OECD Review: Skills Beyond School Background Report for England*, London, UK: UKCES.

UK Government (2014), "Register of Training Organisations", *www.gov.uk/government/publications/ register-of-training-organisations*.

What Works Centre For Local Economic Growth (2015), "Evidence Review 8: Apprenticeships", London: London School of Economics, Centre for Cities and Arup.

Wolf, A. (2015), "Fixing a broken training system: the case for an apprenticeship levy", UK: Social Market Foundation.

Chapter 3

Apprenticeships in a hyper-rural setting in Nordland, Norway

This chapter assesses the apprenticeship services available to young people in the hyper-rural Norwegian county of Nordland. Challenges associated with the county's geography and density are also analysed with respect to their impacts on youth participation in employment and vocational education. Two case studies of a local employer and vocational education provider are described as a lens for the broader implementation of the Norwegian apprenticeship system.

Key findings

- Nordland is a hyper-rural Norwegian county that features a diversified economy with active agricultural, mining, tourism and research industries. Many of the county's enterprises employ fewer than ten people and experience seasonal or variable demand.

- Nordland faces specific challenges to developing, attracting and retaining skilled labour, including aspiring apprentices. These include Nordland's particular geographical and logistical constraints associated with its hyper-rural geography, suggesting a need for flexibility in programme design and implementation to address local challenges.

- Despite current skills shortages and projected increases in the demand for skills in the county, there is also a consistent number of aspiring apprentices who are unable to find suitable training places. This can also exacerbate drop-out from vocational pathways in upper secondary education. This suggests a need to engage employers in local apprenticeship delivery to better align vocational course offerings to meet market demand.

Introduction

Norway is a unitary state that is divided into nineteen first-level administrative counties (*fylker*). The counties are administrated through directly elected county assemblies who elect the County Governor. Additionally, the King and government are represented in every county by a *fylkesmann*, who effectively acts as a Governor. As such, the Government is directly represented at a local level through the County Governors' offices. The counties are then sub-divided into 430 second-level municipalities (*kommuner*), which in turn are administrated by directly elected municipal council, headed by a mayor and a small executive cabinet.

Norway has a total area of 385 252 square kilometres (148 747 sq mi) and a population of 5 165 800 people (2015). The country shares a long eastern border with Sweden (1 619 km long). Norway is also bordered by Finland and Russia to the north-east, and the Skagerrak Strait to the south, with Denmark on the other side. Norway has an extensive coastline, facing the North Atlantic Ocean and the Barents Sea.

Nordland is the second largest of Norway's 19 administrative counties. It is divided into 43 municipalities and covers an area of 38 460 km². The county has many islands and features twelve airports, while railway systems only reach half of the county. It is located in the north of Norway, and has around 241 000 citizens. Bodø, located just north of the Arctic Circle, is the largest urban area and city in Nordland county, and the second-largest in North Norway. Bodø is the regional capital city, with 50 000 inhabitants. The county is divided into traditional districts, including Helgeland in the south (south of the Arctic Circle), Salten in the centre, and Ofoten in the northeast. The archipelagoes of Lofoten and Vesterålen lie in the northwest. Nordland extends about 500 km from Nord-Trøndelag to Troms and is one of the least polluted areas of Europe.

Policy context

Nordland is one of Norway's leading exporting counties with a small number of key industries, notably fisheries and offshore petroleum. Nordland is well known for codfish fishing and salmon farming. Its main export markets are Germany, Scandinavia, Britain, Netherlands, Italy, Spain, France, Russia and Japan.

Coastal Nordland has many small businesses but few larger ones, with only 115 companies employing over 100 workers. The rate of unemployment (at the end of October 2015) was at 2.7%, and was not rising at the same rate as elsewhere in Norway. As well as the unemployed there are others that are not available for work or working less than they wish. This includes:

- Work assessment allowance   7 700
- Sickness benefits   7 500
- Unemployed   3 500
- Partially vacant   1 700
- Jobseekers at measures   800

Figure 3.1 sets out the sectors of employment in Nordland. Tourism is important, mainly in the summer season, although there are some winter visitors for skiing or Northern Lights trips. Tourists are attracted by the scenic coast, especially Lofoten, which is also visited by many cruise ships in the summer, while the rest of the county is often ignored by tourists. Mountain hiking is popular among natives and some tourists. Whale watching attracts tourists to Andøy and the Tysfjord /Lødingen/Svolvær area, and fishing is also popular along the coast and in the rivers.

Figure 3.1. **Employed persons in Nordland in Quarter 4, 2014 by industry**

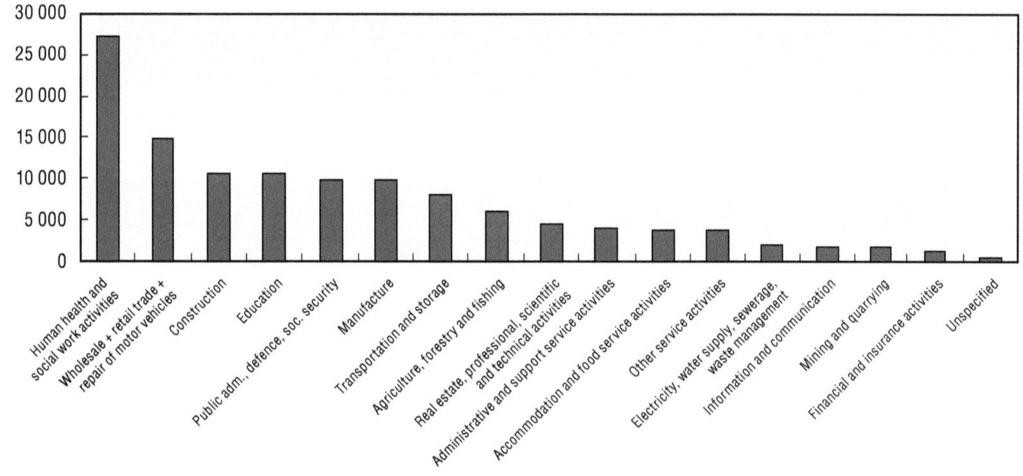

Source: Statistics Norway (2014).

Norway has significant numbers of hydro-electric plants and Nordland has the largest hydroelectric potential among Norway's counties. There are many dams to provide hydroelectric power to the power-intensive factories in the region and across Norway.

Farming is important to the regional economy and consists mainly of dairy farming and livestock such as sheep and domesticated reindeer, which graze the inland highlands. There is also some forestry, particularly in the Helgeland district, and further north.

There was once a long history of mining but this has been discontinued for economic reasons. There are several limestone, marble, and dolomite quarries in Vefsn, Fauske, Sørfold and Ballangen. The port of Narvik has a direct rail connection to the well-known and profitable Kiruna-Gällivare iron-ore fields in Sweden.

Nordland has an increasingly diverse economy, with fledgling research and development in aerospace and space exploration at the Andøya Rocket Range, which primarily is known for its satellite launches. Nordland has been traditionally important for NATO, and the Royal Norwegian Air Force has stationed two squadrons of F-16 fighters at Bodø Airport and all of its P-3 Orion maritime surveillance aircraft at Andøya Air Station. The decommissioning of military bases has led to a regional shift towards a more knowledge-based economy. Bodø Airport is the busiest airport, and a hub for many smaller airports in Nordland.

Problems associated with education and apprenticeship in rural areas

Young people living in rural areas face a number of uniquely rural barriers, particularly concerning access to transport, careers advice, employment and training support, and youth services.

Most apprenticeship positions can be found in larger companies, which tend to be concentrated in urban areas. It can therefore be difficult for young people in rural areas to find suitable places, and they are often forced to follow more "academic" educational routes. However, traditional academic pathways may not suit everyone and does not always prepare young people for the world of work. A lack of apprenticeship opportunities locally could also limit the broader rural agenda and economy, which may force people to move to urban areas for their careers. Rural areas also tend to have more seasonal employment, which can affect the ability of employers to provide continuous apprenticeships.

There are a number of elements that affect access to education, employment and training for young people in rural areas. These are discussed briefly below as they impact the availability of apprenticeships. Despite improved communications and transport technology, the population of Nordland has decreased slightly since 1990, as many young people have moved to larger cities in Norway. Bodø is the only municipality in the county that has experienced a significant growth in population. Between the period between 2006 and 2016, Nordland had the lowest annual average rate of growth in population among all Norwegian counties.

Transport

Young people in rural areas are more dependent on public transport to access education and training than their urban counterparts. However, the cost and low availability of public transport in rural areas can be a significant challenge for young people, and can act as a barrier to their educational choices and overall progress into employment. In Nordland, the local authority provides subsidised transportation to combat this.

The impracticality of young people commuting from the most rural areas and from the islands to school is addressed through housing schemes with local families. A number of youth and education centres also hold regular events (almost every night in Bodø) to meet the needs of the school-aged children.

Employers in rural areas often believe that working with apprentices is unappealing to training providers because of the distances and consequent costs. Travel is a particular challenge for young people who attempt to access apprenticeships (Commission for Rural Communities, 2012).

Careers advice and guidance

The provision and availability of good quality, independent careers advice for young people while in compulsory and post-secondary education or training is crucial to enable them to make sound choices about their futures. Careers advice providers are less likely to engage more isolated areas of the country because economies of scale are more difficult to achieve. There are inevitable concerns that advisers will have insufficient knowledge of local economies, local labour markets and the range of employment, education and training opportunities available within rural areas. Some advice is available online but some young people living in rural areas have limited access to broadband.

There are several measures that aim to enhance the attractiveness and career guidance in VET in Norway. Norway has a twofold counselling service which includes both career guidance as well as guidance in social or personal matters. The Education Act (Opplæringsloven) states that all pupils have an individual right to both types of guidance according to their needs. Guidance counsellors in primary and secondary education provide guidance to pupils in school, whereas counsellors in the County Follow-up Service (Oppfølgingstjenesten) provide guidance to youth from 16-21 who are out of school and/or do not have an occupation (CEDEFOP, 2014).

There are careers advisors in school and available elsewhere to help young people to understand where careers may lie and what apprenticeships may be best for them. Inevitably, parental and family influence over career choice is considerable. Careers advice and guidance in secondary schools is typically delivered by teachers who have either taken professional short courses or have received extra formal training (30 or 60 credit points) to become professional career advisers.

Employment, training and progression

Young people in rural areas are more likely to be in low paid work, insecure employment or working within smaller firms than their urban counterparts. An acute issue for young people is the difficulty in progressing in work, particularly due to questions over the range of employment in rural areas, and concentration of small firms which offer limited opportunities for young people to upgrade their skills and take up training (Commission for Rural Communities, Ireland, 2012) (Institute for Employment Studies for CRC, 2008).

While the level of education and training opportunities affects many rural residents, it has a particularly strong impact on poorly qualified youth. For those who dropped out of a particular course, there are also problems in re-engaging as the choices of alternative courses or institutions tend to be limited. A number of young people who attended courses outside of their home area find that they are unable to continue due to financial pressures, and those who dropped out of courses tended to drift into low skilled employment or Government training schemes (Joseph Rowntree, 2000).

Young people in rural areas who are part of the low wage and low skill economy are more vulnerable to downturns in the economy and many therefore exist in a state of insecure employment (EOTEC, 2006). Evidence also suggests that there is a lower uptake of benefits by eligible young people in rural areas due to the perceived complexity of claiming benefits by those in seasonal or irregular employment (EOTEC, 2006). Consequently, employment programmes are at particular risk of not reaching such individuals (IPPR, 2006).

Employment and training providers experience a range of difficulties when delivering programmes in rural areas. These are often related to transport and small numbers of customers and businesses. As a result of higher delivery costs, the provision of employment and skills services in rural areas is more limited and sometimes of a lower quality than in urban areas.

Technology offers apprenticeship providers greater potential to support learners, especially in rural areas. While this is sometimes restricted by limited access to broadband, this approach can address some of the issues faced by small businesses and their apprentices in striking a balance between job experience and classroom work. For example, IT can be effectively used to enable learners to submit work, hold group discussions with assessors, and record evidence of work. In Nordland, apprenticeship providers utilise e-portfolio systems to enable closer links with apprentices.

Box 3.1. **Flexible programme delivery in Nordland**

In Nordland, apprentices are now able to complete training requirements, provide documents and access government assistance through specialised e-platforms. One popular system known as OLKWEB has been optimised for use by training offices, who are able to follow up on their apprentices and generate reports that document the apprentice's activities and outputs. Training providers are able to perform a number of key functions, including:

- Access the contacts and details of member companies.
- Analyse and monitor the apprentice's progress through curriculum goals provided through traditional means or through the use of films, images and mobile apps.
- Access details of grants and general accounting.

Apprentices are also able to interact with each other through the system, and can use the interface to record meetings and receive information. The employer is also able to monitor the apprentice's progress in off-the-job training.

In the context of Nordland, the customised apprentice interface allows apprentices to fulfill their training requirements without travelling vast distances. E-platforms also remove administrative burdens and allows young people to flexibly complete their apprenticeship requirements.

Employer engagement

The greatest challenge facing most apprenticeship schemes is maintaining and expanding employer demand for apprenticeships (Evans, Dean and Crews, 2011). Often sectors that have the greatest modelled potential for expansion are also the sectors with the largest number of existing apprenticeship learners. Sectors with a tradition of taking on apprentices are the sectors with the highest proportions of existing apprenticeship delivery. An issue for those planning and delivering provision within Nordland County Council is whether to focus on these successful sectors or try and build interest in sectors where penetration is currently weak, but where there is potential for expansion.

There is no difference in apprenticeship support for SMEs and larger companies. All training companies receive a grant. In 2014, the grant equals approximately Kr 23 990

(USD 2750) for each apprentice, and covers the whole training period. New companies who take on apprentices receive an additional grant of Kr 10 000 (USD 1147). In some cases, extra grants are given to companies either offering apprenticeships in small trades/crafts worthy of preservation (*små og verneverdige fag*) or for taking on apprentices with special needs.

In order to reduce the administrative burden of the individual enterprise and ensure that apprentices are given the correct training, groups of SMEs often establish umbrella organisations – Training Offices (*opplæringskontor*) – which assume responsibility for the training of apprentices and formally enter the contractual agreement with the Training Office at the county authority. The county authority must still approve each individual training enterprise that is to take on apprentices.

Norway has a long-standing tradition of close co-operation between education and training authorities and the social partners at the secondary level. The overarching aim of the tri-partite co-operation is to train Norwegian VET students to meet expectations about working life. Through the tri-partite co-operation structure, changes in technologies and labour market and their implications for training needs are communicated from the market actors to the decision-making bodies. The social partners give advice concerning a wide range of topics for upper secondary VET. According to the legal framework, the social partners have representatives, most often the majority, in all important advisory bodies at national and county level for upper secondary VET.

Rural enterprise skill needs

Rural enterprises need to be able to source and retain the right skills. The OECD (2012) recognises that this is one of two important skill issues facing the rural economy which contend fewer available skills than urban areas due to a smaller labour force and less diverse employment. Not all rural businesses experience skill shortages or deficiencies but those that do may encounter specialist or industry-specific skills gaps. Other skills shortages may be temporary and out of a need to retrain or recruit as employees leave (Frost, 2014). The needs of enterprises in rural locations proximate to urban centres will also differ from the needs of those rural locations which are remote and beyond commuting distance. Many rural businesses operate in the hinterland of urban areas and can access the local labour supply or source labour from the commuting population within the catchment of the urban area.

Those responsible for identifying opportunities for employers in Nordland recognised that companies tend to be smaller and it can be difficult to get predictable apprentice intake. On the positive side, they felt that attitudes towards apprenticeship provision were moving in a positive direction.

Policy context

Norway's education system

Education in Norway is mandatory for all children aged 6-16. Norway has the third highest spending on education among OECD countries, with a cumulative expenditure per student between 6 and 15 years at USD 123 591. The OECD average is USD 83 382. The Norwegian school system can be divided into three parts: Elementary school (Barneskole, ages 6-13), lower secondary school (Ungdomsskole, ages 13-16), and upper secondary school (Videregående skole, ages 16-19).

In Norway, a growing share of the population has a higher education. The share has been rising steadily for many years and now almost 1 in 3 people have a higher education.

Women aged 25-39 years have higher educational attainment than any other demographic, with more than half with a tertiary education degree.

The number of women pursuing higher education has been increasing for many years, and the share has increased more among women than among men. The share of men with a higher education is now generally lower than for women. Approximately 28% of men and 35% of women aged 16 years and over have completed higher education.

However, a higher percentage of women complete higher education degrees of shorter duration, namely 27% in comparison to 19% of men. Additionally, the share of men with an upper secondary education as their highest level of education (45%) is larger than for women (38%). The share of men who have completed higher education courses of a longer duration is two percentage points higher (10%) than for women (8%) (Statistics Norway, 2015).

The Norwegian VET system

All young people leaving compulsory school have a statutory right to attend three years of upper secondary education over a five year period. They may choose from three general studies programmes and nine VET programmes. The majority of the pupils who embark on upper secondary education choose a vocational programme. Norway has a well-developed upper secondary VET apprenticeship system, which enjoys a high degree of confidence among stakeholders. The upper secondary VET usually leads to a trade or journeyman's certificate (*fag- og svennebrev*). The majority of upper secondary VET pupils are in the age group 16-21 years (CEDEFOP, 2014).

Upper secondary VET normally includes two years at school, followed by two years of formalised apprenticeship training and productive work in an enterprise or public institution. This is known as the 2+2 model. The first year (upper secondary level 1) consists of general education and introductory knowledge of the vocational area. During the second year (upper secondary level 2), VET students choose specialisations and the courses are more trade-specific. In addition, an in-depth study project offers hands-on training in workshops at schools and in enterprises during the first two years. The priority of VET education is to provide a large portion of the training in a company. The current government policy emphasises providing even more opportunities for training in a company during the tuition hours of the In-Depth Study project. The subject accounts for 20 per cent of the teaching hours during the first year, and 35 per cent of the teaching hours of the second year.

During the two last years of apprenticeship training, the apprentice has one year of training and one year of productive work. The training is provided according to the National Curriculum for Knowledge Promotion. Should the pupil be unable to sign an apprentice contract with a company, the county authorities is obliged to organise a year of hands-on training in an upper secondary school. In the school year of 2013/14 there were 37 469 apprentices in Norway.

By international standards, the system is relatively inclusive and little stigma is attached to VET pathways in upper secondary education (Kuczera et al., 2008).

Not all VET programmes follow the 2+2 model. A small group of programmes are organised differently with either one year in school followed by three years of apprenticeship training, or the other way around. In general, the programmes that follow a 1+3 model are often small crafts courses where the schools have difficulties providing relevant training. The programmes that follow a 3+1 model are often programmes that include more theory of the trade (UNESCO-UNEVOC, 2013).

Another deviation from the 2+2 model is the Programme of Electrical Trades, which follows a 2+2.5 model, with two years in school and two and a half years in a private or public company or enterprise. In addition, some programmes are entirely school-based and do not lead to a trade or journeyman's certificate, but so-called "other vocational qualification".

IT has been incorporated into the mandatory schooling in many counties who offer laptops to general studies students for free or for a small fee.

Apprenticeships in Norway

The Ministry of Education and Research has overall responsibility for education and training at all levels. For upper secondary VET, the curricula and structure are established in regulations and all providers are required to comply with them. The county authorities are responsible for the volume of school and VET provision, dispensing VET financing provided by the State budget (including apprenticeships) and providing apprenticeship placement and supervision.

All young people leaving compulsory school in Norway have a statutory right to three years of upper secondary education and around half follow one of 9 vocational programmes. Students can choose between many different professions/occupations in one programme, including:

- Building and construction;
- Design, arts and crafts;
- Electricity and electronics;
- Healthcare, childhood and youth development;
- Media and communication;
- Agriculture, fishing and forestry;
- Restaurant and food processing;
- Service and transport;
- Technical and industrial production.

Upper secondary VET is normally completed by a practical-theoretical trade or journeyman's examination (*Fag- og svenneprøve*). Successful candidates are awarded a trade certificate (*Fagbrev*) for industrial and service trades or a journeyman's certificate (*Svennebrev*) for traditional crafts (CEDEFOP, 2014).

Apprentices receive a wage negotiated in collective agreements that ranges from 30% to 80% of the wage of a qualified worker, with the percentage increasing over the apprenticeship period. Employers that take on apprentices receive a subsidy, equivalent to the cost of one year in school. After the two years vocational school-based programmes, some students opt for a third year in the 'general' programme as an alternative to an apprenticeship. Both apprenticeships and a third year of practical training in school lead to the same vocational qualifications. Upper secondary VET graduates may go directly to Vocational Technical Colleges, while those who wish to enter university must take a supplementary year of education.

Each autumn, stakeholders including schools, politicians, and employers gather to discuss the following year's course structure for the county. The final decision on what is to be maintained, expanded or closed is completed by December of each year. Many considerations have to be taken before a final decision is made. A pupils' right to get onto one of their three choices carries considerable weight. Demographics, regional policy and economy are also considered when planning school places.

The county is divided into three regions, and it is of great importance that most teaching/training venues are within each region. Because of the county's size and shape, Nordland's education system requires many young people to move to take advantage of educational opportunities.

The social partners participate actively in the development of policy. The National Council for Vocational Education and Training advises the Minister on the development of the national vocational education and training system. The Advisory Councils for Vocational Education and Training are linked to the nine vocational education programmes provided in upper secondary education. They offer advice on the content of VET programmes, trends and future skill needs. The National Curriculum groups assist in deciding the contents of the vocational training within the specific occupations. The Local County Vocational Training Committees advise on the quality and provision of VET and career guidance (Kuczera et al., 2008).

Adults over 25 also have, on application, a statutory right to upper secondary education and training. Education should be adapted to the individual's needs and life situation. Adults also have a right to have their prior learning assessed towards national curricula. The process may result in exemption from parts of training. The experience-based trade certification scheme gives adults the right to sit a trade or journeyman's examination upon proof of long and relevant practice. The candidate must demonstrate comprehensive experience in the trade or craft, normally a minimum of five years (CEDEFOP, 2014).

The lack of large employers in Nordland is typical of most very rural areas. Local government is the characteristic exception. In terms of apprenticeships, the limited capacity and flexibility of many small enterprises and micro businesses can often reduce their capacity to take on full-time apprentices. "Shared" apprenticeship schemes can be an effective model in rural areas for overcoming some of the associated barriers, although these are unusual and are often more prevalent in land-based industries.

Close and effective working between training institutions and rural businesses requires time and flexibility, both of which can drive up costs. The distribution of national apprenticeship funding in Norway does not account for the additional costs associated with transport that can be incurred by providers delivering to more geographically remote parts of the country.

Norway also has relatively few examples of social enterprises or voluntary and community organisations that are active in the apprenticeship system in rural areas.

The County Council recruits organisations that will then host and employ apprentices. The lack of medium-sized and large employers (or indeed any organisations other than micros) means that there is a need to recruit smaller organisations and to broker more relationships. The Council does not employ specialised staff to build these engagements but rather aims to maintain this focus throughout all of their activities with employers. This is a hallmark of the tri-partite system favoured in Norway and other European countries. Interestingly, apprenticeship employer recruitment is viewed as an aspect of business engagement as much as it is viewed as education system support. The County Council is responsible for trying to match young people to apprenticeship opportunities.

During the apprenticeship, the organisation/company is responsible for delivering the in-work training. The County Council supports employers with training such as day courses and issues license certificates. The trainers in the company must have a professional background appropriate to the apprenticeship. Recently the licensing arrangements have changed and if employers do not have an apprentice for two years they need to re-apply for a license. Failure to meet obligations can also result in a loss of a license.

The workplace must be approved as a training establishment by the County administration and a qualified person from the enterprise has to take a training course given by the county authority. The enterprise must be familiar with the purpose of the training and the national curriculum and is responsible for the nature and quality of the training. Many enterprises choose to become a member of local Training Offices, which act as umbrella organisations for groups of SMEs to assume responsibility for the training of apprentices and formally enter the contractual agreement with the county authority.

Though there is a prevailing impression may be that many young people seek to leave very rural areas, this is not accurate in Nordland. Many seek to stay and build careers, but the availability of jobs and progression opportunities aligned with higher salaries in the large urban areas will always result in vacancies. The perception is that girls are most tempted to leave the region, perhaps reflecting the nature of the labour market, and the professions and careers available locally that offer progression opportunities.

At the end of the apprenticeship, there is a trade or craft examination which gives the final grade to the apprentice. If the apprentice is successful, they receive a certificate showing that they are a licensed craftsman in their chosen trade. The final testing phase is assessed by an examination board in each subject. The examination board consists of individuals who have a professional qualification within the subject. Members of the examination board are appointed by the county and the Board has duration of four years. County Council is responsible for making sure that the examination board has the assessment professional expertise needed to assess a qualifying examination.

To help attract new companies, Norway has begun offering an additional financial incentive to the existing subsidy for companies willing to support and mentor apprentices. This equates to an extra NKR 50 000 (USD 5 730) for business that are new to recruiting apprentices. The apprentice receives a salary that will rise as their experience in the job increases. These rates are set nationally.

Apprentices apply to employers for vacant training places, usually during the second year of their in-school education. The employers then choose the candidates that they would prefer. Over time, the preferences for apprenticeships have changed. Certain careers have gone into and out of favour, chefs and the oil industry being two prominent examples. There are gender differences in the career choices with many girls seeking careers in healthcare and childcare while boys favour engineering and mechanical careers.

To ensure quality training, the county authorities organise courses for professional managers in companies, and one (or more) qualified people have to take the course. The managers are expected to attend, and the county is obliged to ensure that they receive the training via another method if they do not. Regional authorities can organise special training events for "no-show" companies. Not participating in formal training can eventually lead to loss of license, but this is a generally unusual occurrence.

Micro and small enterprise approaches to apprenticeship support

Internationally, there are a number of approaches which seek to address the issues of scale, including:

- *Apprenticeship Training Agencies*, which directly employ and hire out apprentices as a flexible workforce to other employers, known as "host companies"; and

- *Group Training Associations*, apprenticeship training providers set up on behalf of, and governed by, groups of employers from within particular industries.

Models also exist that allow small businesses to share apprentices, usually when single businesses are not able to commit to taking on a full-time apprentice themselves. These are often associated with certain developments/localities such as business parks and supply chains.

There are some apprentice sharing schemes in Nordland but these are rare. The apprentices have one employer, but sometimes they need to practise in another enterprise because their own enterprise cannot fulfil the goals in the national curriculum. This can be for a few weeks, or longer. Due to study plan adjustments for apprentices, the need to use different companies has decreased in recent years.

The use of Training Offices in Norway has increased a great deal during the last 20 years, and now account for 70-80% of all training companies. The Training Offices have the legal status of a training company, but operate between county authorities and the training company. The Training Offices often take responsibility for recruiting new host employers and coach staff involved in the tutoring of apprentices. A recent research report (Høst et al. 2014) on the role of the Training Offices concluded that the Training Offices also carry out the county authority's tasks and actively work to assure the quality of the apprenticeship training (CEDEFOP, 2014).

The national authorities also offer support to training companies and Training Offices by developing guidelines on the training companies' legal obligations and practical examples on how the training can be done. These guidelines include topics such as the role of the training company, how to work with the national curricula at a local level, how to continuously document and assess the training and how to best carry out the trade and journeyman's test.

Larger Training Offices may have employees who mentor the apprentice in a closer relationship than smaller offices are able to provide. Smaller Training Offices (especially those covering many branches in their local municipality) have to rely more on the professional instructor within the company itself.

Governance framework and delivery

Nordland County Council

Nordland County Council contributes to the development of local societies and business within the county, and focuses especially on international business links. It seeks to create a vigorous county with a population influx, growth, employment and welfare. In order to contribute the development of business in the county, it aims to strengthen skills, innovation, entrepreneurship and infrastructure.

The Department of Education is responsible for all high schools in Nordland. This includes 16 high schools, 12 000 pupils, apprentices and intern teachers, three special institutions, workplace training and about 1 500 companies approved for workplace training. The department also includes Nordland Youth Affairs Office, which has the responsibility, among others, for the Youth County Council, the Sami information service *Infonuorra Sápmi*, the counselling service *Klara Klok* ("Clara the Wise") and the Pupil and Apprentice service in Nordland.

The 19 county authorities in Norway are responsible for all aspects of public upper secondary general education and VET, including apprenticeship training. The counties receive financial support from the central government. The apprenticeship training takes place with an employer or employers and follows the national curricula. The apprentice is offered a standardised apprenticeship contract, which is signed by the apprentice, the manager of the enterprise, the appointed training manager and a representative of the county authority. The counties are responsible for approving training companies, and have a right to revoke the company's status as a training company if the training is not provided in accordance with the training agreement and the national curricula.

The rights and obligations of apprentices in Nordland

The pupil may find an apprenticeship placement individually or, as in most cases, utilise the assistance of the county authorities. There is no statutory right to an apprenticeship placement. However, should the pupil not succeed in finding an apprenticeship place, the school is obliged to provide and organise a year of hands-on training which will result in the same final trade or journeyman's examination. This is a costly alternative for the county authorities, and statistics show that pupils who complete upper secondary level 3 in school achieve poorer results on their trade or journeyman's examination than apprentices (CEDEFOP, 2014).

The County Council sets out the following requirements for apprentices in Nordland:

- You must actively participate in both training and value creation in the training establishment.
- You are entitled to receive the training that the curriculum stipulates, but you are also obligated to participate actively to reach your training goals and to participate in the planning and evaluation of your own learning and work.
- You are to help create a good working environment and good working conditions.
- You must sit for the craft or journeyman's examination that the training establishment signs you up for.
- Your period of training is determined in your apprenticeship contract based on normal working hours for your trade.
- You are an employee of the training establishment, with the rights and obligations determined by legislation and by the collective bargaining agreement, for example working hours and holidays.
- Like all other employees, in addition to your apprenticeship contract, you are entitled to a written working agreement with the training establishment (VILBLINO, 2015).

Budget and financing

Apprenticeship funding

Rural counties spend proportionately more on supporting learners and apprentices than other areas because of geographical constraints. The costs of learning delivery are higher in rural areas but funding is not typically distributed on the basis of density or size. While some enterprises may collaborate in rotating apprentices to meet the framework requirements, there is insufficient funding to employ facilitators to establish and maintain a network of SMEs. SMEs often do not have the capacity to establish such networks themselves.

In practical terms, Nordland County Council receives an annual sum of NOK 130 million (around USD 14.5m) for pedagogical support for apprentices from the state government. This equates to NOK 130 000 (around USD 14 500 for each apprentice) for the two years they are in school/college. The money from central government is intended to defray the costs associated with the training provided to the apprentice and the supervision of an instructor. It also covers administration and the running of the training.

There is some flexibility associated with the distribution of this funding. Host companies will receive the whole sum if they have employed the apprentice directly and not through a Training Office. In the majority of cases, funding from the state is transferred to the County Council. The County Council then transfers a sum of money to the Training Offices for each apprentice managed by the Training Office. The Training Offices, which are themselves owned by several companies, will then transfer money to their members/ enterprises. The precise split is decided by the individual Training Office's board, meaning the Training Offices do not have the flexibility to vary the offer. Nonetheless there are major differences in the allocation of funds between Training Boards, which allows the Boards some scope to prioritise certain sectors and occupations.

The Training Offices are responsible for providing and organising a training system/ schedule for each apprentice, and make sure the apprentices are monitored, mentored and assessed. Larger Training Offices may have employees who mentor the apprentice in a closer relationship than the smaller offices are able to provide.

Impact of the initiative and programme

Evidence of success

The clearest evidence of the success of the programme is the County Council's increasing difficulty of finding additional places for apprenticeship candidates, despite the lack of traditional apprenticeship providers, such as large businesses in the manufacturing and engineering sectors, in Nordland. Consequently the County Council has had to work actively at all levels throughout the year to provide more opportunities.

Although the main model for the apprenticeship scheme is two years in school, two years in business and the successful completion of all theoretical examinations, it is not uncommon to follow other models. The council offers more flexible solutions to those who cannot follow the main model for various reasons. Some start apprenticeship training after one year at school, but others have four years of apprenticeship training, combined with some days in school to follow lessons in common subjects. In addition, there is a model for students who for various reasons cannot achieve the goal of successful curricula/certificate.

The decision to choose a more flexible option is driven by a number of factors. There may be some that are bored and want to get into employment immediately after elementary school, some who have weak results and others in more remote areas who may not want to leave home when they are 15-16 years of age.

The tri-partite system is primarily implemented by the Vocational Training Board, which is an advisory body to promote vocational education in the county. The Board brings broad insight into business and employment issues in the county and works to improve the quality of all vocational training by promoting the needs and viewpoints of the labour market to the county.

SKS hydro-electric plant, Nordland

The Salten Krafsamband (SKS) hydro-electric plant lies several miles south of Bodø. There are a few small villages surrounding the plant, including the small college at Gildeskal. The plant only has a handful of permanent staff responsible for the daily upkeep of the plant and the nearby power supply. They also have one apprentice. SKS recognises that there are major recruitment and retention challenges associated with the particularly rural setting in Nordland. Even those who have power generation experience in Nordland or Norway tend to train in hydro-electric plants located between mountains and fjords.

In many respects, there are similarities in the way apprentices are hired and supported in a very rural setting compared to a more urban one due to the fundamental underlying system. While in principle the scheme is similar, there are several additional challenges associated with a rural environment located away from an urban centre. Interestingly, SKS recognise problems both for interaction with the company and with the local community and the need to support young people to thrive outside working hours.

SKS recognise the importance of hiring apprentices, particularly given what has been a very tight labour market at times. They also recognise the importance that new faces can make to a small rather isolated workforce.

"In connection with the recruitment of new workers to the power production industries in Norway, we consider apprentices to be very important. These youngsters come from school with fresh ideas and they help ensure that everyone else in the workplace sharpens up. Our company searches the media for trainees wanting an apprenticeship in the subject." – Bjørn Ågnes (Instructor at Salten Kraftsamband) Produksjon AS

The company actively seeks apprentices using its links to the Training Boards and the various online and new media in Norway where young people post their interest in careers and apprenticeships. They typically directly contract with the apprentice candidate.

As there are genuine challenges associated with providing long-term accommodation for the apprentice, SKS prefers to employ apprentices from the local area. Apprentices are supported through the training school or college and both apprentices and employers attempt to deepen their connections with other stakeholders.

"Our apprentices co-operate with service training schools. When it comes to electrical apprentices (as many are in SKS) they travel to a secondary school (which is often placed in a more urban setting) and it is here that they learn the underpinning basic theory required during the apprenticeship/training period of apprentices and required for the theoretical examinations." – Bjørn Ågnes, SKS Produksjon AS

Almost all apprenticeships in the energy sector are located outside of urban areas. Technology ensures that the company has all it needs to provide in-work support and training.

The link between business and education is valued and SKS expressed a desire for closer institutional links with feeder schools and a greater opportunity to pass on details of the job opportunities that exist. SKS also felt that the most valuable lessons to pass on to others seeking to embed apprenticeships in similar very rural areas is to adequately demonstrate:

● The practical application of their everyday training;

● Willingness to support apprentices in identifying out-of-work and leisure opportunities and integrate them into the community.

To help improve apprenticeship take-up and success in Nordland, SKS recognises the critical need for more apprenticeship places, particularly within the smaller enterprises that are over-represented in Nordland.

Eirik, the current SKS apprentice, recognises the troubles in identifying enough apprenticeship places for the numbers of applicants. He also expressed an interest in more vocational training in school at an earlier age. His other main concerns were the problems of finding apprentice accommodation and the need for more apprenticeship places:

"When it comes to helping students who want to continue their education as an apprentice I think the County/Government should make it more attractive to firms to take in more apprentices. Today we have a lack of places for the apprentices as most firms want people who are finished with their education, they don't want to teach apprentices themselves. I also think the County should contribute further with a place to live for the apprentices who have to move from their parent's house. Just as students in universities have the opportunity to rent a dorm at a student house." – Eirik Willumsen (Apprentice at Salten Kraftsamband)

Gildeskal School, Inndyr

By the time students reach the school at Gildeskal, they have already decided that they want to work in aquaculture or fisheries. When they start on the first of their two years, they undertake practical work experience within a company for one day a week. Their work is intended to give students insight into the profession and is ideally designed around their career aspirations. They should also learn something about workplace expectations and requirements.

Labour market intelligence is a real issue at the local level and statistics and data do not necessarily offer much evidence of trends. Students therefore tend to gain information on employer expectations and job opportunities through close personal contacts. Kjersti Meland who works as a teacher at Meløy videregående skole, Inndyr, Nordland, states:

"My contact with the labour market has been built up over several years. When students are out in practice, we visit them. We also have the opportunity of maintaining contact with the academic environment. The visit may take the form of meetings, but usually we visit the apprentice in the workplace and observe their practical work. Here we meet staff and engage in professional dialogues with them."

Students also take classes from employers to get acquainted with the business environment and but also to help the businesses deepen connections with the school and students. During the second year, the students in the fisheries and aquaculture schools experience different elements of the business both to get a broad understanding of the sector and to allow them to target their desired apprenticeship.

The school is well-known in the business of aquaculture but not necessarily in other spheres. While many of the fishing boats know about the school and its facilities, not all parents and primary school students are aware of Gildeskal college.

Kjersti recognises that the hyper rural location is an issue:

"Our challenges as a rural school are that some students don't want to study here just because of the location. Many of the students have to move away from home and it can be difficult to get dormitory places. We can offer our students some practical education at the school, but we also want them to have practice in other locations that can prepare them for their apprenticeship. The long distances and the fact that some of them are out at sea are, of course, a challenge. But I think that because of this we have learned to be creative and flexible, and that is a good thing."

There is a network of practitioners in Nordland who liaise with businesses and schools to assist apprentices to find suitable placements.

The school and country stress the importance of both flexibility of work placement provision and the need to find experience placements across a large geographic area. This latter necessity can be difficult for apprentices as they may need to travel considerable distances or find affordable accommodation.

In recent years, Kjersti reports that despite the increase in the size of students studying fisheries and aquaculture, the school has remained successful in offering most apprentices a placement with an employer in the sector.

Kjersti stresses the following as critical lessons to pass on to those looking to work in such a rural setting:

● Get an overview of all possible businesses in the area;

● Ensure quality work-focused academic support;

● Motivate students to be mobile;

● Visit businesses regularly and ensure they are happy with the apprenticeship process;

● Be open to suggestions from the companies;

● Be flexible in your own work.

The interviewees both stressed that government support in connection with apprenticeship placement activities would help to drive up apprenticeship numbers. While there is initial funding to cover the cost of student accommodation and travel at the school, there is no additional funding for students while they are on placement in firms. This can negatively influence the desire to place students because the school does not have the funds to cover the accommodation for students.

Strengths of the programme

Apprenticeship schemes have the potential to integrate young people into the labour market if the VET provision meets the needs of the employers. High employment figures for candidates with a VET qualification indicate that VET competence is generally appreciated in the Norwegian labour market. The link to the labour market is considered to be strongest in the traditional VET sectors. These are the building and construction sector, the electrical trades and in industry. In the sectors where the link is weakest, the VET qualification has been established more recently and is not necessarily the only qualification needed for employment. These sectors typically also recruit adults without a formal qualification, but with long experience in the field (Høst et. al. 2014). Høst et. al (2014) conclude that a VET qualification to a varying degree establishes a strong and lasting link to the labour market. VET graduates generally find a job after completing their apprenticeship period, and their employment situation is apparently stable.

A number of interviews were conducted with the Training Office for Fish Farming, which has member companies in Ballangen, Tysfjord, Steigen, Hamaroy, Sorfold, Fauske Saltdal, Beiarn, Bodø, Gildeskal, Meloy, Rodoy and Traena. The Training Office offers apprenticeships in aquaculture but also in fishing, motoring, child and youth work, health work, ICT services and laboratory technical services. The Training Office can also assist students to obtain an apprenticeship within other disciplines associated with fisheries and aquaculture, including office and administration.

Despite the fact that the county is rich in natural resources and has a diversified and export-led economy, it can be difficult to recruit and retain labour in Nordland. Consequently, the Training Office recognised the need to innovate and differentiate their recruitment methods. For example, new projects at Kigok, Gildeskål Kommune aim to inform young people from kindergarten to high school about the career options available within the local area. The Training Office is also developing and piloting new education models, including some that were developed for specific locations and communities.

In order to help overcome the problems of distance associated with the hyper rural setting, training providers in Nordland use an electronic training system to communicate with apprentices for the length of their placement. The apprentices document the training they receive including any tests given by the employer. They can include drawings, photographs, clips of the performing tasks and a log. The supervisor can control their work, and communicate with the apprentices through this system. It is voluntary for the companies to follow this mechanism but it helps with support maintains a regular link with the apprentice.

The challenges associated with the rural setting can be further mitigated by easing access to transport. All inhabitants in Nordland below the age of 20 have a youth card (price NOK 300 (USD 34.50 per month) and this gives free access to all public transport (apart from trains) all over the county. All apprentices can also get 40-50% discount on all of the county buses and boats.

An additional strength within the system is the existence of many possibilities for transition to higher education from upper secondary VET which can be achieved through:

● By completing the third year of supplementary studies qualifying for higher education, comprising the six key common core subjects (Norwegian, maths, English, natural sciences, social sciences and history);

● After completion of a trade or journeyman's certificate:

  ❖ one-year course in the six key common core subjects;

  ❖ direct admission to certain specially-designed programmes notably, but not exclusively, in engineering (Y-veien);

● Applicants aged 23 or above with at least five years' work experience and/or education, and who have successfully passed a course in the six key common core subjects;

● Based on individual assessment of relevant formal, informal and non-formal qualifications for applicants aged 25 or more, who do not meet the general entrance requirements.

A final strength of the system is the close consultation with the needs of employers. County council regularly plans vocational priorities in partnership with the tri-partite system and local politicians. While the shift to a more demand-led system has undoubtedly been popular with local businesses, it has been difficult for some schools who have had to change their offer and to hire new and re-train other existing staff.

Key factors underlying success

The co-operation between the Training Office and the school is one hallmark of successful recruitment. The Training Office meets prospective apprentices at schools to inform them of local opportunities and possibilities. The reputation and history of apprenticeship delivery in Norway is also a strength as the overall approach is well known to parents and employers, while training and support is already embedded into many organisation.

The factors that underlie the success of a Training Office include:

● Co-operation between school, companies and authorities.

● Systematic and close support throughout the apprentice period.

● The ability to find and develop new models of delivery when it is necessary.

Nordland County Council has engaged with its education partners to offer bespoke provision of the vocational education model wherever possible. This ensures that young people considering dropping out of education are given the flexibility to remain in their studies, including the option of working in lieu of education for a short period on the understanding that studies would resume in the future. Local flexibilities such as this are important tools in tackling drop-out from education.

While apprenticeship acceptance regulations should be determined nationally, they should be implemented with local flexibility. Norway's employers receive relatively substantial subsidies for apprenticeship training. Employer involvement in the apprenticeship system is paramount in very rural settings, so this should be reflected in monitoring, training and quality control regulations. A very formal system may have negative impacts on overall apprenticeship numbers as employers find the systems too onerous.

Weaknesses of the system

The current unemployment rate in Nordland is 2.7%, below the national unemployment rate of 2.9%. However, both national and local demand is shrinking for workers who have not completed their education. The modern labour market increasingly requires a higher proportion of young people to have obtained higher education qualifications. Despite this, three out of every ten pupils end their studies before completing full secondary education. Consequently there is a need to change the measures and instruments that target people who have not completed education and/or those with complex problems. This will require close co-operation between the labour market administration authorities, education providers, the health sector and employers.

Education is therefore increasing in importance for those looking to enter the world of work. In 2013, 40% of Norway's unemployed workforce had not completed secondary education.

While Nordland seeks to find suitable employers for all apprenticeships, this is not always possible. In 2014-15, 360 of the 1 500 applications were unsuccessful. For these applicants, the system provides alternative resources and support, including;

● Traditional academic subjects;

● Work (followed by re-application for an apprenticeship);

● In school courses with exams;

● Schools that have taught the first two years may keep the young person with them until they get an apprenticeship placement; a craftsmanship certificate or a job.

Many young Norwegians are confident of finding work in a relatively buoyant labour market with good support from education and training, which has resulted in a relative high rate of dropout from secondary education pathways, including vocational routes. Statistics show that about 60 per cent of the VET learners complete their upper secondary training successfully within 5 years. The critical point for completion is the transition from the second to the third year. For most VET programmes, this is the transition from school-based training to apprenticeship placements in a company.

Nordland has a larger percentage of students in vocational courses and a higher drop-out rate than any other Norwegian county. There are also some shortages in apprenticeship places, which is a key factor for dropping out of secondary education for those pursuing vocational pathways. Training Companies are often able to decide the volume and nature of accepted apprentices, which depends on employer needs rather than the shifting popularity of vocational education. Inevitably, some subjects are more popular than others and have many applicants, while others have decreasing volumes of applicants. For example, the chef training course has recently declined in popularity after several years of growth.

The discrepancy between available apprenticeship placements and the number of applicants has been described as a structural flaw in the VET system in a recent report (NISU 2014). Companies are responsible for determining their own apprenticeship intake, and this may not always match the number of active candidates. While there are some difficulties in matching apprenticeship supply to demand, Nordland actively seeks to respond to current local skills shortages. For example, the Council is currently seeking to train more electricians and childcare places than there are vacancies. While there are jobs for these professions available in the country, there are not enough apprenticeship places. This suggests that the emphasis should be on engaging and recruiting more employers.

In the 2015 Enterprise Survey, Nordland had stable demand for qualified workers though optimism had decreased since the following year. The survey found that firms could have hired another 1 775 more workers if they had been suitably qualified, indicating that training and apprenticeships are important to stem higher unemployment. The survey also recognised recruitment problems in 32 of the more than 240 occupations that are advertised positions. Health and social care workers, craft and trade occupations (e.g. plumbers, concrete workers) and industry top the list of professions with recruitment problems. 12% of companies reported recruitment problems with 9% of companies reporting serious recruitment problems within the last three months. There is continued demand for persons with higher education qualifications, but the greatest need is for individuals with practical vocational training.

An important challenge is how such communities can be developed in rural areas where there are often long geographical distances. Modern information technology makes it possible to reduce the challenges associated with distance. Nordland consists of 43 municipalities and many of these have a population of under 3 000. Many small municipalities are often competing for the same skilled labour, rather than working together to create stronger academic environments. It would certainly benefit Nordland if funding criteria could be re-balanced to take into account the additional costs that can be incurred by providers delivering to more geographically remote parts of the country. Similarly 'shared' apprenticeship models for smaller businesses in rural areas can materially impact apprenticeship rates, but typically require financial or other incentives to encourage the establishment of organisations like Apprenticeship Training Agencies and Group Training Associations. The Training Companies are the logical route for establishing other organisations, or could adopt responsibility for the co-ordination and sharing of apprentices.

The Fish Farming Training Office recognised that the biggest challenge both nationally and locally is the relatively low apprenticeship completion rate. They further note that it can still be difficult to find enough, and the right, students and this is exacerbated by the reputation that fish farming is low paid and low status work.

What are the main lessons for other OECD countries?

In October 2013, Norway had a change of government which has emphasised increased impetus on VET. This includes counteracting drop-out, increasing the number of apprenticeship placements, making VET provision more flexible and increasing the state grant given to companies that provide apprenticeship training. The findings of this study offer valuable lessons for the establishment and maintenance of effective apprenticeship programmes.

Apprenticeships and VET has a key economic function in up-skilling and integrating young people into the labour market and in providing high quality technical skills. But VET has been surpassed by academic and tertiary education as a focus of education policy research and reform. Stakeholders interviewed from both education and industry wished to see greater emphasis on transferable skills and employer-friendly provision within schools.

In Nordland, local autonomy is clearly an important aspect of the education system. The County Council is responsible for the training provision and is required by law to define and implement a quality training provision system that is adapted to local needs. The national authorities do not specify its content. Flexibilities of this kind are important.

The Training Companies have the operational responsibility for the apprenticeship training during the last two years in the 2+2 model. To ensure that the apprentices receive training which meets the requirements outlined in the curricula, the training companies are obliged by law to develop a training plan for each apprentice. Though supported to a degree, they would benefit from additional help and relationships with other similar companies could be reinforced through virtual or other networks.

Most local practitioners who work with apprentices and companies rely on local contacts and their knowledge of local businesses and employers. This local knowledge is pivotal to maintaining apprenticeship numbers. This business and labour market intelligence could be expanded in order to broaden access to the apprenticeship system. Improved labour market information could help to ensure that funding and support is being targeted to the appropriate sectors and meets the needs of employers.

Inevitably, when seeking to increase engagement in the apprenticeship system, there will be challenges to overcome, including:

● The maintenance and expansion of employer demand in the current, difficult economic climate;

● The significant inequalities within sectors;

● Maintaining the balance between quality and quantity.

There is a sense, also reflected in previous studies, that the emphasis on the right of Norwegian pupils to choose their VET programme may limit the responsiveness of upper secondary VET to the labour market. National efforts to boost the input from employers are needed. It is positive and significant that Nordland's employers continue to make practical commitments to recruiting and supporting the future workforce.

Around 20% of 20-to-24-year-olds have not completed upper secondary education in Norway, which is well above the general Nordic average of approximately 10%. Leaving upper secondary school before completion is more common among VET than among general students. Dropout occurs for a variety of reasons, including the availability of work and the lack of apprenticeships in some sectors. Careers guidance and better labour market information for schools and parents may help in countering this. There is also a need to organise course offerings to balance the pressure from students and parents while meeting the needs of employers.

Despite having few employers that employ more than ten people, Nordland achieves a surprisingly high rate of apprenticeship placement. Difficulties in finding apprentices for particular firms or types of work may occur either because the relevant information does not reach students or because they find the type of work or workplace unattractive. Nordland could consider reducing programmes that attract few apprenticeships. A stronger link between the availability of apprenticeship places and the dimensions of VET programmes would promote better labour market outcomes.

The positive relationship between training bodies, employers and the County Council is critical to underpinning apprentice support. It is also important that Nordland offers training for trainers. Not all Councils do this and the employers interviewed valued the support.

The role of Training Offices in administrative and training matters is pivotal to deepening links between schools, young people and employers. Ensuring schools and potential apprentices are informed of opportunities requires flexibility and close partnership. This model is transferable and successful in placing increased power with the demand side of the labour market. Nordland could benefit from innovations such as developing new models of collaborative apprentice sharing between sectoral and geographically related organisations.

Information advice and guidance on careers is very important within the model and though all young people receive this, more could be done to formalise independent advice and guidance, possibly utilising the existing skills within the Training Offices. Local labour market intelligence can also help young people to choose the right careers, particularly with respect to a strong or emerging industry.

An easily overlooked but critically important factor is the provision of significantly subsidised transportation for young people in Nordland, including apprentices. Nationally, apprenticeship funding in Norway does not account for the additional costs associated with transport that can be incurred by providers delivering to more geographically remote parts of the country. Ideally, this would be factored into provision of funding for very rural places.

Commuting for education is a factor in many young people's lives in the most rural areas and islands of Nordland, including commuting to school. This is overcome through housing schemes with local families and through a number of youth and education centres. This model of local support is important. The need for apprentices to feel a part of the local community and to enjoy rural living should not be underestimated when attempting to attract and maintain apprentices in hyper-rural settings.

Critical transferable lessons identified by the Training Office for fish farming include the need to support apprentices outside of work. They have recognised that they need to maintain a focus on the apprentice's activities outside of work and on their community life. Students in rural areas often live in dormitories, while those in urban areas tend to live at home. The chance of drop-out is higher for those away from home. Apprentices must enjoy living in a rural area for its own sake or they may not choose to remain in their apprenticeship industry over the longer term. Consequently, institutions should focus on helping apprentices integrate into the local community outside of their work competences.

To help improve the retention of students, the Fish Farming Training Office stressed the need for:

- Better conditions for follow-up students that live in dormitories.

- The potential of greater financial and other advantages to companies that take an apprentice. The Training Office suggested removing labour taxes on apprentices (labour taxes are between 5-15% of wages in Norway).

They also noted the potential to increase apprenticeship intake in local voluntary and community organisations in rural areas. Similarly, seasonal employers, including those in tourism and hospitality, could be explored for further apprenticeship opportunities.

References

Bates et al. (2008), *Working in 21st Century Rural England – A scoping study*, Institute for Employment Studies for CRC.

Cartmel, F. and A. Furlong (2000), *Youth unemployment in rural areas*, Joseph Rowntree Foundation.

CEDEFOP (2013), Spotlight on VET Norway, European Centre for the Development of Vocational Training, Brussels, *http://dx.doi.org/10.2801/50807*.

CEDEFOP (2014), *Apprenticeship-type schemes and structured work-based learning programmes*, Norway, European Centre for the Development of Vocational Training, Refernet.

Commission for Rural Communities (2012), *Barriers to education, employment and training for young people in rural areas*, Ireland.

EOTEC for CRC (2006), *Research into the aspirations of young people in the rural West Midlands*, ECOTEC for CRC, March 2006.

Evans, C., A. Dean and A. Crews (2011), "Delivering Apprenticeships: The Challenges for the South West", *Employment and Skills Partnership Alliance Briefing Paper*, April 2011.

Frost, D. (2014), *Barriers to Rural Enterprise Growth in Rural Economic Development in Ireland*, Rural Economy and Development Programme, Teagasc.

Høst, H., A. Skålholt, R.B. Reiling and C. Gjerustad (2014), *Opplæringskontorene i fag- og yrkesopplæringen – avgjørende bindeledd eller institusjon ute av kontroll?* Oslo, NIFU, Rapport 51/2014.

Vilblino (2016), *Apprentice rights and obligations*, *www.vilbli.no/?Lan=3&Fylke=18&Forside=Radgiver&Artikkel=021811*.

Kuczera, M. et al. (2008), *OECD Reviews of Vocational Education and Training: A Learning for Jobs Review of Norway 2008*, OECD Reviews of Vocational Education and Training, OECD Publishing, Paris, *http://dx.doi.org/10.1787/9789264113947-en*.

Michelsen, S. (2012), *Apprenticeship, Youth and Labour Market Outcomes – A Diachronic Investigation into the Norwegian Case*, Nordisk Instiutt for Studier av innovasjon, forskning og utdanning.

Midgley, J. and R. Bradshaw (2006), *Should I Stay or Should I Go? Rural youth transitions*, Commission for Rural Communities.

OECD (2014), *Innovation and Modernising the Rural Economy*, OECD Publishing, Paris, *http://dx.doi.org/10.1787/9789264205390-en*.

OECD (2013), *PISA 2012 Assessment and Analytical Framework: Mathematics, Reading, Science, Problem Solving and Financial Literacy*, PISA, OECD Publishing, Paris, *http://dx.doi.org/10.1787/9789264190511-en*.

OECD (2012), *Education Today 2013: The OECD Perspective*, OECD Publishing, Paris, *http://dx.doi.org/10.1787/edu_today-2013-en*.

Statistics Norway (2015), *www.ssb.no/en/utdanning/statistikker/utniv*, downloaded December 2015.

UNESCO-UNEVOC (2013), *TVET in Norway*, International Centre for Technical and Vocational Education and Training.

Chapter 4

Targeting young people – work-based training at the local level in Germany

This chapter investigates the opportunities for work-based training for young people in the context of the dual vocational education system of Germany. The transition from school to work for young Germans is smoothed by a strong apprenticeship system and mechanisms that target government and employment services to young people at risk or with low qualifications. Specific examples of employer engagement in youth employment initiatives are also explored.

Key findings

- Germany has a long history of vocational education, and vocational education pathways are seen as of equal or greater standing than traditional academic routes. The German vocational education system is characterised by its "dual" nature, which features a combination of "on-the-job" training in an enterprise and theoretical training with a local training provider.

- Young people in Germany have the ability to transition into the world of work through a number of diverse pathways. Young people who choose to pursue apprenticeships through the dual vocational system can use them as a means to transition into high quality and desirable employment.

- The German employment authorities have pursued a number of new initiatives to improve the integration of young people into the labour market. These range from improved matching of apprentices for small and medium-sized enterprises to improving access to introductory work-based training opportunities.

- While the system is diverse and complex, and involves an array of programmes that occur at both the national, regional and local level, some concerns remain about the flexibility of the system to adapt to circumstances at the local level. There are also concerns about potential path dependency associated with pursuing vocational education pathways.

Introduction

The German technical and vocational education and training (TVET) system is one of the most developed in the world. Germany has a long history of vocational education and work-based training programmes as a pathway to high quality employment in a range of occupations. This is partially due to strong institutional support from employers, who provide relatively more training places than employers in other countries. Employers also enjoy a number of opportunities to contribute to the design and delivery of TVET policies at the national, regional and local levels.

Young people in Germany have a diverse array of options when transitioning from compulsory education to the world of work. This report explores some of these pathways through the lens of work-based training opportunities available through the vocational education system. It investigates a variety of initiatives from government actors, employment agencies at both the national and federal state level and employer groups.

Policy context

After fulfilling compulsory schooling, young people can work, undertake an apprenticeship or tertiary education or some mixture of these activities. In Germany, the tertiary education system can be separated into classical universities and universities of applied sciences ("*Fachhochschule*"). Classical universities cover a range of academic disciplines and features theoretical and research-oriented education. In contrast, teaching at the "*Fachhochschule*" is usually more practical and work-oriented. There are also co-operative study programmes ("*Duales Studium*"), which combine practical studies at university with on-the-job training at private companies. Dual education students are primarily employees with fixed-term contracts who also receive regular social insurance payments.

Outside of the different types of universities, young people in Germany can enter the dual vocational education system ("*Duales Ausbildungssystem*") and begin an apprenticeship after leaving school. Within the OECD, Germany has one of the largest shares of young people in upper secondary education pursuing dual vocational training (OECD, 2015).

The dual vocational training system has a long history in Germany and many professions that require a college degree in other countries can be pursued after completing an apprenticeship, such as occupations in the fields of nursing or physiotherapy. Thus, there has been a relatively large share of apprentices in Germany in the past, although an increasing share of young people have pursued tertiary education over the last 30 years. Trends in the number of apprentices and university students in Germany since 1980 are illustrated in Figure 4.1.

Figure 4.1. **Trends in total numbers of apprentices and tertiary students**

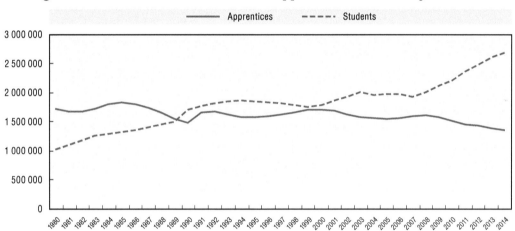

Source: Statistisches Bundesamt (2015).

The increasing numbers in tertiary education reflects expanded access to universities. In recent decades, the freedom to choose between educational paths has vastly increased. In the past, tertiary education was predominantly reserved for a small fraction of students who graduated from the most advanced level of secondary education. Nowadays universities and universities of applied sciences are more accessible for the majority of youth, which reflects the German political desire to increase the levels of skilled workers in Germany.

Figure 4.2 shows the converging trends in enrolments in apprenticeships and tertiary education. The abolition of compulsory military service and the shortening of the "*Abitur*" (the final secondary school exam) in some federal states have also contributed to the strong recent rise in new tertiary students. At present, the number of new students and new apprentices are almost equal, which is remarkable in the context of the last 20 years (see Figure 4.2).

Figure 4.2. **Trends in enrolments for apprenticeships and tertiary education**

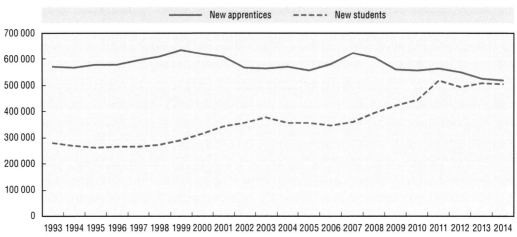

Source: Statistisches Bundesamt (2015).

Overview of the German apprenticeship system

The German training system is considered "dual" because it combines both practical on-the-job training with theoretical education in vocational schools ("*Berufsschule*"). The duration of the apprenticeship typically varies between two and three-and-a-half years, depending on the profession. There is no formal requirement for starting an apprenticeship, although most training facilities require a secondary school leaving certificate from a secondary education school. A better certificate can improve the chances of successfully gaining an apprenticeship and can also reduce the duration of the apprenticeship. For example, the "*Abitur*", the highest leaving certificate, shortens an apprenticeship by up to a year. After completing the training, apprentices receive certification that outlines the skills acquired, an evaluation of performance throughout the apprenticeship and the vocational school.

Apprentices receive monetary compensation throughout the job training, which increases every year. The vocational training pay varies substantially across professions as well as between German regions. For example, a West German construction mechanic receives 879 Euros per month in their first year while a West German first year apprentice in the hairdressing sector will only receive 374 Euros per month (BIBB, 2014a). Similarly, the average payment in West Germany is 767 Euros per month, but only 708 Euros per month in East Germany (BIBB, 2014b). As the compensation in many occupational fields is exceeded by living expenses, there are additional vocational training grants available from the German Federal Employment Agency, depending on the apprentice's living situation. These grants vary depending on the apprentice's living circumstances, rent, parents' income and apprenticeship payments.

Apprentices typically spend three to four days per week at a training facility to gain work experience and acquire practical job-relevant skills. The training facility will typically offer resources and guidance to the apprentice. Apprentices can also choose to attend vocational schools on a part-time basis, for either one or two days a week or in blocs of several weeks. The vocational school is compulsory for apprentices younger than 21 years, while older apprentices are not obliged but retain the right to regularly attend vocational school. The subjects in the vocational schools include job-specific studies like technical and medical courses as well as general education in subjects like German and politics. The Chambers of Industry and Commerce (*Industrie- und Handels-kammer*, "IHK") are responsible for monitoring the quality of the apprenticeship in the training facilities and establishing guidelines. This guarantees that the successful completion of the apprenticeship will be recognised throughout Germany, which enables graduates to move between regions.

The dual vocational training system is based on the voluntary involvement of the employers. There is no specific obligation for employers to train students, nor is the system heavily subsidised by the government. Employers choose to opt into the vocational training system because it is viewed as a major investment in their future workers. This attitude has a long tradition in Germany as well as its neighbouring countries. In general, employers view vocational training as an opportunity to train young people according to their business needs.

Three legal documents (Berufsbildungsgesetz, Handwerksordnung and Jugendarbeitsschutzgesetz) administer the eligibility of employers and training companies to offer vocational training. Under these laws, over half of German employers are eligible to offer apprenticeships. Since 2000, around 50% of eligible employers have participated in the vocational education system. The participation rate of eligible employers is positively correlated with the size of the workforce of the enterprise.

The content of the training is determined by vocational training regulations that are approved by the Federal Ministry for Labour and Social Affairs with advice from the Federal Institute for Vocational Education and Training. Social partners and employers may also propose changes to these regulations or even the introduction of completely new training occupations. Through this mechanism, local stakeholders are able to influence the development of vocational training curricula. The training regulations define the name of the apprenticeship and its duration. The regulations also include the minimum skills and proficiencies to be developed, as well as a time schedule for teaching and the examination requirements of the apprenticeship.

The nature of the apprenticeship can differ widely. Training facilities provide training in approximately 400 different professions, ranging from administrative positions such as bank clerks to technical positions such as dental technicians and carpenters. Besides companies in the industrial, commercial, trading and agricultural sectors, it is also possible to complete an apprenticeship with administrative authorities and freelance professionals like physicians and lawyers.

There were 1.35 million apprentices in Germany in 2014, and approximately 500 000 sign new training contracts each year. In 2014, the most popular apprenticeship was an office clerk role, 75 000 apprentice positions, 75% of whom were female. 62% of all apprentices were male (see Table 4.1), but the nature of apprenticeships varies between the genders. On average, male apprentices favour more technical positions while female apprentices tend to take apprenticeships in medical and commercial roles. For example, while there are almost 61 000 German motor vehicle mechatronics apprentices, only about 2 000 of them are female. In contrast, over 37 000 women take apprentice positions as medical assistants in comparison to just 550 men (Statistisches Bundesamt, 2015).

Figure 4.3 shows a relatively constant trend in apprenticeship drop-outs until 2010, when the rate increases despite a strong decline in the stock of apprentices. The nature of the education before the apprenticeship appears to be a factor in completion rates. In 2012, 34.6% of apprentices with a secondary school leaving certificate from lower secondary education providers ("Hauptschule") did not complete their apprenticeship and training programme. In contrast, only 13.4% of apprentices with a higher standard of secondary education ("Abitur") terminated their training without a certificate (Statistisches

Bundesamt, 2013). The increase in drop-out rates may also be driven by increased freedom to choose between educational paths, as those who fail to complete their apprenticeships are able to more easily apply for other forms of education.

Table 4.1. **Most popular apprenticeships in 2014 by gender**

Total	Percentage of total apprenticeships	Male	Percentage of total male apprenticeships	Female	Percentage of total female apprenticeships
Office clerk	5.6	Motor vehicle mechatronics	7.2	Office clerk	10.9
Motor vehicle mechatronics	4.6	Industrial mechanic	5.3	Medical assistant	7.1
Retail salesperson	4.5	Electronics technician	4.1	Retail salesman	6.4
Industrial clerk	3.8	Mechanic for sanitary, heating and air conditioning	3.7	Industrial clerk	6.0
Industrial mechanic	3.5	Retail salesmen	3.4	Dental assistant	5.7

Source: Statistisches Bundesamt (2015).

Figure 4.3. **Trends in dropout rates for apprentices**

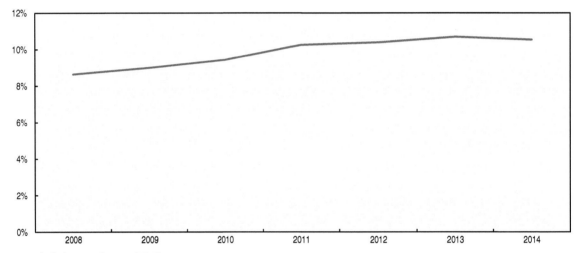

Source: Statistisches Bundesamt (2015).

Work-based training programmes in Germany – The role of active labour market policies

In 2013, the German Federal Employment Agency ("*Bundesagentur für Arbeit*", BA) had a budget of 1.5 billion euros for active labour market policies (ALMP), many of which feature work-based training programmes. Of these, almost EUR 300 million was spent on measures targeted towards young people (BA, 2014a). In each month of 2014, over 300 000 young people took part in ALMP (BA, 2014b). In addition to targeted ALMP, young people are able to take part in general services provided by public employment services, including computer software training, foreign language courses and general job application training. In June 2014, over 39 000 participants aged below 25 years participated in publically funded training programmes (BA, 2014b).

Figure 4.4 summarises and illustrates the policies that target German jobseekers below the age of 25. The overwhelming majority of youths (188 000) who receive in employment services participate in programmes that offer career guidance and vocational training. For example, over 49 000 persons participated in programmes that provide guidance for young people entering a profession (*"Berufseinstiegsbegleitung"*) and a further 11 000 participated introductory training courses (*"Einstiegsqualifizierung"*) (see Figure 4.5).

Figure 4.4. **Labour market measures targeted towards young people under the age of 25, 2014**

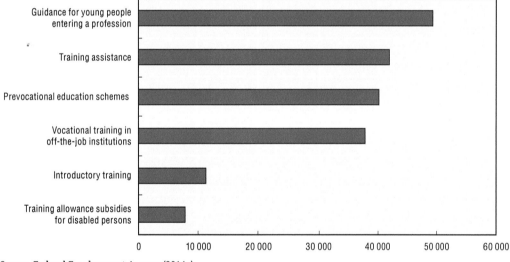

Source: Federal Employment Agency (2014a).

Figure 4.5. **Specific programmes for young jobseekers**

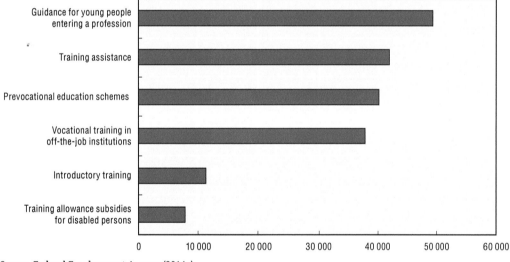

Source: Federal Employment Agency (2014a).

Over the last few years, the number of unoccupied positions and unplaced applicants for apprenticeships has increased due to spatial and occupational mismatch. In response, the BA introduced the *"Berufliche Ausbildung hat Vorfahrt"* initiative in 2014 which features a campaign that encourages employers to provide apprenticeships to disadvantaged young people. The initiative also targets policymakers to increase access to training assistance, arguing that measures that support vocational training (*"Ausbildungsbegleitende Hilfe"*, ABH) should be offered to all jobseekers in order to prevent breaks in vocational training. These measures include exam preparation assistance, private tuition in German, counselling or mediation between apprentices, teachers and parents. The BA's initiative aims to further co-operation between employers and vocational training institutions and promote additional external training for regions with a high level of skills mismatch.

Some ALMP are designed to improve skills match between aspiring apprentices and employers, thereby improving apprenticeship outcomes while also broadening access to the system. Others attempt to improve the employability and skills among young people through work-based training. Some of these initiatives are discussed further below.

Customised apprenticeship placement services for SMEs

In 2007, the Federal Ministry for Economic Affairs and Energy (BMWi) introduced a new programme to improve the placement of trainees in enterprises (PV). The aim of the programme was to ensure that small- and medium-sized enterprises (SMEs), particularly those in the craft and services sector, were able to obtain suitable talent for dual vocational training. Without support from third parties, SMEs have more difficulty attracting apprenticeship candidates in comparison to the public sector or large enterprises.

The programme provides funding to agencies that assist the placement of apprentices into suitable positions. These agencies are typically not-for-profit organisations who aim to find placements for enterprises and intermediate agencies that provide assistance to SMEs. There are a number of intermediate training placement companies and chambers of commerce who are supported by the PV placement programme in order to help SMEs recruit suitable trainees.

PV agencies and implementation of the PV programme

In Germany, it is the norm for businesses seeking apprentices to liaise with third party placement organisations to find a suitable apprentice. PV placement is the only significant alternative to the mediation services offered by the Federal Employment Agency. Very few companies (< 5%) seeking apprentices negotiate private arrangements with potential trainees.

The PV services are provided by a range of not-for-profit organisations, including chambers of commerce, chambers of craft, chambers of liberal professions and other business organisations, which tend to offer more personalised services to SMEs than alternative services offered by the Federal Employment Agency, job advertisements and internet portals.

The model of implementation varies, but these organisations generally work closely with local SMEs to determine their particular skills needs. They also recruit aspiring apprentices from local technical education schools and recruitment events, such as career fairs, and assess their training needs, wishes and living conditions. The PV agencies also typically arrange the initial interaction between employers and apprentices.

Since a preliminary study in 2008-09 funded by the BMWi (Salman and Vock, 2009), the PV programme has expanded both its scale, in terms of funding, number of beneficiaries and reach. In response, the number of PV agencies that receive funding has risen from 70 in 2011 to 105 in 2013. These organisations provided counselling, possible workplace-related training and placement assistance in 159 continuously manned offices throughout Germany.

Employers and PV agencies

There is also a pool of trainees who use PV services to find apprenticeships, with each organisation averaging 250 to 700 "informational interviews" to interested candidates throughout 2014. There is also a large number of known and potentially interested companies that offer training places for trainees and apprentices. The PV agencies in the commercial and industrial chambers have the largest pool of companies who are willing to host an apprenticeship, usually between 2 000 and 3 000 enterprises. These organisations are also often responsible for vocational training within their field and are aware of placement opportunities. They also typically maintain databases of the nature and requirements of their member enterprises.

However, the pool of places is significantly smaller among PV organisations that are not affiliated with a particular commercial or craft chamber. The PV projects of major chamber organisations such as the trade and industrial chambers typically offer an average of 100 to 250 apprenticeship places per year. The PV projects of craft-related organisations, other business organisations as well as the chamber of liberal professions do not typically deliver the same number of apprenticeship places.

Outcomes

From 2010 to 2013, participants in the PV service seeking apprenticeships were approximately 60% male and 40% female. Around 90% were under the age of 25, and just 11% were under the age of 15. Around 45% of those advised were students from general schools, while more than half had already left school. PV counsels a relatively small proportion of A-level students (10%). The majority of participants who sought apprenticeship placement assistance were youths from lower secondary education and middle school. Around one-quarter were from an immigrant background.

According to the PV placement statistics, thousands of apprenticeships are placed through the PV programme (see Figure 4.6). In 2010, 5 726 mediations (81.8%) into training were achieved, which increased to 9 016 mediations (88.0%) in 2013. At the same time, the PV agencies became the largest external actor of the Federal Agency for Labour and mediated the "Einstiegqualifizierung" (EQ, see section below) internships for several thousand candidates. From 2010 to 2013, the PV initiative mediated between 41% and 47% of all apprenticeship vacancies. During the period between 2007 and 2013, the PV projects were able to place 56 594 apprentices with SMEs and mediated 5 357 operational EQ internships with a total funding disbursement of EUR 30.2 million.

Figure 4.6. **Placement of the PV support programme in training and EQ-internships, 2010-13**

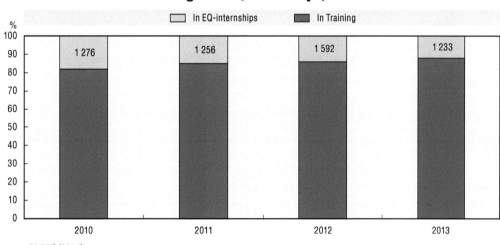

Source: BMWi (2014).

The agencies that provide PV services tend to work closely with regional employment agencies. A survey of PV services in 2014 found that 82% of chambers of craft and 71% of chambers of commerce work closely with regional employment agencies. The chambers of liberal professions and other economic organisations co-operate with the employment agencies on a case-related basis. When evaluated in 2014, regional employment agencies positively assessed the work carried out by the PV agencies, but noted that the PV initiative does not necessarily create additional places for trainees and apprentices.

The PV projects have set up a rapid and flexible process that is appreciated by SMEs. Around 40% to 50% of the SMEs surveyed in 2014 noted that their use of intermediate PV agencies had resulted in cost savings in the search and recruitment of trainees. Around 30% to 50% of the companies perceive the benefit of ensuring the competitiveness of their business. About 90% of those searching for a traineeship or apprenticeship appreciate the PV mediation offer as "largely helpful" and about 68% to 78% as "very useful".

Broadly speaking, a survey of the organisations that use PV services in 2014 found that they provided added value. The PV projects of craft chambers and craft-related organisations achieve a high placement rate, whereby 16% to 19% of all apprenticeship applicants are assessed and advised through "informational interviews". The "accuracy" of placement was considered satisfactory in more than half of the companies surveyed in 2014, indicating that the proposed candidates mostly fit the requirements of the apprenticeship vacancy. Only a small proportion of companies – between 9% and 17% – were disappointed by the candidates for apprenticeships that were provided by PV organisations.

However, the analysis also showed that gaps can emerge among SMEs that are not specifically affiliated with a single industry or profession, as they will not necessarily receive services from a particular chamber of industry or craft. Similarly, PV services offered by an intermediate organisation outside of the chambers of commerce or industry will typically offer their services to particular member companies or a set of company circles. PV services reach around 44% of companies associated with a particular craft, while only 17% of service companies make use of PV placement services.

Because the PV funding guidelines provide no detailed instructions to beneficiaries regarding consultation and conciliation, the PV agencies have developed a variety of local structures and practices over time. There is a wide degree of local diversity in the implementation and nature of PV services, and there has been some criticism that the initiative has not developed an overarching brand.

Around 87% of the PV agencies use the key concept of "accuracy" ("*Passgenauigkeit*"), while other PV projects use terms such as matching or coaching. A survey of PV agencies in 2014 found that they tended to exhibit systematic and goal-oriented consulting and mediation between enterprises and aspiring trainees. However, there were differences in the degree of professionalisation (structuring of business processes, targeted and standardised instruments) that was observed among PV agencies.

Einstiegsqualifizierung (EQ)

"*Einstiegsqualifizierung*" (EQ) is a work-based training programme that provides a form of introductory training for those aged under 25. It comprises a 6-12 month internship combined with vocational education. It was developed in order to provide basic vocational competences and company-based qualifications to jobseekers that have been unable to secure apprenticeships. After the successful completion of the EQ internship, the company is able to take on the candidate as an apprentice for a shortened duration. The EQ intern receives a payment of 216 euros per month from the BA. In June 2014, more than 11 000 adolescents took part in the introductory training scheme (BA, 2014b).

Participants in the scheme discuss their desire to achieve a diploma or a professional qualification with trained mediation professionals, who determine whether academic or pre-vocational programmes are more appropriate than EQ. The majority of young people and companies learn about EQ through public employment services. The Chambers of Crafts and Chambers of Commerce mediate 67-73% of EQ positions in their member companies. In particular, chambers will actively recruit companies with training experience (such as PV agencies, see section above) to mediate EQ positions.

Over a three-year period from 2009 to 2011, companies were asked to provide information on their EQ programme and applicants. The surveyed companies tended to offer 1.8-2.4 EQ places but only tended to fill 1.4-1.8 of these places. While the number of applicants exceeded the number of offered positions in all surveyed years, the total number of occupied EQ places has been in decline over the surveyed period and the average number of applicants for each position has fallen from 6.7 to 3.3 (see Figure 4.7). This reflects the falling number of early school leavers, with fewer applicants available for the EQ scheme as a result.

Figure 4.7. **Average number of provided and occupied training places per surveyed company**

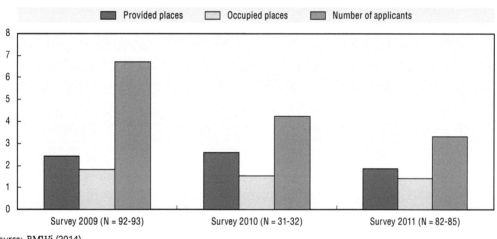

Source: BMWi (2014).

The assessment of participating companies found there was good alignment of expectations between the programme's participants and employers. The vast majority of EQ participants surveyed found that the majority of EQ enterprises shared their expectations with respect to social skills, external appearance and grades in subjects like German. The survey found that the majority of chambers of commerce, job centres and social security agencies found EQ to be either a very good or good method of supporting job applicants with limited placement opportunities and those without previous experience in the vocational training system. More than three quarters of the surveyed firms noted that EQ participants and conventional apprentices completed similar content in the first year of learning, namely guided job-related activities and auxiliary activities.

Participants reported largely positive outcomes from the introductory training. In 68% of cases, the participants note that they were better able to assess future career goals after the introductory training. More than half of respondents agreed that the introductory training corresponds to the desired training occupation, whereas only 11% of the participants were unsatisfied. However, surveyed participants noted that EQ is terminated before completion in 29% of reported cases. The job centres and social security agencies report an average drop-out rate of 25%, commensurate with the general rate of drop-outs for German apprentices. Some employers who are considered more conservative, such as the Chamber of Crafts, have high drop-out rates, while more liberal institutions tend to have higher rates of completion.

Early terminations could be attributed to several reasons. Firstly, dissatisfaction with social behaviour, motivation and reliability of the participants could be an issue. Another reason could be the early achievement of objectives – for example, participants may gain an apprenticeship during the EQ programme and opt to pursue that option instead. Young participants may also drop out due to personal problems with superiors and colleagues. In addition, very few businesses allow participants with learning difficulties or social disadvantages to use external support, which can seriously restrict the success of participants with learning disabilities to the EQ progamme.

In some German federal states, vocational schooling during the EQ programme is mandatory, whereas in others it depends on the age of participants. This is relevant because the inclusion of vocational training in the EQ phase can shorten the duration of any subsequent apprenticeships. The surveyed stakeholders noted that the handling of vocational school attendance was a prominent issue, and some advocated for a unified national vocational education scheme. Apprenticeships can be shortened for a number of reasons. The young people surveyed noted that 45% of apprenticeships had been shortened due to the completion of the EQ programme. In a further 42% of these cases, the apprenticeship was truncated due to professional school attendance or the successful completion of qualifications.

After the successful completion of the EQ programme, participants are eligible to receive a company certificate that outlines the acquired knowledge, skills and abilities. Participants can also receive a certificate from the relevant Chamber of Commerce. These documents then allow young people to enter the dual vocational training scheme. Over a three-year period, the practice of company-based certification increased to 62%. In 2011, 24% of participants received certification of the successful completion of EQ from chambers of commerce. This low rate of certification is because few training agencies and EQ participants apply for the relevant documents.

The majority of the chambers of commerce, job centres and social security agencies have assessed operational introductory training as either a very good or good support tool for those with limited placement opportunities or lack of training maturity. The evaluation shows that EQ participants experience an easier transition into training or employment. In each year of the three-year evaluation period, three-quarters of young people end up in vocational training or training in the profession of their EQ internship. This research provides a reasonable basis for the continuation of EQ programmes. However, the programme could be improved in a number of ways.

Entry qualifications should target the core demographics of young people with low maturity or individual placement constraints. Furthermore, the success of individually or socially disadvantaged young people should be taken into account throughout the allocation process. This could be supported by re-designing the application process to better determine whether the young person has a disability or is otherwise at-risk. Focussed measures can help the programme to reach the target group and smooth the transition between the EQ programme and further vocational education.

The stakeholder involved in the EQ process, particularly the Chambers of Commerce and employment agencies, could streamline their operations to better deliver services to disenfranchised youth. In addition, a clear and uniform definition across Federal States (published in the form of an action guideline or recommendation) and competent authorities could enable national recognition of training and allow graduates to move between regions. In order to boost the utility of the EQ programme, a stakeholder-led process should aim to significantly raise the certification ratio by emphasising the importance of obtaining a certificate or directly sending the application forms to the participants. Recruiting firms with more experience with the TVET system could also ensure that participants in the operational EQ programme have a more valuable experience.

The JOBSTARTER initiative

In 2006, a training structure programme called "JOBSTARTER" was introduced by the Federal Institute for Vocational Education and Training ("*Bundesinstitut für Berufsbildung*" – BIBB). The goal of the programme is to promote local projects that deepen the relationships between companies, chambers of commerce and employment agencies to create new apprenticeship places. Between 2006 and 2013, the projects of this programme created more than 60 000 new apprenticeship places (BIBB, 2013).

Since 2014, the JOBSTARTER initiative has entered a new programme period, named "*JOBSTARTER plus- für die Zukunft ausbilden*", which aims to support SMEs in the acquisition of skilled labour. The second iteration of the JOBSTARTER initiative has two main goals: to better integrate young people into job training, and to intercept and integrate university dropouts. The existing KAUSA ("Koordinierungsstelle Ausbildung und Migration") service centres aim to increase participation from young immigrants. The project also attempts to improve the mobility of young people in order to address supply and demand within and between regional training markets (BIBB 2014c, BMBF 2015).

One aspect of the JOBSTARTER initiative is the project "CONNECT", which is based on the idea of fulfilling several elements (modules) to obtain a vocational certificate. These modules represent different occupational competences. At present, there are fourteen occupations divided into these elements ("*Ausbildungsbausteine*"). Participation in one or more of the modules is intended to count for subsequent firm-led training. The JOBSTARTER initiative also encourages part-time apprenticeships, whereby working hours are reduced to at least 20 hours per week. This should increase the number of companies willing to offer apprenticeships that may not have enough work for a full-time apprentice. In North Rhine-Westphalia, this initiative is accompanied by the "*ModUs*" project, which supports parents in the application process, organises childcare and mediates between the apprentice and employer in case of conflicts.

Jugendberufsagentur

In January 2011, the Senate of the Free Hansa City of Hamburg established the goal of giving every young person the opportunity to undertake vocational training, with a stronger focus on retaining youth who might have dropped out of the previous system. Hamburg was chosen as a model region to test the improved co-operation between stakeholders and jurisdictions of different Social Codes (SGB II, III and VIII).

In response, Hamburg established special job agencies for young people ("Jugendberufsagentur") in 2012. The Youth Employment Agency (YEA) is a coalition of institutions that support adolescents under the age of 25 and provide guidance concerning vocational training or study, employment, entitlement to benefits and assistance in overcoming educational problems.

The co-operative partners of the YEA include:

● The Employment Agency of Hamburg, which offers vocational and academic guidance as well as orientation and placement into available vocational training opportunities;

● The Job Centre 'team.arbeit.hamburg', which supports youths who receive unemployment assistance;

● The Authority for Schools and Vocational Training (BSB) and the Hamburg Institute for Vocational Education and Training (HIBB), two organisations that provide guidance about vocational schools and further education;

● The Federal Agency for Labour, Social Affairs, Family and Integration (BASFI);

● The district offices that assist disadvantaged youths with special needs.

The economy and the trade unions (Chambers of Crafts, Chambers of Commerce, UVNord and DGB, GEW and ver.di) are also represented on the Board of Directors (HIBB, 2012).

All young people in Hamburg must either finish the A-level schooling or receive vocational training to eventually take part in the labour market. Depending on their performance, Hamburger students can choose to attend upper school or start a vocational track educational training after the 10th grade. This results in a large number of young people searching for suitable pathways into training and employment. This transition may not be smooth for young people for a variety of reasons, including low academic performance, lack of housing, debts or a lack of information.

To combat this issue, the YEA provides consolidated information and personalised consultancy and mentoring services in one organisational unit. The YEA operates between and within governance levels to ensure joined up thinking. At the local level, the YEA directly advises students of school-leaving age while also acting to ensure the efficient provision of information at the district level. The YEA also works at the federal level to co-ordinate measures, monitor the labour market and transfer information between partner institutions. At the local level, the YEA and its co-operative partners arrange career counselling in schools from the eighth grade onwards in order to understand the students' professional goals and the optimal pathways between education and work. All students who receive advice are registered with the Employment Agency, which allows the YEA to provide continuous supervision and support until they have found employment or vocational education opportunities.

Similarly, the YEA and its partners work at the regional level in all seven districts of Hamburg. Young people aged below 25 can opt to have their data shared between different institutions in the YEA framework, which facilitates integrated and specialised assistance. Young people can seek personalised guidance from offices that combine the services of employment agencies, Job Centre team.arbeit.hamburg, the Hamburg Institute for Vocational Education and Training (HIBB). This includes providing information about new educational or employment paths alongside services that address social disadvantage. The programme also empowers employees to actively seek out young people at home or elsewhere if they have repeatedly missed school, training or counselling appointments.

At the state level, the YEA's Board of Directors and other economic and social stakeholders meet regularly to discuss and clarify significant issues of co-operation between institutions. They also co-ordinate publicly funded measures and test the accuracy, effectiveness and efficiency of employment services to young people. The YEA has also established a networking department at the state level that collects the data of students to assess the achievement of the YEA's objectives. This department co-ordinates the commitment of the HIBB employees who participate in the career and study orientation procedures. In addition, they administratively manage the planning team and provide necessary data for forecasting their work by monitoring the activities of the YEA. In co-operation with the planning management, they also support the national action plan of the Board of Directors (HIBB, 2015).

During a survey period between October 2013 and September 2014, 9 221 young participants made use of the measures offered by the Employment Agency. Among them, 37.1% have their first degree, while only 4.7% are without any qualifications. With the support of the YEA, the majority of the supervised candidates – namely 4 031 applicants – were able to access to dual training. Only 162 candidates began to undertake tertiary education (Freie und Hansestadt Hamburg, Jobcenter team.arbeit.hamburg, Agentur für Arbeit Hamburg, 2014).

Significant challenges are forecast to affect the YEA in the future, including providing better educational outcomes for young immigrants and refugees, and improving the permeability between vocational and academic education streams.

Employer-driven initiatives for German youth

There are a number of initiatives to improve employment services for German youth that have been piloted by employer groups in the private sector.

For example, the employers' association "*Nordmetall*", which covers 250 firms in the metal and electronics industry in northern Germany, developed a model called "*Nord-Chance*". Young people interested in a metal or electronics job who have not found a vocational training opportunity within the placement period are offered the opportunity to gain a relevant qualification. They are trained and prepared by an educational institution for up to five months and subsequently placed in a firm. If the apprentice is subsequently found to be suitable for the job, he/she is eligible for vocational training opportunities. Within the firm, young people acquire basic knowledge and take part in firm-specific training modules. Furthermore, an allowance is paid during the preparation (150 Euros per month) and introductory training (300 Euros per month). The goal of this initiative is to engage about 1 000 young people with vocational training.

Another model called "*Zukunft durch Ausbildung und Berufseinstieg*" is carried out by the employers' association "BAVC" of the chemical industry. Between 2014 and 2016, the programme aims to offer 9 200 vocational training opportunities each year. The collective agreement also includes a measure to prepare young people for training maturity ("*Start in den Beruf*"). It is targeted to young school leavers and qualifies them for vocational training for up to twelve months within an operational promotion scheme. In addition, the new agreement also allows for the participation of long-term unemployed persons over the age of 25.

Similarly, the foundation "*Senior Experten Service*" (SES), in co-operation with the umbrella organisations of the industrial and craft sectors and liberal professions, has introduced the "*VerA*" initiative to address the trend of discontinued or terminated vocational education. VerA organises about 1 000 retired volunteer professionals who guide young people in vocational education in times of crisis. Based upon trainees' demand, SES appoints experts as training companions to offer support on issues ranging from technical questions about exam preparation to strengthening personal qualities such as motivation and self-confidence (Ies, 2013). VerA is also responsible for smoothing the transition from school to work as well as promoting the initiative to other partners.

VerA is free to use and can be initiated by employers, vocational schools or the apprentice and is carried out through support via telephone or mail. In more than 60% of cases, ongoing support is required for six months or less, while intensive support can extend for over two years. In about half of the cases, the reason for accompaniment was the monitoring and optimisation of the training. After six months, around one-third to half of all trainees improved in the area of "learning". In 20% to 30% of cases, positive changes in "personal factors" like motivation or social skills are observed. Rare improvements are documented in the "external conditions" such as financial problems or diseases. In about two-thirds of all completed accompaniments, the objectives are fully met.

While the evaluation found that that surveyed trainees, training companions, regional co-ordinators and regional actors had similar opinions of the VerA initiative, there were still significant differences in outcomes based on gender, education and the number of meetings that occurred during the monitoring process. However, more meetings tended to improve the outcomes for female youth participating in the programme. It was also found that the migration background of trainees had no influence on the targets. Overall, 90% of trainees and attendants would recommend the VerA programme.

The initiative could be improved through increased evaluation and better matching of training companions and programme participants. To become or remain a competent actor, the training companion should strengthen their own experiences and skills. Since there are interfaces between the tasks of SES and regional co-ordination, the tasks and responsibility of regional co-ordination should be more clearly defined. In order to increase the acceptance of the VerA initiative and enhance the volunteer work, appropriate resources for a professionalised work could be introduced. Finally, it is also important that trainees are approached through number of media, including social media.

Other groups have focussed on improving the quality of vocational education. For example, the IHK and the Central Agency for Continuing Vocational Education and Training in the Skilled Crafts (ZWH) introduced the project "*Stark für Ausbildung- Gute Ausbildung gibt Chancen*", which is supported by the Federal Ministry for Economic Affairs and Energy. This project focuses on the quality of the training staff. The scheme offers specific qualification and training to develop the special needs of disadvantaged young people.

Pathways from school to work – Broadening educational options for young people

After leaving secondary education institutions, most students decide to pursue dual vocational education or study through a tertiary institution. While tertiary education requires at least a secondary education certificate from a vocational secondary educational institution, there is no formal minimum requirement for starting dual vocational education. However, the completion of vocational education does not qualify learners for further tertiary education, which increases opportunities for those without a satisfactory secondary education degree but may reduce educational pathways after vocational education. This is significant because 76.9% of participants in the dual vocational education system did not meet the minimum secondary education standard for tertiary education and a significant minority (26.8%) were 17 years old or younger. A number of policy responses have been developed to address concerns about path dependency and limited future work opportunities for young people who enrol in the dual education system.

In 2009, the Conference of the Ministers of Education and Cultural Affairs announced that those with an advanced level of vocational education ("*Meister*") or three years of professional experience would be eligible for tertiary education. Private colleges also offer shorter courses for persons with corresponding professional experience. Although universities are able to shorten tertiary degrees for applicants with professional experience, in practice this option is not widely exercised.

The federal state of Baden-Württemberg has piloted a programme to provide alternative pathways for young people. Those with an intermediate school leaving certificate will be eligible for a "*Fachhochschulreife*" after the successful completion of three years of the programme. The "*Fachhochschulreife*" entitles participants to study at universities of applied sciences.

Other states are developing early personalised vocational guidance and counselling through the school system to reduce drop-outs of schools and colleges and mitigate the issue of path dependence. A new initiative called "*Berufswahlsiegel*" awards schools with outstanding vocational guidance and counselling services. A similar project called "*Starke Schule*" is supported and managed by the Hertie-Stiftung, BA, BDA and the Deutsche Bank Stiftung.

Other initiatives exist to support the transition from education to work. In 2010, the Ministry of Education (BMBF) founded the "*Bildungsketten*" (education chains) programme to assist young people with special needs who are likely to drop out of school without a certificate. The programme has three elements: analysis, career orientation and support for starting careers. Qualified teachers conduct interviews with children in seventh grade and analyse their strengths and weaknesses with respect to technical competence (e.g. problem solving competence), personal motivation and social skills (e.g. communicative ability). In the following year, personal guidance counsellors help participants to orient career goals through personal advice and assistance with finding internships and apprenticeships. Guidance counsellors continue to assist participants until the completion of their first year of the vocational training (BMBF, 2013a). Over 50 000 people aged 25 years or younger were involved in the programme in each month of 2014, a rise from previous years (BA, 2014b).

Another programme called "*Berufsorientierungsprogramm*" aims to assist students in the eighth grade with career orientation. Over a two week period, students gain practical experience from qualified trainers in three occupations in order to determine the occupations that best fit their personal aptitudes and motivations. Since its inception in 2008, over 450 000 school students have participated in the programme (BMBF, 2013b). The Federal Employment Agency supports these efforts by organising over 90 000 information events at school and universities. Job counsellors talk to students, ask them about their interests and aptitudes, present career paths and point out sustainable apprenticeships and study programmes.

The accessibility of apprenticeships is a challenge for the German vocational education system. The most vulnerable youths, particularly those with only a basic or no school leaving certificate, face major barriers to entry to the regular vocational training system. In order to mitigate this, it is possible for those interested in vocational education to take a training year ("Berufsvorbereitungsjahr") prior to entering the regular dual vocational education. The Berufsvorbereitungsjahr is compulsory for adolescents under the age of 18 who have not completed any type of lower secondary education and have been unable to find an apprenticeship. Students completing the training year complete general education and training in a chosen occupational field on a full-time basis at a vocational school. In 2012, 49 000 students chose this route towards vocational education. Successful graduates are awarded with a basic lower secondary school leaving certificate at the level of "Hauptschule", and are then eligible for an apprenticeship or further basic vocational training through a "Berufsgrundbildungsjahr". This is an additional year of occupational training in fields such as construction technology or domestic management. Upon the successful completion of the Berufsgrundbildungsjahr, students may be awarded a lower secondary school certificate or have the opportunity to reduce the duration of future apprenticeships. In 2012, over 28 000 students participated in this pathway towards vocational education. Although students are not eligible for payment during the "Berufsvorbereitungsjahr" or the "Berufsgrundbildungsjahr", they can receive financial support through the BAFöG (§ 2 BAföG) if they do not live with their parents.

There are other methods of bridging school and employment in Germany. Secondary school graduates can choose to complete a voluntary social year ("Freiwilliger Soziales Jahr", FSJ) through a state-funded civic engagement programme for 6-24 months. Applicants must be under 27 years old and must have fulfilled attended all compulsory secondary education. The successful participants receive free lodging and board, work clothes and additional pocket money (approximately 350 Euros per month § 2 JFDG) in order to enable them to work at German or foreign public interest organisations such as charities, hospitals, church communities or human rights organisations. Other options available include a more environmental programme known as the "Frewilliges Ökologisches Jahr" (FÖJ), and state-funded voluntary work programmes like the federal volunteer service ("Bundesfreiwilligendienst", BFD). Approximately 100 000 young people in Germany participated in one of the three programmes in 2014 (BMFSFJ, 2014). School graduates can also choose to join the voluntary military service ("Freiwilliger Wehrdienst", FWD) for a period of 6-23 months. Volunteers receive free board, lodging and a salary that ranges from 777 euros to 1146 euros per month. In 2014, there were approximately 8 500 young people in the voluntary military service (Bundeswehr, 2014).

In 2013, approximately 250 000 young people participated in one of these alternative pathways to employment, which was roughly half the amount of trainees participating in the dual vocational system. However, interest in these transitions from education to work has declined since 2005, when over 400 000 young people took part in an alternative programme or scheme.

Conclusion and key findings

This Chapter has a number of key findings which reflect the structure and nature of the broader German vocational education system and its impacts with young people.

One key finding is that employers throughout Germany are systematically involved in the provision of vocational education. They provide training positions and partially fund the system. They also have a strong influence on the development of curricula and examination through collaboration at the federal level with the Federal Employment Agency, and ongoing discussions with regional chambers of commerce, regional employment agencies and social services. Employers who provided training places through the federal PV initiative and the EQ programme reported that their expectations with respect to the skills and attitudes of apprentices were largely met. Ensuring ongoing employer engagement in the vocational education and training system can help to align the needs of business with the requirements of young people, and may contribute to the general level of success of initiatives targeted towards German youth.

This Chapter has been strongly shaped by the significance of the vocational education system in Germany and the importance of vocational education to youth-related labour market policy. In most cases, the vocational education system is continuously reformed by policy innovations that aim to improve the transition from school to work for the most vulnerable young people.

This Chapter has also found that active labour market policies, including preparatory training schemes, personalised placement of apprentices and trainees and employer-led initiatives have been broadly successful in Germany. These programmes often specifically target vulnerable young people who may otherwise face serious obstacles when trying to access the vocational education and training system. In these cases, a focus on personalised assistance and the development of competences through workplace embedded training has appeared to increase the opportunities available to at-risk youth. Deepening co-ordination between different layers of governance and different stakeholders, including employers, training providers, employment agencies and chambers of commerce, are also a feature of a number of regional youth-focussed active labour market policies.

Improving the number and placement of apprenticeships has also been a focus of a number of federal and regional initiatives for at-risk youth. While Germany has a long history of dual education and around 50% of those enterprises that are eligible to offer apprenticeships do so, there are still a large number of young people who fail to find a suitable training place. In response to this problem, the PV programme has aimed to improve the placement of apprentices with SMEs while the JOBSTARTER initiative has attempted to increase the number of apprenticeships available by facilitating part-time or shorter duration placements. Expanding the opportunities for vocational education across Germany can help young people bridge education and employment and boost the overall performance of the German labour market.

While the vocational education system is often a part of the solution in addressing youth unemployment, it can also cause problems. The inclusion of disadvantaged young people and removing path dependencies for those with higher abilities are two major issues facing the German youth labour market.

For young people leaving compulsory education, embarking on a vocational education pathway can be an obstacle to future tertiary education. Some attempts have been made to improve this issue by recognising vocational attainments as qualifications for tertiary education. However, the German labour market is still relatively segregated between young people with tertiary qualifications and those with vocational qualifications.

Access to the vocational education system is not guaranteed for all young people, not least because employers are not obliged to employ apprentices. Young people with low or no levels of secondary educational attainment or with specific disadvantages and disabilities often have trouble finding a training provider or apprenticeship place. These youths can either receive further school-based training in the transition system or, as in the framework of the JOBSTARTER initiative, they can receive several modular elements (modules) to obtain a vocational certificate. While some programmes aim to improve outcomes for disadvantaged young people, others do not make specific provision or assistance for young people with specific issues. For example, while the EQ programme aims to support young people with social disadvantages and learning disabilities, the relatively high drop-out rate may reflect a lack of customised support and assistance for vulnerable participants.

Other public initiatives target separate weaknesses of the vocational education system. For example, the Hamburger *Jugendberufsagentur* specifically aims to provide integrated employment services to youth who may have disengaged from the broader vocational education and training system. On the other hand, the PV programme customises the placement of trainees in small to medium-sized enterprises and aims to address skills mismatch while strengthening the SME sector in the medium- to long-term.

Employer groups have also developed initiatives to target young people. The "*Nord-Chance*" programme developed by the North German metal and electronics industry allows young people who have not found a vocational training opportunity within the placement period to pursue an industry qualification. Accordingly, they are trained and prepared by an educational institution for up to five months and subsequently placed in a firm. Similarly, the VerA initiative by the foundation "*Senior Experten Service*" (SES) aims to reduce the rate of early termination rate for vocational education by providing specialised support to young people through a team of 1 000 retired volunteer professionals.

References

BA- Bundesagentur für Arbeit (2014a), "BA-Finanzen – Monatsergebnisse des Beitragshaushalts, September 2014", Nürnberg.

BA- Bundesagentur für Arbeit (2014b), "Arbeitsmarkt in Zahlen – Förderstatistik: Ausgewählte arbeitsmarktpolitische Instrumente für Personen unter 25 Jahre", Nürnberg.

BIBB- Bundesinstitut für Berufsbildung (2015), "Neue Wege in die duale Ausbildung- Heterogenität als Chance für die Fachkräftesicherung: Ergebnisse, Schlussfolgerungen und Empfehlungen", Bonn.

BIBB- Bundesinstitut für Berufsbildung (2014a), "Tarifliche Ausbildungsvergütungen 2013 in Euro: Gesamtübersicht 2013 nach Berufen", Bonn.

BIBB- Bundesinstitut für Berufsbildung (2014b), "Tarifliche Ausbildungsvergütungen 1976 bis 2013 in Euro: Übersicht über die Entwicklung der Gesamtvergütungsdurchschnitte", Bonn.

BIBB- Bundesinstitut für Berufsbildung (2014c), "Studienabbrecher für die duale Berufsausbildung gewinnen- Ergebnisse aus dem BIBB- Expertenmonitor Berufliche Bildung 2014", Bonn.

BIBB- Bundesinstitut für Berufsbildung (2013), "JOBSTARTER Monitoring", Bonn.

BMBF- Bundesministerium für Bildung und Forschung (2015), "Auf zu neuen Ufern! Mobilität in der dualen Ausbildung", Ausgabe 1/2015, Bonn.

BMBF- Bundesministerium für Bildung und Forschung (2013a), "Berufseinstiegsbegleitung – die Möglichmache"', Bonn.

BMBF- Bundesministerium für Bildung und Forschung (2013b), "Praxis erfahren! Das Berufsorientierungsprogrammem", Bonn.

BMFSFJ- Bundesministerium für Familie, Senioren, Frauen und Jugend (2014), "Zeit, das Richtige zu tun, Freiwillig engagiert in Deutschland – Bundesfreiwilligendienst, Freiwilliges Soziales Jahr, Freiwilliges Ökologisches Jahr", Berlin.

BMWi- Bundesministerium für Wirtschaft und Energie (2014), "Evaluierung des Förderprogrammems 'Passgenaue Vermittlung Auszubildender an ausbildungswillige Unternehmen' Abschlussbericht der Evaluation und Wirtschaftlichkeitsuntersuchung", Bonn.

Bundeswehr (2014), "Freiwilliger Wehrdienst FWD", downloadable from: *https://mil.bundeswehr-karriere.de/portal/a/milkarriere/ihrekarriere/fwdmp* (date: 10.10.2014).

Freie und Hansestadt Hamburg, Jobcenter team.arbeit.hamburg, Agentur für Arbeit Hamburg (2014), "Zwei Jahre Jugendberufsagentur Hamburg", downloadable from: *www.hamburg.de/contentblob/ 4436922/data/zwei-jahre-jugendberufsagentur.pdf* (date: 01.12.2015).

HIBB- Hamburger Institut für Berufliche Bildung (2015), "Chancen und Übergänge verbessern, Durchlässigkeit erhöhen", in: Berufliche Bildung Hamburg, downloadable from: *www.hibb.hamburg.de/ index.php/file/download/2446* (date: 01.12.2015).

HIBB- Hamburger Institut für Berufliche Bildung (2012), "Jugendberufsagentur – Begleitung von Klasse 8 bis zum Berufsabschluss", in: Berufliche Bildung Hamburg, downloadable from: *http://ftp.hbzv.com/ Schulbehoerde/bbh_Ausgabe_02-2012* (date: 01.12.2015).

Ies- Institut für Entwicklungsplanung und Strukturforschung GmbH (2013), "Evaluation der Initiative VerA des Senior Experten Service", Bericht 10.1.13. Hannover.

OECD (2015), *Education at a Glance 2015: OECD Indicators*, OECD Publishing, Paris, *http://dx.doi.org/ 10.1787/eag-2015-en*.

Statistisches Bundesamt (2015), *Berufsbildungsstatistik zum 31.12.* Wiesbaden.

Statistisches Bundesamt (2013), "Bildung und Kultur: Berufliche Bildung", Fachserie 11 Reihe 3, Wiesbaden.

Chapter 5

Innovative approaches to attracting and retaining apprentices in Western Australia

This chapter explores the impact and effectiveness of enterprise-embedded apprenticeship programmes in the context of the construction industry of Western Australia. The case study features a "whole of life" pathway for apprentices to make the transition from secondary education to full-time work through a range of experiences and opportunities provided through a single company. The relationship between the apprenticeship scheme and the broader economic context of Western Australia is also explored.

Key findings

- The ABN Group is a diversified construction company that has pioneered an enterprise-embedded model of apprenticeship programme delivery in the context of the Australian federal state of Western Australia.

- The programme delivery method embeds a group training organisation into the company's holding structure, which enables the company to manage both on-the-job training and off-the-job training internally. It also provides the ABN Group with the flexibility to shift apprentices to different construction sites according to the company's needs.

- The process of developing the enterprise-embedded model required a protracted process of consultation with relevant stakeholders, including government partners. Direct lobbying and legislative change was required to make this model feasible, even in the context of a well-developed apprenticeship system.

- The merits of a lifecycle model of apprenticeship delivery, wherein the employer is engaged with the apprentice through the process of awareness, recruitment, training, work experience and graduation, are also explored.

Introduction

Enterprise-embedded apprenticeship models are relatively uncommon across OECD countries, even in those with well-developed apprenticeship systems and relative flexibility at the local level. This chapter explores the evolution of an enterprise-embedded model through the example of the ABN Group, a large construction company based in the Australian federal state of Western Australia. The benefits of the model for the ABN Group include increased flexibility, reduced hiring and training provider costs and increased alignment of on-the-job training and off-the-job training. This model was somewhat unprecedented and required regulatory reform before successful implementation.

Policy context

The total Australian population in 2012 was 22.7 million people, with a national labour force participation rate of 65.2%. Nationally, Health Care and Social Assistance and Retail were the top two industries by percentage of employees. The Australian workforce is highly concentrated on the eastern seaboard, with more than three quarters of workers employed in the three most populous states (New South Wales, Victoria and Queensland).

The Australian labour market has been transformed over the last twenty years by the concurrent trends of increased participation of women in the workforce, a much greater focus on skilled jobs, an associated increase in young people participating in education and the ageing of the population. Technological change, greater labour market flexibility and economic reforms have also been associated with a significant improvement in labour market conditions between the end of the early 1990s recession and the onset of the Global Financial Crisis (GFC) in 2008.

Although labour market conditions in Australia deteriorated at the onset of the GFC in late 2008 and the unemployment rate rose to 5.9% at the peak of the crisis, Australia fared much better than most other advanced economies and recovered strongly during 2010. Since then, however, domestic conditions have softened again as a result of ongoing uncertainty and volatility on global financial markets and weaker global growth.

Western Australia is the largest state in Australia (by landmass) and the second-largest country subdivision in the world. The state experienced particularly strong employment growth over the five years to November 2012, driven predominantly by the strength of the resources sector. Employment increased by 175 200 or 15.4% (the strongest rate of any state or territory).

Western Australian workers are slightly less likely to hold post-school qualifications than the national average (61% compared with 63%). Workers in the capital city (Perth) are more likely to have a bachelor degree or higher qualification than those in regional areas, but workers outside Perth are more likely to have Certificate III level or higher vocational education and training qualifications.

Australia experienced a period of substantial expansion of the resources sector during the 2000s (especially from 2005 to the end of the decade), driven by Chinese economic growth and high commodities prices. From March quarter 2005 to September quarter 2010, capital expenditure by the mining industry increased 258% to AUD 11 143 million (ABS, 2010). The largest proportion of mining sector investment occurred in Western Australia, where mining revenue represents the biggest proportion of both gross state product (GSP) and exports (ABS, 2010).

Figure 5.1. **Western Australia: Industry value added as a proportion of Gross State Product**

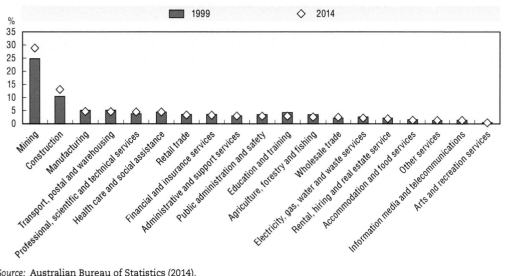

Source: Australian Bureau of Statistics (2014).

Along with strong economic growth, the mining boom led to increased levels of employment in Western Australia. This is reflected by the fact that during the period 2006 to 2011, the number of employed persons grew by 11% in Australia, and by 18% in Western Australia (ABS, 2006; ABS, 2011). The mining industry was a major contributor to employment growth, both nationally, with the number of those employed in the sector growing by 65%, and locally (70%).

In Western Australia, the construction, professional, scientific and technical services and the electricity, gas, water and waste services industries also considerably increased the numbers of employees between 2006 and 2011; by 31%, 34%, and 31%, respectively (ABS, 2006; ABS, 2011).

Figure 5.2. **Employed persons by industry in Western Australia, 2006 and 2011**

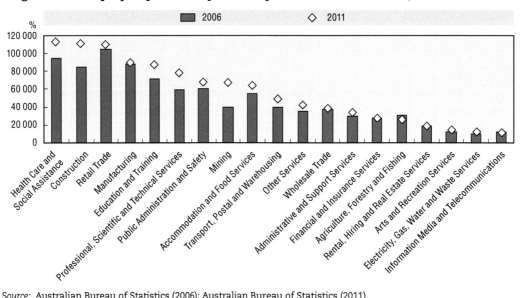

Source: Australian Bureau of Statistics (2006); Australian Bureau of Statistics (2011).

The construction phase of the mining boom had strong flow-on effects to other sectors, particularly the construction industry. A review of 20 years of labour market data published in 2010 demonstrated that sectors relying on trades occupations generally suffered from shortages of skilled workers following strong economic growth; with the construction, and the engineering and automotive trades usually being more severely affected (Oliver, 2011).

Skills shortages occur as a result of an imbalance between demand for qualified workers and the number (supply) of skilled workers available. This may occur as a consequence of a low number of skilled people entering the workforce, aged workers leaving the workforce, or growth in the demand for skills which might result in high competition for workers between growing industries, or employers within these industries.

During the 2000s, low unemployment rates and an increasing number of resource sector projects drove increased demand for skills and resulted in the emergence of skills shortages. The shortage was "exacerbated by a long period of under-investment in apprentice training", following a lower than national average growth in the number of apprentices during the 1990s (State Training Board, 2006).

The strong employment growth in resource-related construction was largely met by skilled workers originally employed in residential and civil construction, who were attracted by the higher wages being offered by the resources sector. This in turn resulted in a high turnover of both skilled and partially trained workers within the construction industry, and created wage pressure (Construction Training Council, 2010). Moreover, the operational side of the resources sector, i.e. the mining sector itself, also posed strong competition for workers. Between 2005 and 2010, the number of workers moving to the mining industry from other industries more than doubled (D'Arcy et al., 2012). It was not uncommon to have teachers, police officers and other professionals, for example, working on mine-sites alongside those with more relevant experience (The Australian, 2010). The impact on the construction industry in Western Australia was significant. For example, 25% of people recruited into mining in 2012 came from the construction industry (Source: interview with Director of Skills Development, CTF).

In Australia, Vocational Education and Training (VET) is the main pathway into trade occupations. The construction industry relies heavily on recruitment of apprentices and employs 40% of all apprentices in Western Australia.

However, although commencements in trades apprenticeships in Australia increased by an average of 6% between 2006 and 2010 (NCVER, 2015), completion rates during this period were low. Across Australia, more than half of apprenticeship training contracts in trade occupations were not completed, whereas in Western Australia, 46% of programmes were not completed (NCVER, 2015). Figure 5.3 outlines the completion rates for Australia and Western Australia.

Figure 5.3. **Contract completion rates for apprenticeships in trade occupations (percentage of contracts commencing in 2006-10)**

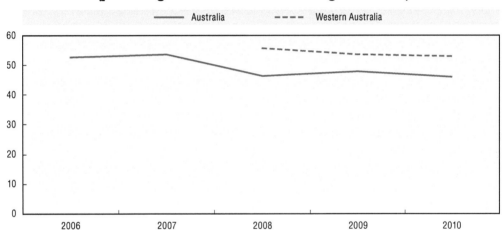

Source: National Centre for Vocational Education Research (2015), "Completion and attrition rates for apprentices and trainees 2014: State and territory data table".

Policy context

Since the 1990s, the Australian VET system has undergone modernisation and harmonisation to ensure that training delivered by the states and territories is consistent and meets the needs of a changing economy. These reforms were achieved through the introduction of legislation and regulation, and were accelerated in the context of an economic boom during the early 2000s, which raised concerns about a shortage in the supply of skilled workers.

In response, the Council of Australian Governments (COAG), comprising the heads of the Commonwealth and all state and territory governments, decided to speed the introduction of competency-based training to achieve a skills pipeline that would be able to meet areas of pressing demand (NCVER, 2011). The National Skills Framework (NSF) was established and included the following initiatives:

● The VET Quality Framework (VQF) – the nationally agreed quality assurance arrangement that ensures the quality and consistency of VET training delivery and assessment;

- The Australian Qualifications Framework (AQF) – a comprehensive framework that provides a unified system of national qualifications in schools, vocational education and training and the higher education sector (mainly universities); and

- Training packages – nationally endorsed standards and qualifications used to recognise and assess people's skills in a specific industry, industry sector or enterprise.

The competency-based training packages are endorsed by industry-specific national Industry Skills Councils to ensure that training meets the needs of industry (Hodge, 2007). Under this arrangement, apprentices demonstrate that they have achieved a minimum standard skill level in order to attain completion, which means that some are able to finish earlier than usual, dependent on their assessed competence.

A more recent initiative of COAG is the *National Agreement for Skills and Workforce Development* (2012), designed to ensure Australia has a productive and highly skilled workforce in to the future and in the context of a changing economy (COAG, 2012). Key targets are to "strengthen the capacity for public and private providers and businesses to deliver training and support people in training", and to, "strengthen, streamline and harmonise the Australian Apprenticeships system", (COAG, 2012).

Within this context of reform, and with a stronger focus on developing a productive, skilled workforce that responds to the needs of industry, Australian Apprenticeship programmes now include a greater focus on the needs of employers. While some apprentices are directly contracted by employers, others are contracted by Group Training Organisations (GTOs) and then hired out to a number of different host employers during their training programme. This way, GTOs provide apprentices with access to multiple worksites to develop their work experience through on-the-job training. Off-the-job training is delivered by organisations known as Registered Training Organisations (RTOs), which deliver Vocational Education and Training (VET) that results in qualifications of statements of attainment that are recognised and accepted by industry and educational institutions throughout Australia. RTOs can be government bodies or privately owned organisations. Figure 5.4 provides an overview of the relationships between parties in the delivery of apprenticeships, within the National Skills Framework.

Australian apprenticeships can be undertaken by any Australian older than 15 years, and some may also be offered as a school-based apprenticeship from Years 10 to 12, the final two years of secondary school. A training contract must be signed by the employer (when hiring independently) or GTO (when hiring through group training schemes), the employee (the apprentice, or the parent/guardian if under 18 years of age), and the relevant RTO.

Training plans, determined in collaboration with RTOs, identify how the course and training will be delivered and how competence will be assessed. The latter is often connected to wage progression, where achievement of competence against the requirements of the training package is assessed and reflected in wages. A Level III (VET) Certificate is granted to those who successfully complete their apprenticeship programme.

The Western Australian Department of Training and Workforce Development (DTWD) administers training contracts and regulates the apprenticeship system within the state. DTWD is responsible for auditing training plans, assessing employers' suitability to train apprentices, and ensuring that regulatory requirements are maintained across the apprenticeship system.

Figure 5.4. **Overview of the National Skills Framework
as it relates to apprenticeships**

Source: Author's own elaboration.

Apprentices in the Western Australian construction sector

In the early 2000s, there were major concerns about the Western Australian construction industry's capacity to ensure development and supply of a skilled workforce in the face of growing demand for construction projects. This was compounded by the increasing attrition of workers from construction to the lucrative mining industry.

Long-term planning set in place by the Western Australian government, as well as the benefits of the competency-based, employer-focused approach to modernise Australian apprenticeships, were key factors that enabled the construction industry to maintain the supply of skilled workers despite ongoing skills shortages. The Construction Training Fund (CTF), which is specific to Western Australia, was established via legislation in 1990 to support skills development within the construction industry by extracting a 0.2% levy from all construction projects within the state, where the value of construction is higher than AUD 20 000. The levy is intended to be used to incentivise employers to train apprentices and to up-skill their existing workforce. It is also used to support the provision of school-based work experience and pre-apprenticeship programmes, which are seen as strategic initiatives to ensure the development of a future workforce pipeline within the construction industry. Over 48 000 apprentices and trainees have been supported by the CTF since its inception (CTF, 2016).

The construction sector is highly dependent on the availability of a skilled workforce in order to meet demand for projects. As companies can only sell what they can build, their capacity to operate is undermined by a lack of skilled tradespeople. Hence, a commercial problem is created and the capability to plan and grow is compromised.

Increasing capital investment from mining companies drove increased wages and population growth (derived from the increasing influx of workers from other states and overseas), and resulted in growing demand for building and construction projects in three markets:

1. Mining infrastructure;

2. New housing stock; and

3. Housing renovations and expansions.

The ABN Group, as a leading operator within the building and construction sector, primarily services the new home and home renovation markets in two of the four largest Australian states (by population) – Western Australia and Victoria. As a large organisation and employer, the ABN Group was significantly affected by the availability of skilled tradespeople, especially in a context of expansion during the mining boom.

Beyond training newcomers to the industry, it is also crucial for companies to be able to access a pool of graduated tradespeople within their workforce. In the construction sector, graduating apprentices typically become self-employed contractors. This means that, after completing an apprenticeship programme, there is no guarantee that tradespeople will either continue working for their host employers or be able to find employment in the industry. In GTO arrangements, where apprentices rotate between different, unrelated employers, the links and commitments between these parties is even weaker.

Prior to 2004, contractors working within the ABN Group would host apprentices hired through a very small number of external GTOs. The rotation of apprentices between host employers outside ABN Group translated into apprentices that did not genuinely see themselves as part of the ABN Group of companies. As the ABN Group's interaction with RTOs was mediated by the external GTOs, ABN Group also had limited control over the apprenticeship training programme and its ability to meet the company's skills needs and broader values. A third significant issue was the high leakage of apprentices to other employers, and other industries, before and after training was completed.

This led to the creation of an enterprise-embedded apprenticeship programme to meet the expectations of the ABN Group with respect to training standards, recruitment of talented candidates, apprenticeship completion, and retention of skilled workers.

A key outcome of this new approach to workforce development was a decision by the ABN Group to adapt the usual group hiring services provided by GTOs by creating its own internal GTO, ABN Training. This new company was established by the ABN Group in 2004, when investment in the mining sector was peaking and expected to keep growing, and demand for skilled tradespeople in the construction sector was soaring.

The enterprise-embedded apprenticeship model

Objectives

The main goal of the enterprise-embedded apprenticeship programme developed by the ABN Group was to achieve the highest possible retention of graduated apprentices within the company, with the broad aim of guaranteeing future accessibility to tradespeople that meet the ABN Group's standards of skills and align with their organisational culture. Underlining this was the aim of achieving generational change in standards relative to core issues such as safety, work readiness and quality of work.

The following key performance indicators underlie the work of ABN Training:

- 70% of each intake complete apprenticeship programme
- 80% retention rate as a tradesperson six months following graduation
- 60% retention rate as a tradesperson two years after graduation

The internal GTO ABN Training also attempted to attract mature-aged workers to their apprenticeship programme. While mature-aged people are generally underrepresented in the Australian apprenticeship system, over a third (34.5%) of apprentices hired between by the ABN Group from 2012 to 2015 was mature-aged. The organisation also attempts to attract apprentices from other underrepresented groups.

Activities

As illustrated in Figure 5.5, the enterprise-embedded apprenticeship strategy developed by the ABN Group has a "whole of life" approach, and consists of three phases:

1. Work exposure: promotion of career paths in the construction industry to Year 10-12 students;

2. Apprenticeship: in-house delivered apprenticeship programme; and

3. Career progression: a "graduation" programme offering employment solutions both within the ABN Group and the broader building and construction industry to maximise the retention of graduated apprentices.

Figure 5.5. **The ABN Group's workforce development strategy**

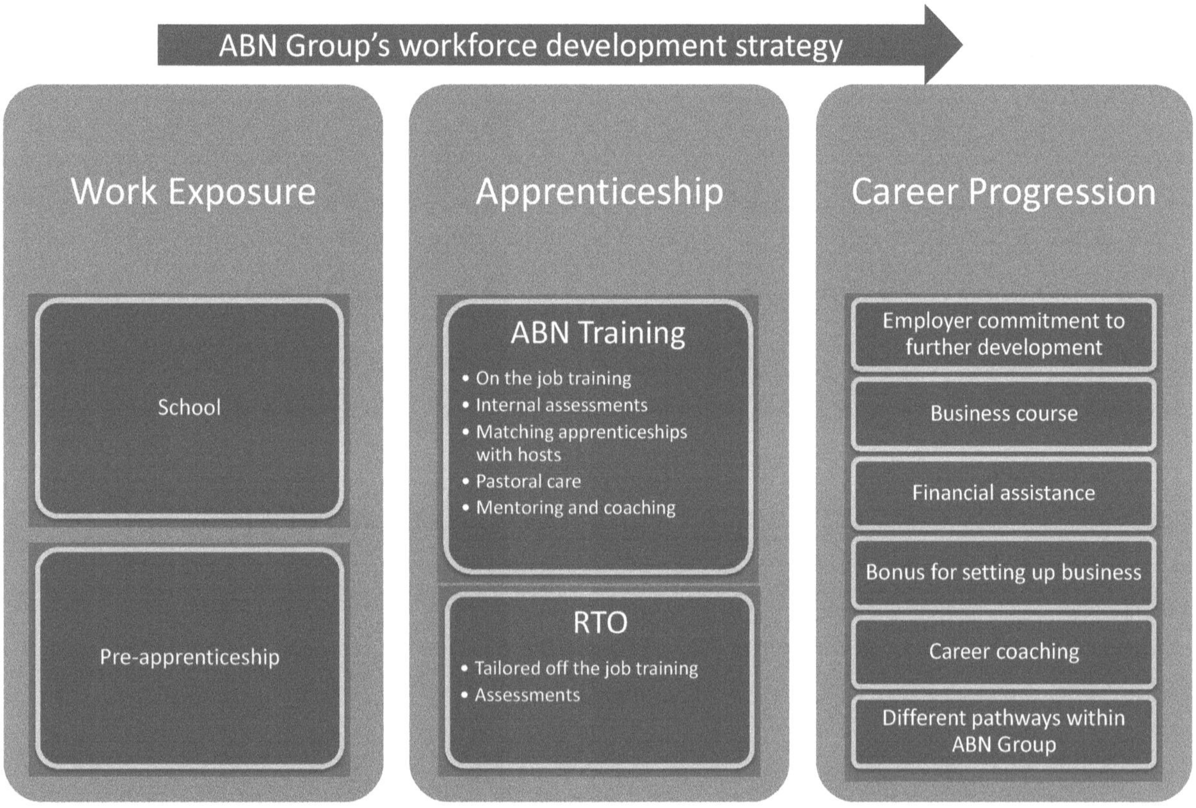

Source: Author's own elaboration.

The programme features:

- A ratio of one training manager to approximately 25 apprentices, well below the general industry practice among building and construction GTOs of one training manager to 50 apprentices (Source: interview with a project manager from the Construction Training Fund);

- Tailored training and career plans; and

- Coaching and mentoring programmes from the commencement of apprenticeship through to post graduation.

Work exposure

As part of this first phase of the "whole of life" workforce development strategy, ABN Training works in collaboration with the CTF to promote careers in the construction industry to secondary students. The Group contributes to career fairs and schools-based "try-a-trade" short courses where secondary school students in Years 9 and 10 can participate and receive an overview of each trade. As part of this same work exposure phase, ABN Training also provides Years 11 and 12 students with on-the-job training as part of CTF's "Schools2Skills" pre-apprenticeships programme. Each year, the ABN Group hosts around one third of the approximately 1 500 Western Australian students that participate in "Schools2Skills" programmes.

ABN Training works with schools and RTOs to recruit apprenticeship candidates that have been involved in the school-based programmes funded by the CTF, as these have a better understanding of the industry, and therefore a lower risk of non-completion. Many of these students have already achieved Level II certification as a result of successful completion of the "Schools2Skills" programme, which can then accelerate completion of their apprenticeship. These candidates also tend to have a better understanding of the industry and a lower risk of non-completion. In addition to this, the ABN Group also seeks to recruit mature-age participants. Although mature age apprentices are entitled to higher wages that school leavers, the ABN Group has found that they tend to be more committed to the programme and able to advise and mentor younger apprentices.

In 2014, ABN Training received 1 000 applications for 100 apprenticeship vacancies. These apprenticeships are offered in particular trades on the basis of market and skills demand, the company's strategy and workforce planning

Apprenticeship

Successful candidates are hired by ABN Training as apprentices under a training contract, and then hosted by different subcontractors working across the 23 subsidiaries of the ABN Group, each of which specialises in a different area of construction. In 2015, apprenticeships were offered in 13 trade areas. On commencement, apprentices have the opportunity to experience all trade areas before specialisation. Upon appointment as an apprentice, they continue to be exposed to other trade areas to enhance their understanding of the industry.

The ABN Group also creates special internal training teams for trades where the workload within the ABN Group is too restricted to justify a host employer taking on apprentices. For example, in 2015, specialised training teams were created in the areas of wall and floor tiling, carpentry and joinery, concreting, and commercial construction.

Almost all of the ABN Group's companies have a "training manager" that is responsible for the recruitment and management of the apprentices allocated in that company (in some instances, smaller companies within the Group share a Training Manager). Training managers are also responsible for providing apprentices with tailored training plans and mentoring. The ABN Group's Apprentice Training Manager oversees the training managers working for the Group's various companies, ensuring apprentices receive the appropriate training and level of pastoral care required to keep them fully engaged in the apprenticeship programme.

The ratio of Training Managers to apprentices in the ABN Group is around 1:25, which compares favourably to the general industry practice of one GTO training manager to around 50 apprentices. This lower ratio is designed to allow apprentices to develop a stronger relationship with their training manager. In comparison, most GTO training managers tend to focus on finding host employers instead of offering support and pastoral care (source: interview with Director, Skills Development from the CTF). Apprentices are internally assessed prior to any formal assessments undertaken by the associated RTOs, and will receive extra support to address any learning difficulties that might lead to failing RTO training units.

The ABN Group also holds annual Apprentice Awards to recognise the top-performing apprentices in that year's cohort. The categories for awards include leadership, excellence in their chosen trade and safety awareness. ABN Group apprentices have also featured strongly in broader State and National Apprenticeship Awards over recent years.

Career progression

The final part of this phase is the career progression phase, during which apprentices are mentored by a Trade Development Manager to set both short- and long-term career goals. Graduate apprentices attend a short business course, where they learn about the legal and financial aspects and obligations of operating a business, and hear from graduates from previous years who share their business experience.

Each successful graduate also receives an AUD 1 000 voucher from the ABN Group to use with a local accounting firm to assist them to register their business name, obtain insurance cover and process their first taxation return. Graduates are also coached on how to establish their own business as a sub-contractor and create their own team, or have the option of joining other contractors' teams as a subcontractor. As a contractor, successful graduates work for one of ABN Group's companies according to the skill sets developed in the apprentice programme. Graduates are also offered interest-free loans to assist them to buy tools and equipment and establish themselves in the market if starting up their own contracting business to work for ABN Group. The loan is then paid back through direct debits on construction contracts. Apprentices can also access finance packages from the ABN Group for home and car loans, either upon graduation or later as a contractor or employee.

Feedback and mentoring support from the ABN Group continues indefinitely after graduation, and graduates may be guided towards further training and education if moving into a more high-skilled or managerial position is part of their longer-term career goal.

The graduation programme is crucial to the success of the apprenticeship as graduates are offered financial and pastoral support, with the possibility of employment within the ABN Group. Alternatively, graduates who choose to establish their own contracting business are guaranteed contracts from relevant ABN Group companies. This aligns with the ABN Group's workforce development strategy and integrates with the company's planning process to meet current and forecasted future workloads.

Programme, governance framework and delivery arrangements

The enterprise-embedded apprenticeship model takes place in the broader context of the ABN Group's business activities. The ABN Group is an integrated construction, property and financial services company comprising 23 businesses – one of which is ABN Training. A high level overview of ABN Group industry profile is outlined in Figure 5.6.

Figure 5.6. **The ABN Group's industry profile**

Source: Author's own elaboration.

ABN Training is a registered GTO that is responsible for the design, development and implementation of the apprenticeship programme at the ABN Group. It works closely with the ABN Group's board of directors to identify medium to long-term strategies, and to monitor and evaluate the progress of apprentices.

As a registered GTO, ABN Training is also responsible to the following external organisations:

● The Western Australian Department of Training and Workforce Development (DTWD), which provides funding, assesses GTOs against the *National Standards for Group Training Organisations* for membership of the National Group Training Register, and conducts biannual compliance audits;

- The Construction Training Fund (CTF), which provides funding, supports recruitment planning and strategy through market intelligence, and supports school-based training programmes and promotional activities for skills development in the construction industry;

- Registered Training Organisations (RTOs), which assess work-based training opportunities, provide off-the-job training and assist in the development of training models suited to business needs;

- Construction and Property Industry Skills Council, which collaborates with ABN Training and other GTOs to improve relevant training packages.

Figure 5.7 provides an overview of the governance arrangements within the ABN Group.

Figure 5.7. **Overview of the programme governance arrangements within the ABN Group**

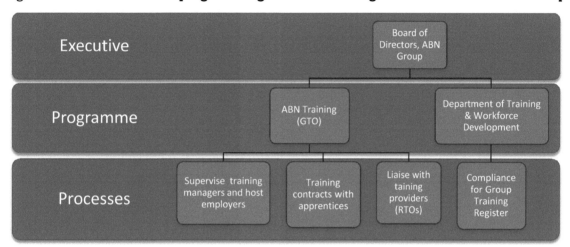

Source: Author's own elaboration.

As Figure 5.7 shows, ABN Training is an organisation housed within ABN Group and reports to its board of directors. ABN Training supervises the host employers, namely contractors that work for the ABN Group, and the Training Managers that are responsible for the overall management and mentoring of apprentices.

The overall performance of both the programme and all the training managers is evaluated annually through surveys disseminated to apprentices and host employers, and the results are used to inform continuous improvement.

Due to the volume of apprentices, the organisation is able to negotiate training package delivery with RTOs to minimise off-the-job training where possible. For example, apprentices within the carpentry apprenticeship pathway would usually attend an RTO for five days of off-the-job training to complete the roofing unit of competency. As apprentices are able to develop this competence on site, and apply related skills almost daily, the ABN Group was able to negotiate with the relevant RTO to provide only relevant off-the-job training over the period of a single day. This maximises the development of practical workplace skills for apprentices while meeting the national minimum standards for units of competency. The ABN Group also collaborates with external companies and suppliers to provide industry training, including with respect to safety, tools and materials application.

Budget and financing

Figure 5.8 provides an overview of the financing arrangements that apply to ABN Training's apprenticeship programme.

Figure 5.8. **ABN apprenticeship programme governance**

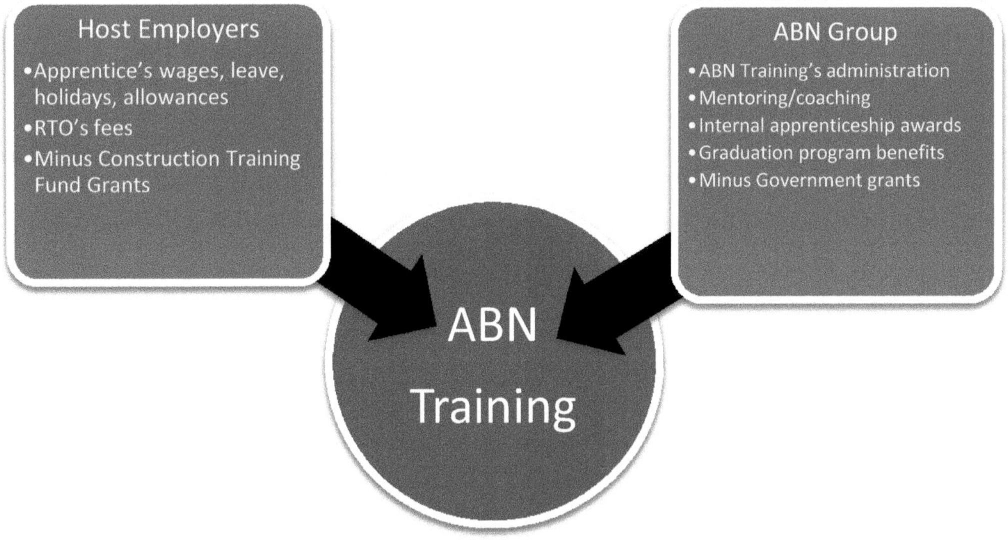

Source: Author's own elaboration.

ABN Training receives government funding of AUD 1 500 for each apprentice upon commencement, with a further AUD 1 000 provided if participants are based outside of Western Australia's capital city (Perth) or are over 21 years of age. On completion of the apprenticeship, ABN Training receives a further AUD 2 500 per apprentice from the Commonwealth government.

As a GTO, ABN Training also receives funding from the CTF and the Australian Brick and Blocklaying Training Foundation. Unlike other GTOs, ABN Training passes these funds onto their host employers.

Discounting all the costs that are covered by host employers, and government and CTF incentives, the programme costs ABN Group around AUD 5 000 per apprentice. The ABN Group begins to observe a return on investment after the apprentice completes 32 weeks of work.

One of the features of a GTO is that the host employer pays a fee to the GTO to cover the cost of the apprentices' wages, workers' compensation insurance, superannuation etc. As part of the programme costs are absorbed by the ABN Group, this enables ABN Training to charge lower fees to host employers (within the Group) while paying apprentices above the relevant minimum (industrial award) rate.

Strengths of the programme

Innovation

The main innovation illustrated in this case-study has been the enterprise-embedded model developed by the ABN Group whereby the traditional GTO arrangement has been adapted into an internal programme. By doing this, the company has been able to utilise the apprenticeship programme as part of its workforce development strategy and can offer apprentices the chance to experience work across the breadth of the ABN Group. Apprentice retention rates have remained high due to the specific features of the programme, including continued coaching after graduation, business training and access to in-house loans.

The Programme has three core features. Apprentices:

- Are contracted and receive on-the-job training within a single company (compared to other GTO arrangements, where apprentices are contracted to the GTO and "subcontracted" to a variety of host employers throughout their apprenticeship);

- Receive thorough support to fulfil their career pathway aspirations; and

- Experience an environment that enables fulfilment of a career pathway as tradespeople. The "whole of life" strategy of the programme enables apprentices to access pastoral care and support not only during training but also after graduation.

Both the ABN Group and the CTF have noted that, to the best of their knowledge, this is a unique approach that does not occur elsewhere in Australia, in or outside the construction industry (source: interview with the Director of Skills Development, CTF).

Table 5.1. **Innovative aspects of the ABN Group's apprenticeship programme**

Innovation	Impacts
Apprentices are hired by and hosted/trained within one single entity (ABN Group).	Model fosters organisational citizenship. Graduated apprentices are more likely to meet ABN Group's quality standards, and become a loyal, reliable workforce. ABN Training is directly linked to ABN Group's board of directors, and the whole programme is designed and implemented to pursue ABN Group's strategic priorities.
Apprentices are guaranteed work, and may choose between different career pathways within ABN Group, while continuing to receive ongoing mentoring and support.	ABN Training is able to attract candidates who are the 'cream of the crop', as apprentices have the opportunity to explore multiple trades as well as look forward to more than just completing a trade certificate.
High volume of apprentices provides greater flexibility in embedding the company's needs and standards when negotiating tailored training delivery with RTOs.	Training can be adapted to business needs and internal standards, leading to: Less duplication of training delivery between off-the-job and on-the-job content. Higher cost-effectiveness. Apprentices able to complete training units in less time. Apprentices able to spend more time on site, resulting in improved productivity.
Significantly lower ratio of training manager to apprentice compared to the average GTO.	Training managers are able to offer more personalised support, and to dedicate more time to each apprentice.
The main role of ABN Group's training managers is to provide mentoring and coaching, rather than focusing on managing the allocation of apprentices between host employers.	Apprentices feel supported, increasing satisfaction rates and strengthening links with the company.
Subcontractors hosting apprentices are prioritised for new contracts offered by companies within ABN Group.	Increased attractiveness for ABN Group contractors to act as host employers for apprentices.
Mentoring and coaching continues after completion of the apprenticeship, when Trade Development Managers stay in contact with the contractors or employees who graduated from ABN Training for an unlimited time. This occurs even if they no longer work for ABN Group.	Apprentices feel supported in their career pursuits, strengthening links with ABN Group brand. ABN Group is able to reach out to qualified tradespeople in times of skills shortage. Former apprentices are confident they will be welcomed back after an absence.

Source: Author's own elaboration.

Outcomes

The enterprise-embedded apprenticeship model has succeeded in achieving high completion and retention rates. According to internal data, 71% of apprentices completed the programme between July 2009 and June 2012. In contrast, the average completion rates for construction apprenticeship programmes were 42% in Australia, and 52% in Western Australia, between 2008 and 2010 (NCVER, 2014).

Training Managers within the ABN Group note that the lack of completion is often a result of a lack of maturity. The ABN Group's willingness to hire experienced candidates, including mature applicants and those that have already completed the "Schools2Skills" Programme, may have also driven the high apprenticeship completion rate. Retention rates for the period July 2011 to June 2015 show that approximately 86% of apprentices who successfully graduate remained with the ABN Group for the first 6 months after completing their apprenticeship. Two years after graduation, 73% of graduates remain with the ABN Group.

Table 5.2. **Measured outcomes for apprentices completing the ABN programme between July 2011 and June 2015**

Target	Benchmark/KPI	Achieved
Completion	70%	71%
Retention rate within ABN Group six months after graduation	80%	86%
Retention rate within ABN two years after graduation	60%	73%

Source: ABN Group.

Impacts

ABN Training's apprentices have been regular winners of regional (state) and national awards over a number of years, which attests to the quality of the training programme.

Internal satisfaction surveys undertaken by ABN Training in the third quarter of 2014 provide further evidence of the positive impact of the programme. The performance of the training managers was rated as "excellent" or "above average" by 96% of apprentices and 98% of host employers. Host employers' performance was rated as "excellent" or "above average" by 89% of apprentices while the performance of apprentices was rated as "excellent" or "above average" by 77% of host employer respondents. There is also strong competition for the ABN apprenticeship programme due to the guaranteed career opportunities offered upon completion, alongside the standard trade certificate qualification.

Over 900 apprentices have commenced the programme since 2004 and have provided a consistent and easily accessible workforce for the ABN Group. Most graduated apprentices continue working for ABN Group as sub-contractors, while many others become employees working as schedulers, construction and site managers and move on to assume other managerial roles within ABN Group's companies. Many graduates also go on to become host employers for new apprentices, which further reinforces the sustainability of the model.

The enterprise-embedded programme also has positive impacts on the supply of skills in the broader Western Australian construction industry. According to ABN data, an estimated 98% of their graduates remain in the building and construction industry six months after the completion of the programme, and an estimated 85% remain in the industry two years after graduation. Although data from other apprenticeship programmes is not available for comparison, these numbers are quite striking in the context of the skills shortages associated with the mining boom that drew workers away from almost every industry in Western Australia.

There are also indirect benefits for the ABN Group, including an improved reputation as a major contributor to skills development in the construction industry and increased ability to attract new clients (source: interview with the ABN Group's Managing Director).

Key factors underlying success

A key factor underlying the programme's success is the full commitment of ABN Group's leadership team to the programme. The programme's successful implementation was driven by the direct involvement and personal engagement of the Group's Managing Director and other senior leaders in pushing for regulatory reforms, developing and implementing innovative approaches to workforce development, and promoting trades as a career.

The ABN Group's willingness to collaborate with apprentices in the long-run by guaranteeing post-completion employment has also had positive impacts on apprenticeship completion and retention rates. The strong pastoral care and mentoring provided during and after the apprenticeship is also crucial to the programme's success.

Some of the unique features of the apprenticeship model include:

- ABN Training offers a wraparound service that is directly linked to the company's operations and strategies;
- The ABN Group partially absorbs management costs, meaning host employers pay a lower fee to ABN Training then they would pay to an external GTO whose sole business is group training;
- The enterprise-embedded model is able to capitalise on some features of the large and diversified company, including greater access to market intelligence (including between its own companies) and the ability to expose apprentices to a wide variety of work;
- There are a number of host employers available within the ABN Group, which allows ABN Training to find the best match for the apprentice's skills and interests;
- As an industry leader, ABN Group is able to facilitate discussion around apprenticeship policy, and lobby for changes in regulation;
- The programme specifically targets mature apprentices and young candidates who have completed other vocational training programmes. The experience of these candidates helps to foster better educational opportunities during the apprenticeship and increased completion and retention rates.

Obstacles faced during design or implementation

Regulation

At the time that the ABN Group started hiring its first apprentices under external GTOs, the Western Australian apprenticeship model was based on time-served rather than achieved competencies. The model was seen to be inflexible in terms of the responsiveness of training providers to industry needs. It also lengthened the average apprenticeship as candidates were unable to receive credits for skills previously learned in other courses or during work experience.

The ABN Group's senior leadership team worked alongside representative of the state government, industry councils and associations and unions to review and reform the regulation of the apprenticeship system of the building and construction industry. After a process of investigation and review, the state apprenticeship model was shifted from a 4-year time-served programme to a competency-based approach (Western Australia Training Board, 2006).

This allowed apprenticeship programmes to be completed in three years (or less, depending on apprentices' abilities). This made apprenticeships more attractive to both young people, who were now able to get credits for skills learned in pre-apprenticeship programmes, and also mature workers from aligned industries who could get credit for competencies learned in previous jobs. The competency-based programme also removed some requirements for extensive classroom-based learning and promoted more practical on-the-job skills development. Developing an embedded, internal GTO meant that the ABN Group was able to ensure that training design is tailored to its business requirements.

Access to talented young people

Prior to establishing their internal enterprise-embedded apprenticeship programme, the ABN Group identified a need to address a perception that apprenticeships were not highly valued compared to university. This perception limited the ABN Group's ability to attract the best candidates.

To address this, the ABN Group worked in conjunction with the CTF to lead discussions on promoting the construction industry to young people leaving school. In 2004, an awareness and careers promotion campaign with the slogan *"One Industry – No Limits"* was developed to provide information on careers in the construction industry. The campaign was targeted towards educators, students and parents and illustrated how students could pursue a VET qualification while at school and demonstrated how different educational pathways could lead to a successful career in the construction industry.

Potential transferability

What are the main lessons for other OECD countries?

This case study provides a number of lessons for other OECD countries. In particular, the case study shows that designing and implementing an effective industry-led and enterprise-embedded group training model is reliant on a range of factors including strong leadership, appropriate financial and non-financial incentives, strong engagement with the education and training sector and enabling regulatory processes.

The following five key lessons learned from ABN Group's experience might be considered and/or adapted within other OECD countries:

● Factors that improve apprenticeship completion and ongoing retention may include:

❖ A high ratio of supervisors to apprentices;

❖ Appropriate mentoring and career development opportunities;

❖ Allowing apprentices to develop broader business skills as well as technical skills.

● Industry engagement is necessary to support the supply of apprentices and a training levy is a valid and proven method for achieving this;

● Financial incentives for employers are effective in enhancing supply of apprentices;

● Those managing apprenticeship programmes should liaise with the academic education sector to develop optimal pathways from education into work. Deeper connections can also address the perception that an apprenticeship pathway is "second best" to university; and

● Flexibility and adaptability in training and assessment delivery can lead to greater cost effectiveness, deeper liaison between employers and training providers and can help stakeholders understand each others' contexts and requirements.

Industry engagement in apprenticeship programme delivery is particularly effective in countries such as Australia and Germany that have dual apprenticeship systems, where training takes place both on and off the job and often commences during secondary education. This enables smoother transitions to employment and can help meet increased demand for workers in industries in which there are either skills shortages or forecast expansion (Steedman, 2014).

It is also crucial that government or industry councils are able to facilitate the transfer of information within the labour market by adopting systematic approaches to identifying areas of skills shortage and planning training policies accordingly. For example, the Western Australian state government's Future Skills policy, for example, embeds a focus on subsidised training for priority courses linked to areas of shortage (Future Skills WA, 2016).

Further, financial incentives underpinned by clear legislation have been found to be a strong factor in encouraging employers to take on apprentices. The success of the construction training levy in Western Australia is linked to the CTF's ability to redistribute monies to initiatives such as apprenticeship training, engagement with schools through programmes such as "School2Skills", incentives to attract and support underrepresented learners including women, Indigenous learners and those in remote areas, and providing support to employers to up-skill existing workers. Because the levy is industry-specific, it can be targeted based on evidence and data collection to better meet the needs of the industry.

Developing a clear transition pathway from education, to apprenticeships and finally to small business ownership and employment was effective for the ABN Group. Vertical and horizontal integration within relevant organisations can also help to boost success.

The volume of apprentices enrolled in the programme delivered by ABN Training allowed them to negotiate targeted training delivery with RTOs in order to support organisational goals. The training context is flexible and apprentice-centred while remaining relevant to employment and the needs of the ABN Group. This approach takes place within an integrated framework of employers, training providers, apprentices and government. Meeting the needs of various stakeholders requires constant dialogue between government and industry around skills and vocational education policies.

This case is an example of how industry can challenge norms and regulations and question whether public policy is delivering as intended, or whether regulation is hampering or encouraging innovation and productivity.

Considerations for successful adoption in other OECD countries

The innovative approach used by the ABN Group reflects the broader Western Australian and Australian vocational education framework. All countries within the OECD possess some elements of the Australian Apprenticeship model.

The enterprise-embedded model developed by the ABN Group is based on its strong links with other parties, including government and the education and training sector. Transferring the model to other contexts would require the establishment of similar connections. The adoption of the enterprise-embedded model in other OECD countries would necessitate consideration of the following factors, including:

● Scalability of the model. The model implemented at the ABN Group made considerable use of its size and horizontal and vertical integration. It is not clear whether the same model would be successful in smaller or multinational organisations;

● A critical factor to the success of the model was access to an industry skills levy that is applied to all Western Australian construction projects valued over AUD 20 000. The levy is an industry-specific approach that establishes a common fund for training, and has similarities to the common funding pools established within the apprenticeships systems in Denmark and France (Steedman, 2014);

- Co-ordinated policy settings are critical, particularly when supported by clear legislation that enables the transferability of competences and confirms the rights of stakeholders. Legislation should enable apprentices to see the value of portable certification that is valid across the country rather than only within a particular organisation. Further, the rights of the apprentice and the responsibilities of employers and training providers should be made clear in legislation.

- Engagement with the schools sector is crucial, particularly with respect to the development of programmes that link the schools sector with industry areas of existing and future demand. This is necessary in dual vocational educations systems, such as those in place in Australia and Germany (Steedman, 2014).

- Apprenticeships should be open to all willing candidates above the age of 18. In Australia, apprenticeships are open to anyone of working age, unlike other countries such as Austria, France, Germany and Turkey where there are maximum age restrictions (Steedman, 2014). Improving access to apprenticeships may be an important consideration depending on the relationship between skills shortages and population demographics.

- Clear and streamlined policy priorities are necessary to remove bureaucratic hurdles to the development of good relationships between employers, training providers and apprentices. Where government acts as a "facilitator and regulator" (Steedman, 2014), and policy as well as training requirements can be continuously improved through consultation with industry representatives, there is likely to be a strong role for employers in the process.

References

Australian Bureau of Statistics (2013), *Population Projections, Australia, 2012 (base) to 2101*, *www.abs.gov.au/ ausstats/abs@.nsf/Latestproducts/3222.0Main%20Features12012%20(base)%20to%202101?opendocument& tabname=Summary&prodno=3222.0&issue=2012%20(base)%20to%202101&num=&view=.*

Australian Bureau of Statistics (2014), 5220.0 Australian National Accounts: State Accounts 2013-14, "Expenditure, Income and Industry Components of Gross State Product, Western Australia", *www.abs.gov.au/AUSSTATS/abs@.nsf/DetailsPage/5220.02013-14?OpenDocument.*

Australian Bureau of Statistics (2014), 5220.0 Australian National Accounts: State Accounts 2013-14, "Chain volume measures and current prices, Annual", *www.abs.gov.au/AUSSTATS/abs@.nsf/DetailsPage/ 5220.02013-14?OpenDocument.*

Australian Bureau of Statistics (2012), 1301.0 Year Book Australia, 2012, *www.abs.gov.au/ausstats/ abs@.nsf/Lookup/by%20Subject/1301.0~2012~Main%20Features~Agriculture~27.*

Australian Bureau of Statistics (2012), 1367, State and Territory Statistical Indicators, *www.abs.gov.au/ ausstats/abs@.nsf/Lookup/by%20Subject/1367.0~2012~Main%20Features~Labour%20Force%20 Participation%20Rate~4.5.*

Australian Bureau of Statistics (2011), Census data, *www.abs.gov.au/websitedbs/censushome.nsf/home/data.*

Australian Bureau of Statistics (2010), 5625.0 Private new capital expenditure and expected expenditure Australia, September 2010, *www.abs.gov.au/ausstats/abs@.nsf/products/CAF7D00DDD667D4FCA257A0E 0012CDA5?OpenDocument.*

Australian Bureau of Statistics (2006), Census data, *www.abs.gov.au/websitedbs/censushome.nsf/home/data.*

Australian Government, Department of Education, Employment and Workplace Relations (2013), "Australian Jobs 2013", *www.cdaa.org.au/ContentUpload/Docs/australianjobs2013.pdf.*

Building and Construction Industry Training Fund (2014), sourced from: *https://bcitf.org.*

Construction Training Council (2010), Workforce development plan for the construction industry, available from *https://bcitf.org/upload/documents/research_reports/Website_Research_Workforce DevReport.pdf*.

Construction Training Fund (2016), *Funding Support Overview, https://bcitf.org/funding-support/apprenticeships*.

Construction Training Fund (2014), "One Industry No Limits – Careers in Construction", *http:// nolimits.com.au*.

Council of Australian Governments (2012), National Agreement for Skills and Workforce Development, available from *www.federalfinancialrelations.gov.au/content/npa/skills/skills-reform/national_ agreement.pdf*.

D'Arcy, P., L. Gustafsson, C. Lewis and T. Wiltshire (2012), "Labour market turnover and mobility", Reserve Bank of Australia's Bulletin, December 2012, available from *www.rba.gov.au/publications/bulletin/2012/ dec/1.html*

Doyle, M. (2014), "Labour movements during the resources boom", Reserve Bank of Australia Bulletin, December 2014, available from *www.rba.gov.au/publications/bulletin/2014/dec/2.html*.

Government of Western Australia, Department of Training and Workforce Development (2016), *www.futureskillswa.wa.gov.au/Pages/default.aspx*.

Government of Western Australia, State Training Board (2006), "Careers for Life: Creating a dynamic and responsive apprenticeship and traineeship system – Report of the Skills Formation Taskforce to the Minister for Education and Training", *www.stb.wa.gov.au/SiteCollectionDocuments/Final_Report-Skills_ Formation_Taskforce.pdf*.

Hodge, S. (2007), "The origins of competency based learning", *Australian Journal of Adult Learning*, 47.2.

Housing Industry Association (2014), available at *https://hia.com.au/~/media/HIA%20Website/Files/Media %20Centre/Media%20Releases/2014/WA/BGC%20Remains%20the%20Wests%20Largest%20Builder %20%20WA.ashx*.

Interview with ABN Group's Managing Director, 17 November 2015.

Interview with ABN Group's Apprentice Programme Manager, 6 November 2015.

Interviews with the Director of Skills Development, Construction Training Fund on 2 December 2015 and 18 December 2015.

National Centre for Vocational Education Research (2011), "Report 1: Overview of the Australian Apprenticeship and Traineeship System", Commonwealth Government, 2011, *www.australian apprenticeships.gov.au/publications/ncver-report-1-overview-australian-apprenticeship-and-traineeship-system*.

National Centre for Vocational Education Research (2013), "Australian vocational education and training statistics: Completion and attrition rates for Apprentices and Trainees 2012", *www.ncver.edu.au/wps/ wcm/connect/b9cce99f-4c94-4bbd-8121-97ea02d024d5/2012-completion-and-attrition-rates-2632.pdf? MOD=AJPERES&CACHEID=b9cce99f-4c94-4bbd-8121-97ea02d024d5*.

National Centre for Vocational Education Research (2015), "Completion and attrition rates for apprentices and trainees 2014: state and territory data table", Average of apprenticeship contracts attrition rates for 2008-2010, *www.ncver.edu.au/wps/portal/vetdataportal/restricted/dataContent/!ut/p/a1/xZFPU8IwEMU_ DcdMtm1oyxH_YECB2uJAe2FCkkqUpiXNMOKnJ9Xx4gyiJ3N7mbdv97eLC7zChWYH9cysqjXbdboI12PPv6aUw GROaQjjaLRIM_oUAI3wEhe44No2dotzzQ_SrNstM1L0QDDLesDrqtnJLg4xLRCz1qgPZZiVLSprg1jTGKmt4k53H muY0tIJHzyCWuuMn__SuNraHFEXjSzb7GTb9W-4Ejj3ykEQyL6HhIhKRMAvUcxFhNgmJrHgJCQgHVDugOD MG8KveJ0loXehf-UsMZ0CjGdZOpreZgHMw-8GGDzeuAx_NqEPiQf3_QsJ8JXww5C5o4jOjpkQnP1xLZNL3G5 v6mW_L4bu2rW28s3i1b-cu6mqODii15S-L8pqOTwBmPQU4g!!/dl5/d5/L2dBISEvZ0FBIS9nQSEh/*.

National Centre for Vocational Education Research (2015), "Apprentices and trainees 2014-annual: territory data tables", available at *www.ncver.edu.au/wps/portal/vetdataportal/restricted/dataContent/ !ut/p/a1/rVHLbsIwEPwajpaX2E3CkT6ooeVRQgXJBW2SpbgFExwLlX49jqpeKlFaqXub1exoZpZnfMEzgwf 9gk7vDG4anIXLfju4UUrCYKxUCP2oN5sm6lmAivicZzwrjKvcmqemOJBd1mu0VLagRIctwKqyZJwuqGZoSu YsakMeBNCWrHbo6HNP1mq3s0fW3DGH-YbqRrwqdMnTQnSoJIhYDgExKUGyWAjJUOYRYZwLwJV3m 3q3cGa68KswnjJR92Fw7SmxGgL0R8m0N7xLBIzD7wToPN16jWA0UI-TNJxcXVCAL4UfTKY-RXTW5kTy5I- 1DC7l9r3p1_0-6_pX7oyjd8cX___LaruNxZG9TdXHbLWdd08IzbnK/dl5/d5/L2dBISEvZ0FBIS9nQSEh/*.

Oliver, D. (2011), *Skill shortages in the trades during economic downturns*, National Centre for Vocational Education Research (NCVER).

State Training Board (2006), "Careers for life: Creating a dynamic and responsive traineeship and apprenticeship system", Report of the Skills Formation Taskforce to the Minister for Education and

Training, Perth Western Australia, 2006, available from *www.stb.wa.gov.au/SiteCollectionDocuments/ Final_Report-Skills_Formation_Taskforce.pdf*.

Steedman, H. (2014), "Overview of Apprenticeship Systems and Issues: ILO contribution to the G20 task force on employment", International Labour Office, Skills and Employability Department, Geneva: ILO.

The Australian (2015), "Mines recruit women drivers on big money", *www.theaustralian.com.au/news/ nation/mines-recruit-women-drivers-on-big-money/story-e6frg6nf-1225829870194*, downloaded 7 December 2015.

United Nations Development Programme (2015), *Human Development Reports*, downloaded 18 December 2015, *http://hdr.undp.org/en/content/human-development-index-hdi*.

United Nations Development Programme (2015), *Human Development Report – Work for Human Development*, *http://hdr.undp.org/sites/default/files/2015_human_development_report.pdf*.

Chapter 6

Youth skills development and retention in Otorohanga, New Zealand

This chapter analyses the impacts of local leadership and consultation in the development of initiatives to address youth unemployment in Otorohanga, New Zealand. Initiatives to support youth through the transition from school to work that are examined include the introduction of local training, mentorship and pastoral care services. The chapter highlights the success of integrated local leadership among actors in government, business, faith and educational institutions to develop solutions to address specific issues in a diversified rural context.

Key findings

- This chapter investigates the impacts of a series of initiatives spearheaded by local community leaders in the small rural New Zealand town of Otorohanga to encourage youth to undertake apprenticeships in the town's trade sector.

- The initiatives in Otorohanga focussed on local leadership, training guidance and pastoral care from respected figures of authority to increase the uptake, completion and retention of apprenticeships in the trades sector. Focussing on a particular industry was found to be effective in the Otorohanga context.

- The process of enacting these apprenticeship initiatives involved addressing related issues, including the provision and proximity of off-the-job training, the status and perception of apprenticeships and vocational education, and the role of careers guidance and information in building a sustainable apprenticeship culture.

- The evolution of the governance and funding structure for the Otorohanga youth initiatives is also examined, particularly with respect to the movement from a grassroots project towards a formal and standardised programme.

Introduction

The Otorohanga youth initiative offers an interesting case study of targeted employment creation in rural New Zealand, where just a few businesses in one sector in a small town catalysed a number of projects to support local youth to enter a trades career in their home town to address a local staff and skill shortage. Youth unemployment rates in New Zealand are marginally higher than the OECD average and have become a matter of national concern (Human Rights Commission, 2014). Unemployment levels tend to be higher outside of the major urban centres, which poses significant social and economic challenges to small rural towns. Although there is a state focus on achieving a school accreditation and training certification in New Zealand, the federal government allocates less additional support to areas of need than many other OECD countries. This means that a greater onus rests with local actors to respond to local development challenges. It is in this context that this research paper presents a study of a locally instigated initiative to address youth unemployment challenges in the town of Otorohanga.

At first glance, the schemes targeting the youth of Otorohanga may appear to have been driven by youth unemployment. However, this is not the case, as unemployment levels in 2006 for this particular town were similar or even slightly better than in the rest of the nation. The true catalyst for local action was the concerns of a specific group of local businesses, which were unable to attract and retain skilled workers because young local jobseekers were failing to successfully complete the appropriate training requirements.

It is often the case that young people who have grown up in a small rural town and have come to know and appreciate the local people and the spaces are the best positioned to stay and contribute to the town's economy and community. However, it is common for this youth cohort to leave for the cities. As in most rural towns, these youth are often obliged to do their training in the larger towns due to the availability of facilities. From there they tend not to return, as they discover other lifestyles and other job opportunities.

Within a nation with an aging population, this urban drift of youth compounds the demographic challenges in small rural towns, which may in turn affect the town's long-term economic viability. In the small town of Otorohanga, there was a need to address skills shortages in the local technical trades industry while also ensuring that local youth were aware of local opportunities, supported in their career development and willing to stay in the town. This led to the establishment of a series of initiatives that nurtured young workers to stay and to thrive at home. This in turn helped to build sustainable local industry that was confident of a continued supply of skilled labour.

For other OECD countries with small rural towns facing similar challenges, this case offers a vision of how the local businesses can address their staff and training needs. The experiences of Otorohanga found that while skills and work readiness training were important facets of the programme, it was also critical to incorporate tuition and pastoral care to facilitate communication with business owners. Personalised care should be tailored to suit the local stakeholders and should be provided by a local person with a deep understanding of the community and the industry.

This Chapter outlines the rationale and context for the youth employment initiative from the national and local perspective, before detailing and assessing the actual interventions which were undertaken. The paper concludes with an overview of the key lessons which can be derived from the experience.

Policy context

New Zealand is a small upper-income country in the South Pacific. It has a relatively small population estimated at 4 659 287 in 2015 (Stats NZ, 2016). The New Zealand economy is dominated by the service sector, but is well integrated into global market networks and also heavily relies upon the export of primary and agricultural produce. Consequently, the country has a strong and labour-intensive rural/agricultural sector. The performance of this sector in recent years has stabilised rural populations in many parts of the country and driven demand for specific technical skills in rural areas and the service centres scattered across them. Otorohanga is one such service centre that has close links with the agricultural activities in its hinterland.

In 2015, the national unemployment rate was 5.3%, while the Labour Force Participation Rate stood at 68.4%. The working population was estimated to be 3 656 000 while those in employment stood at 2 369 000 and the numbers unemployed being 133 000 (Stats NZ, 2016). It is important to note that according to Stats NZ one of the reasons for the low unemployment rate is the falling labour participation rate which hints at changes in the employment patterns within the country. The youth unemployment (defined as the 15-24 year old cohort) rate in 2015 was 10.9%, more than double the national average. The unemployment rate among women aged 15-24 is even higher, at 12.6%. Equally concerning are ethnic difference in the unemployment rate, with Maori and Pacific youth having experienced more rapid growth in the rate of unemployment. In 2011, the national unemployment rate in the 15-25 year bracket was 17% for Maori youth, 14.5% for Pacific and 8.2% for European (Human Rights Commission, 2014). In spatial terms, across all age brackets, rural unemployment is often higher (6.9% in the case of the rural province of Gisborne) compared to the larger urban centres (3.9% in Christchurch) (Stats NZ, 2016b).

Youth unemployment has been recognised as being a particular challenge by the national government, particularly because the New Zealand NEET rate (Not in Employment, Education and Training) for the 15-24 year old cohort was 12.5% in 2011, slightly higher than the then OECD average of 12.2%. The situation has deteriorated since 2008 when an OECD report noted that the New Zealand youth unemployment rate was 5% lower than the OECD average in 2006 (OECD, 2008). This concern was identified by the New Zealand Department of Labour (DOL) which noted that these young people are 'disengaging both from formal learning and work, and as such, are considered to be missing the opportunity to develop their potential at an age that heavily influences future outcomes' (Human Rights Commission, 2014). Also there is concern, as noted above, about the over-representation of young Maori and Pacific youth in the unemployment rates. The reasons for disengagement from employment and education are varied and include those who have low educational attainment levels, those who have been obliged to become young carers, the inter-generational impact of poor parenting, low social-economic status, offenders, drug/substance misusers and those with emotional and behavioural difficulties (Human Rights Commission, 2014). The increase in youth unemployment is in part due to the global financial crisis according to the New Zealand Human Rights Commission. The New Zealand Human Rights Commission has called youth unemployment a "ticking time bomb", while the Equal Employment Opportunities Commission has noted that "youth unemployment is an unacceptable problem and is critically embarrassing for New Zealand" (HRC 2014).

The challenges of youth employment and unemployment in the country are exacerbated changes in industrial relations law that have weakened protection measures for youth employment (NZ Government 2015 budget). This may have contributed to the fact that 40% of youth now being engaged in part-time employment. In addition, this cohort experiences very high employment turnover in comparison with the general population (Stats NZ, 2013) (see Figure 6.1).

Figure 6.1. **Worker turn-over rates by age group, 2000-14**

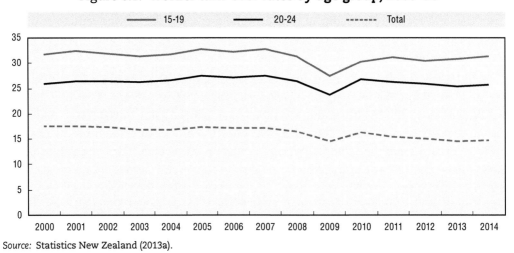

Source: Statistics New Zealand (2013a).

The high levels of youth unemployment have been recognised by social agencies as a significant national concern. The Methodist Mission have noted that one third of youth in some districts being unemployed is an issue that "needs urgent attention" (ODT, 8 August 2011).

Figure 6.2 indicates the differences in the NEET rate between 15-19 year olds compared with 20-24 year old. The high rate in the latter sub-cohort is of particular concern as is the slow upward trajectory of the results.

Figure 6.2. **New Zealand NEET rates by age group, 2005-15**

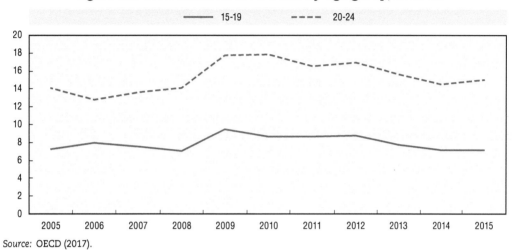

Source: OECD (2017).

The situation in Otorohanga

Prior to the launch of the local initiatives in 2005, the Otorohanga region was facing similar problems with employment as the rest of the country. The general 15 years and over unemployment rate in Otorohanga town was 5.5% in 2001 prior to the establishment of the programmes, which was relatively favourable compared to 7.5% in the rest of New Zealand at the time. In 2006 the unemployment rate in the town fell to 4.3% but rose to 9.9% in 2013, which was higher than the national unemployment level of 5.3% in 2015 (Stats NZ, 2001, 2006, 2013b, 2016). These changes are reflective of broader shifts in the regional economy as the fortunes of farming have waxed and waned. In 2004, the businesses of Otorohanga highlighted a specific skill shortage of apprentices in the trades which encouraged a local response targeted at youth. The subsequent upward trend in unemployment is in an indication that the resulting programme was more focused on creating youth jobs in one specific sector rather than in the creation of large numbers of jobs across all age cohorts. Unfortunately recent data on youth unemployment is not available at the sub-regional level, making it difficult to both gauge the severity of current local youth unemployment and the degree to which the interventions may have impacted on that rate.

Otorohanga is a small rural service town of 2 589 people and is part of a wider rural municipal district of 91 380. In the wider municipal district, there was a small increase in population of 1% between the 2006 and 2013 census counts, and 27.2% of the population identify as Maori compared to a national average of 14.9% (StatsNZ, Census 2013). The only other small town in the Otorohanga district is the very small coastal village of Kawhia with a population of only 390 which is decreasing sharply, while the rest of the district population reside in rural areas (Stats NZ, 2013b). The nearby Waitomo caves in a neighbouring district provide some passing tourism traffic to the town and offer some opportunities for employment in hospitality and tourism. The natural pull for young people in recent years, has been to leave the rural districts and relocate to the nearby provincial city of Hamilton. Hamilton hosts numerous high schools, Waikato University and The Waikato Institute of Technology (Wintec), and its satellite town of Cambridge offers specialist high school subjects such as physics and therefore is attractive to higher achieving youth. The Waikato regional council is composed of 10 district councils, of which Otorohanga district is one, and encompasses the city council of Hamilton.

The economy of the Otorohanga district is based on rural activities. Both the 2006 and 2013 censuses showed that the majority of people were employed in agriculture. In 2006, 1 060 people or 32.2% of people were employed by the agricultural sector, in comparison the national average of 5.7% (Stats NZ, 2006, 2013b). However, despite the dominance of the agricultural and particularly the dairy industry of Otorohanga, the youth scheme was driven by the requests of businesses in the automotive and engineering fields that were experiencing skills and staff shortages. After the agricultural industry, census statistics indicate that the services sector is the second highest employer as 15% of the population are employed in public administration and safety, followed by similar percentages in manufacturing, education/training and retail. The most commonly recorded occupation group was listed in the census was "managers" at 33% compared to the New Zealand average of 18%, but there are fewer people listing their occupation as "professional" than the national average. This could reflect the number of small businesses and franchises that require managers in this small town. The next most common listed occupations were machinery operators, drivers and labourers.

The largest single employers in the town are the lime quarry, which employs about 100 people, and farm supply shops. One farm supply shop that sells large farm-machinery and employs over 75 workers was one of the key businesses that originally indicated its difficulty in finding people with trade qualifications willing to relocate to the town. This business owner was also the individual most willing to work with the project.

Other key businesses in the town include an engineering firm that employs about 80 staff, some large rural freight companies, including one that employs 50-80 people, and some smaller construction businesses focusing on farm buildings. There are also three rural accounting firms that cater to the accounting needs of the surrounding rural population, including one that employs about 50 staff and has a relationship with the local school to assist with advertising and the employment of school leavers. However, the accounting industry was not targeted by the youth employment initiatives detailed below. The town also has retail activities typical of a rural service town including some fast food franchises and general stores. Otorohanga has one high school with 353 pupils in 2015, 191 of whom identify as Maori; the school also includes a boarding school which tends to attract the children of families from the neighbouring beach town of Kawhia where unemployment is very high (Source: based on interviews with the local apprentice support tutor, the Otorhanga youth projects facilitator and former Mayor, the MPOWA tracking co-ordinator and others.)

Pre-programme employment support

Prior to the commencement of the local initiatives detailed in this paper, only national programmes were implemented in Otorohanga. These included nationally available programmes such as apprenticeship support provided by the national Industry Trading

Organisation's (ITO) and schemes that support the tracking of school leavers and ensure that secondary education matched the needs of employers. These schemes are detailed below.

The state was also conducting other programmes in the wider municipal region, including the establishment of the Waikato Institute of Technology's (Wintec) Polytechnic course in the provincial city of Hamilton. This course develops entry-level skills in the engineering and automotive trade and the completion of the course is a prerequisite for applying for an apprenticeship. Wintec also offers courses in basic skills for working as a trades labourer. It was noted by local stakeholders that youth who had completed training in Hamilton were attracted by the lifestyle and employment opportunities and tended not to move back to rural towns.

The New Zealand Government also has a number of broad initiatives to assist youth and provide better support and pathways into post-school education, training or career development (Treasury New Zealand, 2011). Some New Zealand training academies allow students study in the workplace while still enrolled in secondary school. These programmes include the school-based Gateway and STAR programmes (see below for details). The Otorohanga College had both of these programmes in 2004 and followed the Pathways programme where all classes in the school are introduced to one of six career path ways. Prior to 2004, the college also had a part-time careers advisor position and held annual careers days that involved presentations from town businesses and several one day work experience visits to local businesses (Source: based on an interview with the Otorohanga college careers advisor).

The Ministry of Social Development also established a Youth Services unit in August 2012 to provide support to connect NEET youth to employment or training opportunities. This Unit predominately contracts to regional community agencies to provide personalised career services to school leavers, who are then followed up every six months to see how they are progressing through training or employment (*www.msd.govt.nz*) (Source: based on an interview with the MSD Youth Services Unit). In Otorohanga, this service was implemented by a community agency that also helped the larger region.

In summary, national programmes designed to address youth unemployment include:

- Youth Guarantee (Youth Guarantee New Zealand, no date) is a programme run by the Ministry of Education that is designed to reduce the number of youth in the NEET bracket. The methodology was developed in 2010 and has been implemented since 2013. One programme is called Achievement, Retention and Transition (ART) and tracks the career paths and training progress of school pupils and consenting school leavers in a centralised data base. Should concerns arise, a regional agent of education services will contact the participant to suggest education options, or regional agencies sub-contracted by the Ministry of Social Development may advise the participant of other possible activities. If the youth are NEET, they also qualify for courses funded by the government's Youth Guarantee programme.

- Under the Youth Guarantee scheme, the STAR programme makes funding available to schools to provide targeted and job-related short training courses. This also gives some flexibility to secondary education providers to address workplace requirements. An extension of the STAR Programme is the Gateway Programme, which is designed to link school-leavers to workplace and tertiary learning opportunities, including through work experience one day per week.

● The Modern Apprenticeship Scheme was a subsidised apprenticeship for youth aged 16-21, with four support visits made to the trainees per annum. This programme was phased out and replaced by the full adult scheme in 2015 with funding attached to obtaining credits (NZ Government, 2013).

● The recognition of vocational learning experiences in the National Qualifications Framework system.

● The Mayor's Task Force for Jobs (MTFFJs) was set up to encourage Mayors across N.Z. to engage with local businesses and education providers to reduce youth unemployment levels and the Otorohanga Mayor was a member. The Otorohanga initiative however occurred independently from this group, though the project certainly inspired the MTFFJs with the facilitator eventually becoming the chair of the MTFF's in 2008 (Source: based on an interview with the Otorohanga youth projects facilitator and former Mayor).

Currently NZ Apprenticeship training is open to all ages and is co-ordinated throughout New Zealand by national Industry Training Organisations (ITOs). Each ITO designs apprenticeship training to meet the training requirements of specific industries. They also provide training packages that include block courses, correspondence assignments, on-line learning, exams, tutoring and pastoral care, which may necessitate attending a regional centre. The apprenticeship is partially subsidised by the state, but trainees or their employer must pay course-related costs and the ITO fee (NZ Government, 2016). However in Otorohanga, some trainees had learning or personal difficulties that affected their training and work life. Local stakeholders found that pastoral care provided from a distant regional centre was unable to address these issues. The result was a low rate of completion of apprenticeships in Otorohanga in 2004.

While systems of youth support were in place at the national level, the OECD (2008) found that "current labour market policies do not easily reach young people who have disengaged from school at an early age and are not entitled to welfare support". The OECD report goes on to note that "New Zealand presently devotes considerable efforts to trying to overcome this difficulty. However, co-ordination between the national and the community levels requires further fine tuning." It is in this context that the Otorohanga initiative sought to address the needs of both local youth and business in the town.

Local governance considerations prior to the programme being established

Prior to the initiation of the programme, the various forms of governance in the town did not directly interface or collaborate on youth related issues. The town council functioned independently of the school system, while economic development policy was focused on an industrial park and a "Kiwiana" themed programme to promote the town. Youth initiatives from social actors such as the local church were not directly integrated into these processes.

Liaison regarding youth employment did not include local businesses. The local high school did adapt their school training to national industry training needs via the Star and Gateway programmes, but local business liaison was outside of the ambit of the programme. Similarly, regional bodies such as the Industry Training Organisations (ITO's) apprenticeship programmes and the local trades training initiatives were based in the provincial cities and did not provide local or specialised assistance to Otorohanga.

This was the environment and context in which a new initiative to address the local businesses needs for youth skills emerged in 2005.

Description of the initiative

Overview

The launch of the local initiative was catalysed by a series of local events, not all of which were directly associated with youth employment. In 2004, Otorohanga experienced several youth social issues, including two suicides and fighting at the local boarding school. This raised community concerns about the need to ensure that the social and economic well-being of local youth could be enhanced through the provision of support and training. In parallel, local business owners in Otorohanga's mechanical and engineering fields expressed their frustration at not being able to obtain qualified staff or successful apprentices. This and the need to address broader youth concerns inspired the newly elected mayor to make some enquiries to personally facilitate the search for a solution, which subsequently led to the eight projects detailed below.

A critical factor in the success of this facilitation was that it was personally enacted by this new mayor who had himself done his apprenticeship in automotive trades and had his own small local business selling farm bikes. He therefore had a personal knowledge and shared interest with the relevant businesses and the issues and challenges faced by youth training in this field. This perspective and his local connections enabled him to speak frankly with the local business owners and obtain their trust to create solutions that could increase the availability and training of local staff.

The mayor also did not fit the persona of a typical rural mayor due to his personal dynamism. He was prepared to highlight issues and proposed solutions in the media, including via "Ted Talks" published online. This public persona and the resulting initiatives helped to promote Otorohanga as a town with "zero youth unemployment", which may have helped to attract other New Zealanders to the town. The Mayor also helped to inspire others, including the principal of the local high school and a local church, to become involved in broader youth related activities. His role as mayor also allowed him to liaise with the Waikato Training Institute, which set up a local branch in the town to help facilitate training, and other government stakeholders in 2005. In 2008, his efforts in addressing youth employment issues resulted in his election as the chairperson of the Mayor's Taskforce for Jobs, a national network of Mayors that aimed to address youth employment issues.

Local leadership in a number of different institutions was crucial to the successful implementation of the initiatives. For example, a local trainer in the quarry industry was prepared to tutor and mentor trades people and undertook further training as an adult educator. He earned the nickname of "camp mother" by gaining the trust of the youth, which allowed him to offer support if they had personal issues. In addition, a local businessman in the farm equipment retail business was very proactive in supporting and co-facilitating the initiative, while also busy running his growing business. There were also two church social workers who were able to convince their church to set-up and host a youth "drop-in" centre to support their work with the youth in the community. Finally there was the goodwill of the school which managed to develop an effective relationship with the Mayor's newly facilitated team while struggling with the issue of running a school in a rural community with a large low income population.

In summary, the initiative emerged from the engagement and mutual, albeit informal, co-operation between key partners. There was also close liaison with the principal of the local school and the eventual involvement of Wintec which set up an Otorohanga satellite centre for their pre-trades training course to remove the requirement to travel to Hamilton.

Early discussions which led to the design of the programme

The Mayor began by having discussions with the local businesses which utilised automotive and mechanical trades to understand the nature of the employment, training, recruitment and retention blockages. Not all businesses were willing to discuss matters with him and he emphasised collaboration with businesses who wanted an input into the proposed programme. Ultimately, only six businesses were engaged in the initial project discussions, although over thirty now have young employees who receive pastoral care.

The discussion undertaken established that youth from the small town did indeed want to work in the trades in their home town, but were faced with two difficult options. One was to move to the nearest provincial city of Hamilton to complete the pre-trades training course offered by the Wintec. However, exposure to Hamilton's city lifestyle and job opportunities meant they tended not to return to their home town. Or, alternatively, youth who were accepted into apprenticeships in local home town businesses often failed to complete their obligations to the ITO due to the cost of tutoring and travel to attend block courses in Hamilton. Both apprentices and trade labourers also found that, on occasion, they had personal challenges that affected their workplace performance and could lead to them losing or leaving their jobs. Youth were also often unaware of which local businesses were offering employment in the trades. Businesses also noted that skilled migrant workers and their families tended not to settle well into the small rural town environment of Otorohanga and often returned to the larger cities. As a result, youth who had grown up in the town were seen as more likely to stay long term if they could be successfully trained locally (Source: based on interviews with the apprentice support tutor, Otorohanga youth projects facilitator and Mayor and a local Otorohanga businessman and member of the current ODDB).

Programme objective

From the beginning, the programme was organised informally, which created a high level of good-will among the small team of stakeholders from local business, local government, the church and the school. Publicity around the eventual Otorohanga Youth Programme refers to it achieving "zero youth unemployment", but the core focus of the programme was to offer encouragement and support to ensure local youth could be successful in accessing and holding local jobs in the automotive and mechanical trades. (Source: based on interviews with the apprentice support tutor, Otorohanga youth projects facilitator and former Mayor, the MPOWA tracking co-ordinator and a local Otorohanga businessman and member of the current ODDB). The projects undertaken have been successful in meeting this aim.

Projects

From these early discussions, eight projects were identified and established to meet the needs of the youth (Source: based on interviews with the Otorohanga College careers advisor, a representative of Otorohanga Wintec hub and others.)

● A local tutor began to offer evening apprenticeship tuition classes to offer trainees pastoral support and assistance with managing their ITO correspondence paper work assignments during their firm placement. This helped to address any personal issues that may be affecting the youths' work life, and also enabled business owners to identify and resolve any employment challenges. The apprentice tutor was previously a trainer at the quarry and did additional training in supporting adults with learning difficulties. The tutor also offered work-based pastoral care informally to other youth who had graduated from the new Wintec Otorohanga pre-trades course and now work locally as trade labourers. He also separately offers year-long training in quarry management and day courses in forklift driving.

- A youth "drop-in" centre and holiday programme were established at a church venue called the Harvest centre, which also runs a programme to mentor youth two days per week.

- The same church group also tracked the progress of local school leavers to ensure that they were able to access training or work opportunities. This tracking programme is called MPOWA.

- The church also set up a part-time position called the "College Community Mentor" to personally liaise with the high school and these various community opportunities. This was in addition to the college's existing part-time careers advisor.

- Wintec, a Hamilton based trade training intuition, decided to establish a branch of their training institution in Otorohanga to offer entry level courses, including a 10 month course in the engineering and automotive trades, as well as courses in business administration, computing and horticulture. The pre-trades course is a prerequisite for acceptance into an apprenticeship and assists youth to enter the trades industry directly as labourers.

- The Mayor also had an annual celebration for graduates of apprenticeships to provide a sense of achievement and community support to the youth involved.

- The apprentice tutor also works with the local school careers advisor in running an annual careers fair. This originally involved presentations from businesses to the school and a series of one day work experiences, but has now evolved to the youth spending a full week of work experience at a local business of their choice and then a second week at an alternative local business.

- One of the local businessmen also produces a brochure detailing the local Otorohanga businesses offering youth employment opportunities in the trades.

Governance Framework

As noted above, this initiative was initially very informal, and the project never acquired a name other than the "Otorohanga Youth Projects". The initial discussions were private and were only conducted with parties interested in the trades or youth and willing to be involved. This included six businesses which utilised the trades and who were willing to discuss the issue. This privacy allowed people to express their views and concerns honestly and openly and to express their level of interest in personally implementing actions. Discussions with youth regarding their needs were also held on a largely individual basis.

The smallness of the town allowed the various parties to easily identify each other, and the informal nature allowed individuals to get involved only if they wished. While key role-players interacted regularly, the projects or responses were either implemented independently, which allowed them to maintain their autonomy, or with just two parties working together, such as the careers fair or work experience. It is notable that the projects were all established and funded within a short time frame, probably due to the autonomy of the actors.

Ultimately the Mayor acted as the facilitator to personally link and unify the different processes. His background as both an ex-apprentice and as a small businessman who hired youth in the trades was critical as it gave him insight and helped to build the trust of the participants. His authority as mayor also helped the projects achieve quick access to government funding and engagement with external institutions such as the Wintec. His outgoing personality also ensured that the project gained the attention of the nation and changed the perception and reputation of the town.

Concerns emerged over time regarding the longevity of the programme and if it should remain informal, particularly when it was centred on a single individual. When the Mayor decided not to stand for re-election in 2013, he put in place the current formal mechanism to create joint oversight and governance for the programme. He established the Otorohanga District Development Board (ODDB) where representatives of council, business and local interest groups were able to oversee the programme and any forthcoming projects. The board is chaired by the new mayor, a young dairy farmer who had been actively encouraged by the previous mayor to undertake the role. The board promotes the youth employment projects in the Otorohanga town promotion material.

The new ODDB is also considering whether other sectors, such as the substantial dairy sector, should also develop initiatives to meet their youth employment needs. It also seeking to identify opportunities for young women, who have not benefitted from support to the trades industry to the same degree as young men (Source: based on interviews with an Otorohanga businessman and current member of the ODDB, and the current chair of the ODDB and current mayor of Otorohanga). To date, the implementation appears relatively slow with respect to these new foci and the trade brochure has not been updated in recent years.

The ODDB has commissioned several reviews of the Otorohanga youth projects to assess their effectiveness and determine future support priorities, given the reduction in state funding discussed below. The ODDB has sought to solely focus on economic development, which has resulted in the cancellation of funding for social projects such as Harvest drop-in centre. The Centre is now seeking alternative resourcing. The audits, while appreciated for their insight, have led to a situation in which some parties have a sense of being underappreciated. This has had a negative effect and has required parties to rebuild co-operative relations and regain their confidence to carry on their activities independently. The projects that are still under the ODDB umbrella have found it challenging to operate without any input into their own fundraising, as operators do not participate in the ODDB's decision making or fundraising processes.

Formalising the governance process has changed the dynamics of the scheme and has resulted in a loss in direct engagement of independent actors in the town. There is a need to incorporate some of the earlier private and informal aspects if the ODDB wishes to engage independent parties in a new sector or new activities.

Funding

In 2006, the mayor's charisma and position gave institutional weight to a proposal to the NZ Ministry of Social Development to fund the apprenticeship support tutor's part time position for three years to the tune of NZD 60 000 per annum. Funding for additional years was obtained from eight other funding sources including two local businesses, two councils, Wintec, the college, the ODDB and the North King Country Development Trust (no date) which receives electricity power board payments for economic development distribution. The Mayor also secured additional funding of over NZD 70 000 from the Ministry of Youth Development and the Ministry of Social Development to cover the costs of the three part time positions including the College Community Mentor and two staff at the Harvest Centre's youth 'drop in' programme. The donations also funded four years of the MPOWA tracking programme to follow the progress of the college's 80 school leavers per annum and ensure that they had appropriate support for their training plans or new job positions. This programme was implemented as a localised, smaller version of a larger regional tracking programme.

In 2012, the funding from the Ministry of Youth Development and the Ministry of Social Development (MSD) was reduced and redistributed to initiatives in two neighbouring small towns. The remainder of the funding was transferred to the ODDB for distribution. In 2014, further government funding was cancelled and the ODDB has noted that all residual finances will be exhausted by June 2016. Thus, while the ODDB continues to fund tutoring services, it no longer funds social projects not the MPOWA tracking co-ordinator position.

The NZ Government's MSD Youth Services contract for tracking NEET youth in the district has now been allocated to another community trust in a neighbouring small town, which offers dairy and forestry industry training to disengaged, often Maori, youth. This tracking programme operates in a similar manner to MPOWA and liaises with youth and local businesses. This new contractor tends to focus on rural school leavers but supports the voluntary work of MPOWA with urban Otorohanga youth. The NZ government's Ministry of Social Development is expected to continue funding district wide community groups to undertake the tracking and advising of school leavers via its Youth Services unit.

Alongside the one off grants from two local businesses, individual businesses now contribute financially to the apprentice tutor position, which charges a fee to the local businesses of NZD 250 per annum per apprentice. However businesses are often reluctant to pay as they view the apprentice as the beneficiary of the service and note that they already pay a pastoral care levy to their national ITO apprenticeship provider for regional support. Reluctant businesses can apply for a grant from the ODDB to defray the cost. Other businesses are willing to pay the cost but bond the apprentice so they must repay their host business if they leave before completing two full years of their position after attaining the qualification. The full cost of covering the apprentice tutor's costs would be approximately NZD 1 000 per apprentice per annum. The tutor has indicated that this level of support would be unacceptable to local businesses. Nationally, ITO apprentice support continues as previously with block and on-line courses and support available in major rural centres.

The tutor also operates other employment support programmes in the Otorohanga trades which are fully funded by the businesses that benefit from this employee support. This includes year-long training of supervisors at the local lime quarry, which employs approximately 100 workers, and one day courses in forklift operation for the transportation companies. The quarry workers also receive work based pastoral care, although this aspect is unfunded.

The local secondary college has cancelled the college community co-ordinator role after the funding ceased and replaced the position with a school counsellor and the existing part-time careers advisor position. The careers fair and work experience done in conjunction with the apprentice tutor has recommenced. The funding for the Wintec Otorohanga Regional Hub is secure as a high priority under the NZ government's "achieving education outcomes" policy focus. Wintec is independently governed from its Hamilton campus, but workplace support for Wintec graduates after employment is only available through the apprentice tutor's pastoral care programme, which is unfunded for non-apprentices and relies on his goodwill.

Results achieved and key outcomes

Addressing local "trade industry" youth employment

In 2015, the apprentice support tutor offered support to a total of 72 apprentices undertaking their 3-4 year apprenticeship. Approximately 35 of these apprentices required intensive support, with some struggling with literacy and numeracy issues. Tutoring for those that require intensive support includes assistance with completing their apprenticeship papers one evening a week and personalised support on issues that may affect their employment. The remaining 37 apprentices are able to access assistance upon request. In the past, tutoring support has at times also been offered to apprentices in other trades such as building, electrical and plumbing. The tutor is in regular contact with over 30 local businesses in the automotive and engineering trades, and another 20 businesses in other trades, including quarrying. These visits enable businesses to communicate any concerns they have about their young workers and also allow the tutor to offer support to apprentices and informal assistance to graduates of the pre-trades course who now work as labourers. The apprentice support tutor noted that social issues and often need to be addressed alongside formal training issues, as these affect the young person's ability to stay in a job for the long-term.

This includes issues such as:

- Partner, family or social relationships;
- Illegal acts outside of work;
- Substance use;
- Mental and physical health issues.

These issues can affect the performance and dynamics of a young person's experience in the workplace. The tutor felt that social issues could not be separated from the economic issue of job development (Source: based on an interview with the apprentice support tutor).

Very early on in the programme, both apprentices and businesses noted that the trades tutor's more personalised and localised support had increased apprenticeship completion rate to about 90%, compared to the previous 34% completion rate under solely the traditional ITO apprenticeship scheme (Source: based on interviews with the apprentice support tutor and the youth projects facilitator and former mayor). Both the tracking programme and pre-trades training course also report that most youth who complete their apprenticeship stayed in employment long-term, with most graduates of the Wintec pre-trade training going into employment as either labourers or semi-skilled staff or entering trade apprenticeships or further education. However, about 40% of the Wintec pre-trades course applicants do not complete the course, probably due to youth discovering they are not suited to this particular career path (Source: based on interviews with the apprentice support tutor, the Otorohanga youth projects facilitator and former mayor, the MPOWA tracking co-ordinator and a representative from the Otorohanga Wintec hub).

Another economic success occurred when one business that participated in the scheme noted that the support assisted him to grow his business by 450% over nine years by opening branches in the tourism city of Rotorua and a small town outside the city of Hamilton called Cambridge. Though this business owner noted that the key catalyst for this growth was his attendance at an entrepreneurial growth workshop in Auckland, he does credit the Otorohanga training programme and apprenticeship tuition support as the reason that he is able to find sufficient staff to achieve this level of growth. He also indicated that he uses

Otorohanga as his base for training new staff (Source: based on an interview with an Otorohanga businessman, member of the Otorohanga Youth Projects and the current ODDB).

The establishment of a regional branch of Wintec in Otorohanga, which offered an early entry course for the automotive and engineering trades, attracted 8-10 local youth per course. This programme successfully feeds most graduates into the apprenticeship programmes or employment, usually as labourers or semi-qualified staff. The number of course places is very similar to the job capacity in the local town (Source: based on interviews with the apprentice support tutor and a representative of the Otorohanga Wintec hub).

In the cases outlined above, the initial objective of encouraging and enabling the success of local youth in accessing local jobs in the automotive and mechanical trades was successful. This in turn benefits the local economy. Further initiatives could attempt to broadly consider 'general' youth employment, instead of predominately focussing on the trades.

Addressing non-trades local youth employment

The new careers day organised by a partnership between the school and the trades tutor was particularly successful at placing youth into local jobs other than the trades. The lengthened career programme involved the expansion of the work experience programme in 2015 to one full week at each of two local businesses of the high school student's choice (ranging from fast food franchises to a lawyer's office). This was successful in introducing the businesses to the locally available youth and the youth to the local businesses. This model was seen as preferable to the previous one day opportunity for businesses to display their options at the local school which was preceded by a single day of work experience, often outside of the district (Source: based on interviews with the apprentice support tutor and the Otorohanga College careers advisor).

The position of college community co-ordinator (a position based in the local secondary school to link the students with community resources) was initially successful because the first worker was able to gain the trust of the students due to a previous sports-related role. The college co-ordinator then worked with individual students to introduce them to local employment, post-school training and social development options. Subsequent staff in that role had less rapport with students and when funding from the Ministry of Youth Development ceased, the position was replaced by a school counsellor contracted to visit the school 2 days a week to manage social issues. The school also continues to have a careers advisor (Source: based on interviews with the MPOWA tracking co-ordinator and the Otorohanga College careers advisor).

The MPOWA tracking programme is a service available to all graduates of Otorohanga college. MPOWA currently have 160-180 youth on their books who they are in regular touch with. They successfully offer advice on how to attain placements in occupations such as the Navy, Army and nursing and assist in job applications i.e. to local dairy and retail opportunities. Any young people who are interested in the trades are referred to the apprentice tutor. This has assisted in a number of general employment and training placements, although not always in the local area (Source: based on an interview with the MPOWA tracking co-ordinator). Recent changes have seen this contract going to Ngati Maniapoto Marae Pact Trust who offer services to a wide rural area. They however greatly appreciate MPOWA's local knowledge and support, particularly to the more urban township area of Otorohanga and utilise this now voluntary service (Source: based on an interview with the Maniapoto tracking co-ordinator).

The local dairy and forestry industry are not participants in the facilitation work of the Otorohanga youth employment projects or the ODDB. There are two regional dairy farm training providers, including the National Taratahi Agricultural Training Centre based in the nearby rural town of Putaruru, and the Maori operated Maniapoto Training Agency in the nearby rural town of Te Kuiti. The Maniapoto Training Agency offers farm and forestry training for disengaged youth on the trust's Maori land based farms and also provides transport to Otorohanga students. This group has also been awarded the youth services contract to track the progress of local young people.

Both the Taratahi and Maniapoto training projects have helped the youth to access the dairy industry, which employs 35% of Otorohanga's working population. The Maniapoto Trust also works with businesses to ensure that graduates are well matched with empathetic employers. They often place workers on farms in groups of three to give them a degree of empowerment and mitigate isolation. The dairy tutor also voluntarily follows up with the youth once they enter employment and the new employer. Farms with a poor reputation for employee conditions are not referred to graduates (Source: based on an interview with the Maniapoto Trust dairy support tutor). This type of informal support to training graduates appears to be the current state of pastoral care and employer support in the local dairy sector. While there has been a wider national push to improve conditions for dairy workers, there have been no specific programmes to improve work placement completion rates in the dairy industry.

MPOWA, which works with the non-trades youth, have not been required to undertake industry visits and discussions to see how local jobs for young people could be attracted or retained. They prefer to work with individual young people and individual employers (Source: based on an interview with the MPOWA tracking co-ordinator). The Maniapoto Trust, the current provider of local tracking services for young people, also note that providing individualised advice to young people is time-consuming and that they are unable to provide additional resources to developing opportunities for young people in specific industries. They also lack specific industry connections, with the exception of their parent Trust's expertise in the dairy industry (Source: based on an interview with the Maniapoto Trust tracking co-ordinator).

While general youth employment jobs and training programmes were well implemented in Otorohanga, the unavailability of data on regional youth unemployment rates makes it difficult to assess the quantitative benefits of the initiatives. However, in 2013 the overall unemployment rate in Otorohanga was 9.9% (Stats NZ 2013b), which is higher than the national average of 5.3% (Stats NZ, 2016) and has increased alongside the implementation of the programmes. This indicates that the programmes may have been unsuccessful in reducing youth unemployment, or that young people are being hired at the expense of older jobseekers. However, while the initiatives may not have had a discernible effect on the unemployment rate in Otorohanga, the programmes that focussed on improving training and employment options for young people in the trades sector was successful in promoting long-term apprenticeship success and facilitating business growth.

Current challenges and weaknesses of the programmes

The focus of the programme was on the trades sector, as the key actors in the scheme were from this sector. However, the needs of other sectors, particularly industries that are attractive to women such as the hospitality or accounting industry, were not addressed. Similarly, the dairy industry was not included in the initiatives, despite being the largest employer in the town. To address this, the ODDB is considering liaising with businesses in other sectors that have the potential to sustainably employ rural youth. These businesses should have the time and passion to boost skills in the industry and the ability to offer pastoral care and appropriate support to young people.

There also arose an issue of succession for the initiatives as initial stakeholders moved away from their original positions. Although the ODDB was established to replace the initial informal organisation of the participants and evaluate and fund some projects, the evaluation and critique of projects left some participants feeling underappreciated. This was compounded by the board's removal of previous key individuals from the decision-making process and direct engagement in applications for funding. Since then, the formalisation and implementation of new initiatives has slowed. The informal collective of actors from a small town industry may be the more effective method of building trust with the relevant stakeholders.

State funding for the scheme was short-term and the government subsequently withdrew its support from the social and support aspects of the programme. This has negatively affected the local programme. The NZ's government current policy focus on improving qualification outcomes and discouraging youth from entering the NEET criteria (Ministry of Education, 2014) has resulted in the reallocation of funding towards Wintec style training rather than localised pastoral support of youth in apprenticeships or in the workplace.

In addition, the national policy may encourage youth to remain in the school system or to move from one training option to another, rather than seeking long term employment placements. In Otorohnaga this issues has been partially addressed through the pre-trades course, which is a prerequisite for apprenticeships. While placement in the pre-trades course is guaranteed and is fully state-funded if the youth fits the criteria, applicants are interviewed by the tutor to assess their suitability. Tracking of youth vocational outcomes has determined that this has led to a higher number of Wintec graduates moving into trade employment. However, the tracking programme also established that a number of course participants rotated into other courses, often as a time filler while their first choice was not available.

Funding and responsibility for the provision of pastoral care in the workplace is often allocated to regional bodies such as the nationally based ITOs for apprentices or nationally funded school leaver tracking programmes called "Youth Services", which started in August 2012. Youth Services funds are allocated to various community organisations in regions. However these regional bodies often struggle to provide individualised pastoral care to small local business and youth staff in rural towns, due to their need to cover a wider area or a wide range of professions.

A clear success of the local initiatives for youth in Otorohanga was the provision of very personal, workplace based pastoral care to trainees in relevant local businesses by a few dedicated and specialised individuals. This localised and highly focused targeting of a specific industry remains the key to retaining youth in a rural environment. In summary, the challenges which the programme faced include:

- The programme did not undertake liaise with industries outside of the trades, though potential also exists in the dairy and accountancy industries. Incorporating other actors into the initiatives would require input and commitments from stakeholders in other industries.

- The need to rely on the constant commitment and goodwill of key individuals.
- The withdrawal of the Mayor from the town council and the scheme has left a void which is not easy to fill as so much of the dynamism of the programme relied on his personal charisma and ability to link key role-players.
- Loss of state funding for many of the programmes, as government priorities change and finances are allocated elsewhere.
- The current government focus on qualification outcomes may lead to youth remaining in school or rotating around training options, rather than moving into long term employment.
- Changes in governance and control of the programme which left some participants feeling underappreciated and disenfranchised.
- Regional youth support staff are unable to assist specific local industry development, due to their wide client base. This is compounded by their time constraints.

Potential transferability

Some clear lessons emerge from the Otorohanga experience which may be particularly pertinent to other small urban centres losing youth. The Otorohanga style has already been utilised in other New Zealand towns, such as "Porirua Youth 2 Work" scheme, Warkworth's "Future Works" and "Hawkes Bay Youth Futures", although these programmes tend to have a general youth employment focus rather than specific industry sector focus. The primary lessons from Otorohanga are:

- The need to liaise with "local" businesses within a particular industry sector in the rural area, to identify their specific requirements for their workforce. Developing a positive relationship between the employee and the company through work-based pastoral care is also critical to ensure that any training needs or personal issues are addressed.
- The targeted employment sectors should be carefully considered, including with respect to the potential to increase the retention of young employees, the number of jobs to be created, the nature of the skills shortage and finally the degree of aspiration from the local businesses to be engaged in the programme.
- The programme should aim to work with only the interested businesses within the target industry, rather than to liaise with all. Note that this also occurred in the dairy industry training programme which only liaised with "youth empathetic" businesses.
- To find local actors with the time and energy to implement and design youth-focussed initiatives, the stakeholders should have an intimate knowledge of the local businesses in the relevant specific sector and their ability and willingness to relate to their youth staff. This may require different groupings of individuals to work in different industry sectors.
- The promotion and fundraising by charismatic members of a sector group is very important as is their vision and enthusiasm. Endorsement of these individuals by a local Mayor or a local leader is also important. Personal interventions as well as the character of the Mayor and the apprentice tutor were critical to the success of the programme in Otorohanga.
- Activities should be funded through local resources or from assured long term funding so as not to be vulnerable to short term or changeable government funding priorities.
- It appears to be preferable to target the provision of local pastoral care to particular community members, rather than providing pastoral care on a wider regional basis as tends to occur in rural ITO apprenticeship support.

- Pastoral care should be provided to the business operator as well as to the youth involved.

- Informal groups of individuals to address industry needs are suitable to allow natural trust to evolve and independent initiatives to flourish. This can also enable rapid implementation if group consensus is not required. There are benefits to formal evaluations of effectiveness, which should also occur periodically.

- The establishment of more localised training branch institutions for youth is beneficial, but these should include post-qualification pastoral care to ensure movement into employment is successful and long term.

- There is clearly a benefit to liaising with high school youth to enable them to have week-long work experiences in local businesses. This may assist a range of local businesses by allowing them to form a relationship with the local youth who may become eventual employees.

- Pursuing a multi-faceted approach that integrates the school, training, businesses, and youth groups can help to transition youth into long term local employment without creating an incentive to remain in school or training.

- The programme should be driven by the employment needs within a particular local industry sector and not by training per se, or even general employment objectives, although this could be a parallel objective.

More generic considerations of potential value to rural areas in other OECD countries include:

- Programmes should be driven from the employment needs of a specific industry sector of a town rather than a general job creation goal.

- Local synergies and social capital can be maximised by identifying appropriate local businesses and allowing them to network with other interested parties.

- Ensure that branches of tertiary training institutions are locally available and that they have the capacity to undertake training specific to the needs of the local industrial/ business sector. Pastoral care and support should be offered to graduates to help them transition into work.

- As the Otorohanga case clearly shows, youth training can also involve 'work based pastoral care,' such as life-coaching that prepares youth with life skills, alongside more traditional vocational education. This pastoral care needs to involve the business operator and follow young people into employment.

- Having a local champion who personally knows the industry from the perspective of both the business and youth workers will be more likely to gain the respect of and engagement of all relevant role-players. Local leaders who can draw in external support and provide overall leadership and vision will help ensure the success of the programme.

- Youth-focussed programmes should draw on external funding and training where appropriate, including the reallocation of regional pastoral care support funding to more localised and business focused initiatives.

In summary, the initiatives in Otorohanga were similar to other youth-focussed programmes implemented throughout New Zealand, including with respect to providing support, advice, tracking services, training programmes and ITO apprenticeships. However, the difference in Otorohanga was the high degree of localisation and personalisation, including work-based pastoral care and tutoring in the home town. The inclusion of future employers and respected local leaders into the programme was also key to its success. The initiative was also targeted to the automotive and engineering trades and led by invested local stakeholders in the private, government and social sector. The initiative's informality also enabled the programme's leaders to identify the core challenges and develop effective local solutions. The result of the programme was increased retention of young people in Otorohanga, increased apprenticeship completion rates and the mitigation of skills shortages in the local area.

References

Human Rights Commission (2014), *Youth employment problem: A New Zealand Context, www.neon.org.nz/ www.hrc.co.nz*.

www.msd.govt.nz/about-msd-and-our-work/work-programmes/welfare-reform/youth-service/, accessed 2/15/2016.

Ngati Maniapoto Marae Pact Trust, *www.maniapoto.org.nz*.

NZ Government (2016), *www.careers.govt.nz/courses-workplace-training-and-apprenticeship*, sourced 2/11/2016, *www.behive.govt.nz/release-new-zealand-apprentices*.

NZ Government (2015), Budget, *www.treasury.govt.nz/budget/2015* sourced 2/15/2016.

NZ Government (2013), Minister of Tertiary Education and Employment, Steve Joyce 25 Jan 2013 New Zealand Apprenticeships to boost skills and Support Jobs, *www.behive.govt.nz/release-new-zealand-apprentices*, accessed 2/11/2016.

NZ Ministry of Education (2014), Statement of Intent 2014-2018, page 15 Government Priorities. Published by the Ministry of Education New Zealand, August 2014.

North King Country Development Trust, *http://nkcdt.org.nz/whoweare.php*, sourced 1/3/2016.

OECD (2017), Youth not in employment, education or training (NEET) (indicator), *http://dx.doi.org/ 10.1787/72d1033a-en* (accessed on 25 January 2017).

OECD (2008), *Jobs for Youth/Des emplois pour les jeunes: New Zealand 2008*, OECD Publishing, Paris, *http:// dx.doi.org/10.1787/9789264041868-en*.

Statistics New Zealand (2016), Employment and unemployment page, *www.stats.govt.nz/searchresults. aspx?q=youth%20unemployment*.

Statistics New Zealand (2013a), Youth Labour Market Dynamics in New Zealand, *www.stats.govt.nz/browse_ for_stats/income-and-work/employment_and_unemployment/youth-labour-market-dynamics-NZ.aspx*.

Statistics New Zealand (2013b), Population Census 2013, *www.statsnz.govt.nzwww.statsnz.govt.nz/*.

Statistics New Zealand (2011), Youth not in employment education and training, *www.stats.govt.nz/ browse_for_stats/income-and-work/employment_and_unemployment/NEET-paper.aspx*.

Statistics New Zealand (2006), Population Census 2006, *www.statsnz.govt.nz/*.

Statistics New Zealand (2001), Population Census 2001, *www.statsnz.govt.nz/*.

Taratahi Agricultural training centre, *www.taratahi.ac.nz, www.stats.govt.nz/searchresults.aspx?q=youth %20unemployment*.

Treasury New Zealand (2011), Statement of Intent 2011 -2016, Outcome: Improved Economic Performance, *www.ssc.govt.nz/sites/all/files/pif-treasury-review-may11.PDF*, sourced 1/3/2016.

Youth Guarantee NZ (nd), *http://youthguarantee.net.nz/start-your-journey*, sourced 1/3/2016.

Chapter 7

The urban technology project in Philadelphia, United States

This chapter presents the case study of the Urban Technology Project, an apprenticeship programme in Philadelphia that aims to promote IT skills among disadvantaged youth through work-based training in the public school system. The programme is unique in America, where apprenticeships still tend to focus on the acquisition of technical and trades-related skills. The establishment, structure and subsequent evolution of the Urban Technology project are further explored.

Key findings

● The Urban Technology Project aims to build technology skills among urban youth through work-based training in the Philadelphia public school system, alongside off-the-job training with local training providers, including a local college. The apprenticeship programme reflects the make-up of inner city public schools and features more female apprentices and those from a minority background than is the norm among American apprentices.

● The programme's success is partially a result of strong links between the programme's operators and employers from the local Philadelphia information technology industry. Many of the programme's graduates have since joined the local information technology workforce or have pursued technical positions in other enterprises.

● The programme's structure has undergone an iterative process with respect to structure and the optimal combination of off-the-job training and on-the-job training. The programme has also evolved in terms of training provision and the certification of competences.

Introduction

Historically, apprenticeships in the United States have been underfunded and largely disconnected from the country's education programmes and workforce systems. Apprentices make up a much smaller percentage of the nation's workforce compared with European counterparts. The general population's focus on higher education ("college for all"), coupled with the misperception that apprenticeships are only applicable to manufacturing and construction trade jobs sponsored by labour/management agreements, has hindered the growth of the programme. However, there has been a renewed focus on building apprenticeships in recent years. The government, educators and businesses are reconsidering the potential for apprenticeships to transform how the country prepares its workforce, specifically youth, for the future demands of the economy. United States policy makers are reaching out to OECD countries to both learn from their successful apprenticeship models and collaborate around building a truly global apprenticeship movement.

The government is also looking toward successful innovative American apprenticeships to help serve as a guide for new programmes. The Urban Technology Project (UTP), a youth apprenticeship programme located in Philadelphia, Pennsylvania, is an exciting example of what the next generation of government-sponsored registered apprenticeships could look like. Participants are from communities typically underrepresented in American apprenticeships, including younger adults, minorities, women, and lower income populations. The UTP prepares disconnected youth (who are neither working nor in school) to work in the high growth industry of Information Technology, offering a pipeline of experiences that include a strong pre-apprenticeship programme, a certified registered apprenticeship, and carefully structured connections to post-apprenticeship employment through strong partnerships with regional employers, including the thriving local business community. UTP is integrated into the local public school district through both education and workplace experiences, making it a true public/private partnership. As the United States Secretary of Labor Thomas Perez proclaimed, "The Urban Technology Project is exactly the type of model for how we train the workforce of tomorrow", (Education Week, 2014).

This case study will examine the economic and policy context within which current American apprenticeship initiatives have evolved. A description of the UTP will be provided, and the impacts, strengths, and weaknesses of the programme will be considered. Finally, the potential transferability of the programme to other OECD countries will be examined.

Policy context

The United States economy is in the process of recovering from the Great Recession of 2007-2009, and unemployment has been falling and wages have been rising. The unemployment rate for the country continues to decrease from the 2014 rate of 5.6% (US Department of Labour, 2016a). However, youth unemployment is still a concern for the country. In 2014, the unemployment rate for Americans aged 16-24 was 13.4%. In contrast, the youth unemployment rate was 7.8% in Germany, and 8.6% in Switzerland (OECD, 2016). The situation is compounded for lower-income and minority youth, many of whom live in cities. Philadelphia in particular has one of the highest poverty rates among major U.S. cities, with 26.9% of its residents living under the federal poverty level (US Census, 2012), coupled with alarming unemployment: the unemployment rate is 30.6% for youth aged 16-24 who live in the region and are not enrolled in schools (Philadelphia Works, 2016). Many of these youth are disconnected from employment, education or training, or what the OECD terms "NEET". The moniker coined by the White House Council for Community Solutions is "Opportunity Youth", and this population has been the recent focus of federal education and training initiatives.

There is growing awareness in the country that jobs are becoming more technical, requiring specific skills that the current younger workforce does not have. The "skills gap" creates a frustrating scenario in this recovering economy whereby job positions go unfilled while individuals remain unemployed. In 2015 there were 5 million job openings in the country, the largest amount since 2001. President Obama's TechHire Initiative presents an effort to close the skills gap in the emerging field of technology. According to the programme's website, Information Technology jobs are the largest category for open jobs and account for approximately 12% of the country's 5 million current job openings (White House, 2016). TechHire aims to get more Americans trained for well-paying technology jobs, with the simultaneous goal of increasing diversity in the workforce.

Philadelphia is one of twenty localities to host a TechHire programme. The city is a good fit for the programme because the local market has shifted from manufacturing and construction jobs to an increasing prevalence of technology, education and health jobs. Over the last 10-15 years, the technology market has been growing rapidly. While the field reverberates with a palpable and youthful energy, there is limited diversity in the technology workforce. While 45% of the city's population is African American, 80% of the region's IT workers are white, and 70% are male. According to Meg Shope Koppel, chief research officer at Philadelphia Works, TechHire aims to connect employers, educators, and businesses with the goal of developing talent pipelines for a diverse workforce (source: interview with Meg Shope Koppel, Philadelphia Works).

Policy context

The National Apprenticeship Act of 1938 established the registered apprenticeship (RA) programme in the United States. The programme is jointly administered by the Department of Labor (DOL)'s Office of Apprenticeship (OA) and State Apprenticeship Agencies (SAA) in 25 states. Participants who complete an RA programme are awarded a nationally recognised credential. It is difficult to determine the exact number of apprenticeships in the country because there are a number of non-registered programmes, but it is clear that the size of the American apprenticeship system is small relative to the apprenticeship programmes in other OECD countries. At the end of 2015, 451 000 apprentices in the U.S. were working toward certification; in the same year, approximately 52 500 participants graduated from one of 20 910 active programmes (US Department of Labour, 2016b). In 2014, apprentices made up only 0.2% of the United States' labor force (Lerman, 2014). When considering the limited growth of apprenticeship programmes in the US, it is important to examine the convergence of several factors, including a lack of business buy-in, constrained funding, and limited public support for apprenticeships.

Businesses have been reticent to build apprenticeship programmes within their companies. Robert Lerman, a leading scholar on apprenticeships in the U.S. and founder of *The American Institute for Innovative Apprenticeships*, identifies several reasons for this. Primarily, there has been a very limited amount of marketing to businesses, coupled with a lack of technical assistance for companies interested in implementing an apprenticeship programme. Additionally, there is a dearth of research necessary to demonstrate the return on investment (ROI) that apprenticeship programmes can offer a business. Furthermore, unlike other OECD countries, American businesses receive no financial support from the government to set up or run apprenticeship programmes. One result is that the number of applicants interested in becoming apprentices far exceeds the number of apprenticeship openings offered by businesses.

The United States' Office of Apprenticeships has been historically underfunded. Prior to 2015, the government spent less than USD 30 million a year on all aspects of the programme. To place this in perspective, Britain has been spending the equivalent of USD 8.5 billion a year on apprenticeship programmes (Lerman, 2014). Until 2014, federal funds for apprenticeship programmes in the United States had been in decline and comprised a very small fraction of the Department of Labor's workforce development budget.

Business disengagement and the historically limited funding for apprenticeships may both stem from a larger issue: public disinterest. Until recently in the United States, there has been a general lack of awareness of and support for the value of apprenticeships. The programme is often perceived by the public through the lens of its historical limitations – designed for construction trades and manufacturing industries, with minimal diversity. Unlike the emerging workforce of today, apprentices are overwhelmingly male and white, with an average age of 30. Only 6% are women, and only 10% are African American (US Department of Labour, 2014).

Philadelphia and the larger state of Pennsylvania have a strong apprenticeship presence relative to other cities and states. Pennsylvania is one of the 25 states that have a State Apprenticeship Agency that registers and oversees programmes in the state. However, Philadelphia's apprenticeship history has for the most part been limited to the construction and manufacturing trades and the unions that represent them. In general, the high growth industries in the city, such as health and information technology, have been disconnected from apprenticeship programmes.

Painting a portrait of apprenticeships in the United States would be incomplete without an examination of the country's education system, both K-12 (primary and secondary) as well as higher education (post-secondary and tertiary) programmes. Educators, policy makers, and the general public have been focused on the concept of "college for all", often at the expense of other career or life paths for the country's youth. This focus impacts the apprenticeship movement in two major ways. Firstly, the K-12 curriculum is focused on college preparation at the expense of meaningful, comprehensive and coherent school-to-career activities. Unlike other OECD countries, US apprenticeships are for the most part disconnected from the K-12 education experience. A stigma against vocational-technical education is rooted in a history of segregated and unequal education tracks for low-income and minority students, which offered little opportunity to switch between academic and technical tracks. Secondly, federal funding for community colleges, the country's two year publicly funded higher education institutions, reduces the funding available for apprenticeship programmes. Until recently, government funding per apprentice was USD 100-400 per year, compared with USD 11 400 per student at a two year public college (Lerman, 2014).

Yet, the landscape for education and job preparation in the United States is on the cusp of a transformation. Higher education has become extremely cost-prohibitive, while at the same time many disadvantaged youth are unprepared for the rigours of college. Drop-out rates are high for those who do start out in college. Only about 40% of Americans have obtained either an associate's or bachelor's degree by their mid-twenties; for African Americans that percentage is 30% and for Latinos it is 20%. (Harvard Graduate School of Education, 2014). A growing "Pathways Movement", with roots in Harvard Graduate School of Education's *Pathways to Prosperity Report*, recognises that high school graduates are not equipped with the skills that the current workforce demands of them. Education advocates are making a strong case for revitalising and expanding the role of career and technical education in K-12 schools.

A renewed energy for apprenticeships coincides with this call for change in the country's education system and how we prepare youth for the workforce. Other factors that contribute to this focus on apprenticeships include the recognition that filling job vacancies will be problematic due to a "skills gap", despite growth in available jobs due to a growing economy and a surge in retirement. In his 2014 State of the Union address, President Obama announced his desire to double the number of registered apprentices within five years (White House, 2014).

In response, the budget for the Office of Apprenticeships increased by approximately 10% in 2014 and 2015. More notably, the Department of Labor was able to supplement this budget with additional money, including H-1 B discretionary funds. This discretionary fund is financed by a user fee paid by employers to hire foreign workers into the United States under the H-1 B non-immigrant visa programme for speciality occupations. In 2015, USD 175 million of the additional funds were dispersed via competitive grant to innovative apprenticeship programmes across the country, a move described as "the most significant apprenticeship investment in our nation's history" (DOL, 2015). The grant aimed to "support the expansion of quality and innovative American Apprenticeship programs into high-growth occupation(s) and industry(s), particularly those for which employers are using H-1 B visas to hire foreign workers, and the related activities necessary to support such programs". The funding opportunity notice explains that "the department is taking a critical first step in charting a new path forward for innovation in apprenticeship as a post-secondary education and training pathway (DOL, 2015)." The intent of the grant programme is to expand apprenticeships in high growth industries such as IT, while targeting underrepresented populations (female, youth, and minorities) to participate in these apprenticeships. In 2016, the Office of Apprenticeship received a supplemental appropriation of USD 90 million, approximately three times the budget of the previous year.

A variety of exciting initiatives at the US Office of Apprenticeships follows this recent increase in funds. Secretary Perez and his team have been traveling to Europe to study the success of apprenticeship programmes in other OECD countries. Using the United Kingdom's Trailblazers programme as a model, the new Apprenticeship USA LEADER (Leaders of Excellence in Apprenticeship Development, Education, and Research) programme calls on employers to promote and support the expansion of apprenticeship programmes among their business peers. Most recently, the United States has signed Joint Declarations of Intent with Germany and Switzerland to facilitate co-operation around career and technical education, including apprenticeships. In February 2016, the U.S.-EU Working Group on Employment and Labor-related issues met to discuss the advancement of apprenticeship strategies in Europe and the United States.

As the United States looks abroad for support in promoting apprenticeships, the country is also forging ahead on apprentice collaboration across different domestic systems. The Registered Apprenticeship College Consortium (RACC), administered jointly by the Department of Labor and the Department of Education, is a network of colleges and registered apprenticeship programmes working together to promote college to career opportunities. RACC aims to support apprenticeship graduates to earn an Associate's or Bachelor's college degree. Apprenticeships are also being advanced as workforce strategy. The Workforce Innovation and Opportunity Act (WIOA), signed into law in 2015, replaces the country's Workforce Investment Act (WIA) and mandates a shift in focus and funding from short-term training to long-term training aligned with high growth and emerging industries. It advances apprenticeships as a workforce strategy and calls for renewed focus on youth and pre-apprenticeship programmes. Further, the law opens federal workforce funding streams for use in the training component of apprenticeship programmes.

The Urban Technology Project

The Urban Technology Project (UTP) in Philadelphia is an Information Technology (IT) career pathway that is centred around a registered apprenticeship programme within the School District of Philadelphia (SDP), and is at the forefront of the recent apprenticeship initiatives in the United States. The programme was approved as a registered apprenticeship programme in 2005, making it likely the longest running information technology apprenticeship programme in the country today. In 2014, the UTP was used as the backdrop for the Department of Labor's USD 175 million American Apprenticeship Initiative grant announcement and also identified as an Apprenticeship USA LEADER (Leaders of Excellence in Apprenticeship Development, Education, and Research). The UTP is an integral component of the Philadelphia regional collaborative that was awarded one of twenty competitive American Apprenticeship grants in 2015, and is also an essential member of Philadelphia's local TechHire initiative.

The UTP supports apprentices as they participate in on-the-job training while receiving related technical instruction, but the UTP is larger than a discrete apprenticeship programme. As mentioned above, the UTP is a pathway; it includes a pre-apprenticeship programme for recent high school graduates to prepare them for becoming apprentices within the programme, and continues to provide support to apprentices as they graduate from the programme and transition into employment and higher education opportunities. Middle and high school students are also involved in UTP activities and receive exposure to technology through extracurricular interactions with the apprentices.

The typical work placement for an apprentice in the programme is at a school where he or she works alongside a mentor to provide support for the building's technology infrastructure. Apprentices work collaboratively with and mentor other UTP participants, including high school students involved in technology clubs and pre-apprentices working on-site. As they participate in on-the-job training, apprentices and pre-apprentices receive related technical instruction and work on obtaining industry certifications. Upon completion of the apprenticeship experience and obtainment of a journeyperson certificate, participants receive assistance to transition into relevant employment. Some graduates of the programme continue to work for the School District of Philadelphia as employees in various departments, but the majority move into private employment. The UTP builds strong relationships with local technology companies and other employers who have the opportunity to see apprentices in action and are excited about hiring participants who have proven themselves capable.

This public/private model is relatively unique for apprenticeship programmes in the United States. An additional innovation is the ease of transition from the public sector setting of the apprenticeship (public school) to employment in the private sector. Unlike traditional apprenticeship programmes, the intent of the UTP is not necessarily for the apprentice to graduate into employment at the apprenticeship site. Rather, the main focus is to support work and learning experiences that engage participants and prepare them to transition into new work opportunities with the UTP's employer partners while embracing a career of life-long learning.

The UTP is a public/private partnership between the School District of Philadelphia (SDP) and the private non-profit organisation "Communities in Schools Philadelphia" (CISP). A host of other partners are also involved with various components of the programme, including funding, training, support services and employment.

The four categories of partnerships are:

1. *Public Entities*: Philadelphia Works, which provides funding for On the Job Training (OJT) for the Registered IT Apprenticeship Programme; PA Career Link, which provides resources for employment readiness; and the Corporation for National and Community Service (CNCS) which provides funding for AmeriCorps pre-apprenticeship programmes.

2. *Educational Entities*: School District of Philadelphia, which provides hands-on training and didactic support; Community College of Philadelphia, which provides IT-specific classroom instruction.

3. *National Corporate Entities*: They provide funding, in-kind training resources and staff to support OJT and prepare UTP members for industry-standard certification. These entities include Apple Inc., Dell, SMART Technologies and OKI Data Americas.

4. *Employers*: Provide feedback to help improve member workplace performance, as well as hire IT apprentices, include: the School District of Philadelphia, the City of Philadelphia

Office of Innovation and Technology, Apple Inc., Jarvus Innovations Inc., Springboard Media, The Neat Company, Robert Half Technologies, String Theory Schools, Universal Companies, Temple University, Drexel University, The University of Pennsylvania Medicine, The Philadelphia College of Osteopathic Medicine and Bucks County Community College.

Governance – Lead Organisations

Over the past 15 years, the School District of Philadelphia (SDP) has faced significant academic and financial challenges. A report by the Greater Philadelphia Chamber of Commerce characterises the city's underperforming schools and high dropout rates as a leading cause of gaps in the quality of the workforce (Greater Philadelphia Chamber of Commerce, 2015). The district is considering alternative ways to address these issues. Currently SDP is enhancing Career and Technical Education (CTE) programming, and has opened several new high schools that are designed to increase retention and graduation rates through a focus on hands-on learning and apprenticeships. SDP's 2015 Action Plan 3.0 includes a mandate about apprenticeships:

"In partnership with the business community, we will increase the number of students earning industry credentials – reflecting Philadelphia's high-priority, growing occupations – while developing guidelines on effective teaching methods to ensure the highest quality of programming options. We will continue to develop 'career pathways' with employers, which can include pre-apprenticeships and registered apprenticeships." (School District of Philadelphia, 2015)

The School District of Philadelphia's longest running apprenticeship programme is the UTP. The director of UTP, Edison Freire, is also the founder of the programme. He is a school district employee, and a director in the district's Educational Technology Office.

Communities in Schools is a national private non-profit organisation that focuses on dropout prevention. Communities in Schools Philadelphia (CISP) is one of 200 local affiliates and aims to connect youth and their families to community resources. Beth St. Clair, the programme manager of the UTP, holds one of the several management positions at CISP. She oversees both the apprenticeship and pre-apprenticeship programmes of the UTP in conjunction with a programme supervisor for the pre-apprenticeship scheme. The apprentices involved in the UTP are directly employed by the CISP, which then liaises with the SDP to place programme participants at school district sites, such as schools or administrative offices.

Philadelphia Works is a public sector entity that receives both public and private funding. The organisation supports efforts to develop a skilled workforce in the city. Philadelphia Works is the lead agency of the American Apprenticeship Initiative Grant, which aims to grow the UTP. Presently, Philadelphia Works provides training funds to the UTP to allow apprentices to participate in related instruction and IT certification preparation. Philadelphia Works also sponsors Philadelphia's local TechHire initiative, which enables the UTP to engage with a wide range of local tech employers.

Objectives: Engaging, supporting and preparing disconnected youth

The UTP serves urban youth who enter the programme with a variety of educational experiences, including high school graduates from the city's public and charter schools and students who have attained (or are in the process of attaining) their high school diploma (GED[1]). As a group, UTP participants face a variety of challenges. The population of urban schools is 72% African American or Latino, and 87% are from low income backgrounds. The graduation rate of these schools is 1 in 4 students. The majority of students at the schools test below basic levels in reading, math and science. Approximately 53% of the participants of the UTP programme are black, while 18.9% are Hispanic and 19.8% are female. This is in stark contrast to the broader face of registered apprenticeships in America, where only 10% of apprentices are African American and just 6% are female.

The UTP aims to engage these disconnected students and support them as they prepare for career and higher education opportunities.

The development of the UTP was an organic process, built around experiences that demonstrate the engaging qualities of technology and service. In 1997, UTP founder Edison Freire was teaching in a struggling Philadelphia high school and was looking for ways to motivate his Latino immigrant students. Based on their interests, he helped them to organise a technology club that they named LatinoTech. He also helped the students master English while learning technical skills, and encouraged them to view these skills as a resource for their community. The youth became problem-solvers, responsible for identifying and tackling community needs. This culture of service permeates all of UTP's programmes today; the programme aims to capture the interest of the youth, connect them to their communities, and encourage a supportive network among all participants.

As the original Latino technology club evolved over time to include all urban youth, it was renamed the Urban Technology Project. Freire recognised that the members of the club were motivated to join the technology workforce after graduating high school but required further support and guidance. A variety of barriers were preventing these youth from entering a college programme or an IT career directly after high school. Freire realised that the recent graduates could benefit from work experience in a more supportive environment than a traditional IT company, one that would bolster the IT skills of participants while building soft workplace skills. Thus, the UTP evolved to gradually include pre-apprenticeship and apprenticeship components with incentives and resources to allow participants to take advanced courses while working. The Programme also built connections with the local community college and the city's IT employers to help support the apprentices as they completed their apprenticeships.

Today's UTP participants engage in both instructional and hands-on activities in order to learn IT skills and prepare for employment in the field. In addition to building these "hard skills", the youth also develop "soft skills" that are equally essential for job placement. As the youth are placed at a worksite, they gain an understanding of the norms of the workplace and what it's like to be in a position of responsibility. They experience first-hand the importance of communication and dependability. The UTP manager Beth St. Clair highlights how UTP staff support participants in constant reflection, with opportunities to consider personal progress and the relevance of the activities in which they are involved. The participants also develop other competences, including project management, leadership development, customer service, presentation skills, resume and interview skills, interpersonal skills, collaboration and teamwork.

The use of the school environment as the primary UTP worksite fosters the culture of service that has permeated the programme since its inception. The school district lacks resources, including funding and staff, to support the technology needs of Philadelphia schools. For example, at one high school that currently hosts a UTP apprentice, a Teacher Technology Leader (TTL) has only been allocated one school period per day to support the school's technology. The TTL designates some of his limited time to mentoring and providing on-the-job training to the apprentice to improve their professional growth. In return, the apprentice helps to support the technology needs of the school and provide essential day-to-day technology support for teachers and students. The participants of the UTP recognise that their work improves their community, particularly their own secondary schools. The apprentices also serve as role models for the students currently in the school.

Activities

The UTP is a pipeline of experiences that includes:

- exposure to technology in middle school and high school (TechServ clubs)
- a *pre-apprenticeship* programme for high school graduates
- a certified registered apprenticeship experience
- connections to post-apprenticeship employment

The programme has multiple entry and exit points. While there are distinct phases throughout the programme, there is a high degree of integration and collaboration throughout the pipeline.

Pre-Apprenticeship: Digital Service Fellows (DSF)

The UTP is an example of what the US Office of Apprenticeships describes as a "pre-apprenticeship to registered apprenticeship" model. The Department of Labor identifies pre-apprenticeship programmes as a starting point for developing a successful career path for under-represented job seekers. This includes disadvantaged individuals who may not be aware of how to access jobs that offer opportunities for advancement. Many pre-apprenticeship programmes focus on youth, as does the UTP. Activities are designed to help participants meet entry requirements for a partner apprenticeship programme. Other focuses for pre-apprenticeship programmes include developing peer networks, developing soft skills and offered access to support services.

In 2002, the UTP developed the Digital Service Fellows (DSF), which has evolved into today's pre-apprenticeship programme for recent high school graduates. The pre-apprentices are also members of Americorps, a federally-funded service programme under the umbrella of the Corporation for National and Community Service (CNCS). This link between an Americorps programme and pre-apprenticeship initiative is unique among programmes in the US. CNCS engages more than 5 million citizens in a variety of national service programmes, with the aim of improving communities. CISP applied for and received a competitive grant from the programme, which is used to manage the DSF Americorps members. For their year of service, Americorps members, including those in the DSF programme, receive a living stipend from the federal government (USD 12 400) and a post-service educational award of USD 5 730 that can be used to pay tuition at an eligible post-secondary educational institution.

Each DSF member cycles through placements at school sites in the Philadelphia School District. The pre-apprentices build IT skills while simultaneously developing basic workplace readiness "soft" skills. Each DSF member is mentored by a master technician, and also works closely with an UTP apprentice, to learn how to provide technical support for schools. During their year of service, fellows prepare for technical certifications and take a college level course. Fellows have the opportunity to develop customer service, project management, and leadership skills while delivering tech services at the school. Participants pass on their knowledge by training and providing service activities to students, teachers and parents.

The Fellows also prepare for what may be their first experience in a professional work environment by taking advantage of a variety of support services offered via UTP partners, including help with childcare, transportation, financial management, housing and access to social services.

As the DSF complete their year of service and prepare to transition to an apprentice position they are registered with the state's Career Link programme, run by Philadelphia Works. Career Link provides assistance in job search, career counselling, and training.

Registered Apprenticeship: Computer Support Specialists

By 2003, an apprenticeship programme was put into place for DSF who had completed their year of service. This programme became known as Computer Support Specialists (CSS), and in 2005 it was approved as a registered apprenticeship programme by the state of Pennsylvania's Apprenticeship and Training Council. Ronald Leonard, from the US Department of Labor's Apprenticeship Office, explains that the UTP's path to becoming an official Registered Apprenticeship (RA) programme was not straightforward. After initially reviewing UTP's proposal, this governor-appointed council in Pennsylvania noted the UTP was an uncommon and extremely novel programme and did not initially approve it. The council typically reviews construction-oriented apprenticeship programmes. Yet after attending a site visit and presentation about the programme, council members were extremely impressed and voted unanimously to approve the programme. The subsequent success of the UTP has paved the way for additional innovative programmes in the state. Ten years after the UTP's inception, the high tech industry in the state has much more confidence that there will be a positive reception for any RA proposal they put forth (Leonard, 2016).

The Computer Support Specialists (CSS) are full-time staff who work for the Philadelphia School District for a minimum of two years. They are responsible for supporting the technology of their assigned school work site and work more independently than the DSF to meet the technology infrastructure needs of the school district. The apprentices solve problems and fix technology daily at their site. Additionally, they are provided with incentives and resources to take advanced courses and receive industry-recognised certifications and credentials. The programme also offers participants the opportunity to pursue college coursework.

CSS are recruited from the DSF pre-apprenticeship programme, but can also enter the programme through other avenues. Some have come to the programme after completing some higher education or technical school training, while others were employed in another field prior to applying for the programme. Upon completion of the apprenticeship, they are awarded a nationally recognised journeyperson certificate as Computer Support Specialists.

Post-apprenticeship

As the apprenticeship programme matured, programme architects considered how to best launch apprentices into the workforce. The school district was an obvious first step as a post-apprenticeship employer because the traditional trajectory for apprentices is to continue employment at the apprenticeship site. In addition, the apprentices were familiar with the workplace norms and culture and had proven their capabilities to the school district. Accepting full time employment was one way to offer the district a return on investment (ROI) for the apprenticeship programme. The participants had also developed many professional connections throughout the district during their apprenticeship, and as a result were able to find full-time positions in a variety of offices.

However, the financially strapped school district was unable to hire all of the qualified UTP graduates, which led the UTP to consider external employment options for participants. This became an opportunity for the apprentices to specialise in other areas of IT beyond a computer support specialist position. Branching out into employment in the private sector enabled the former apprentices to build on their fundamental technology skills while developing more specialised skillsets. Further, this framework allowed graduates the opportunity to offer their skills to employers beyond purely technology companies. There was a recognition that the skills gained in an IT apprenticeship, including digital competencies, problem-solving, and life-long learning, are valuable in other fields as well.

The UTP initially began to build informal relationships with the employers in Philadelphia's burgeoning technology scene and beyond. Some apprentices were hired by technology companies including Jarvus, a web software engineering firm, and Springboard Media, an Apple authorised company that employs Apple certified technicians to sell and repair Apple products. These employers were impressed with the UTP graduates and, over time, began to approach the UTP for candidates for open positions. Today, there are approximately 30 employers in the city that directly approach the UTP for staffing needs. The employers are often willing to hire UTP participants prior to the completion of the apprenticeship programme, which demonstrates how well the UTP prepares apprentices for employment. However, it would be more idea for apprentices to complete the apprenticeship and earn their journeyperson certificate before progressing to full-time work.

The UTP aims to smooth the transition from apprenticeship to full-time work in two ways. First, the programme is developing a learning plan that involves competency-based skills mastery attainment instead of a model that features timed-based training requirements. This hybrid model allows apprentices to complete the programme sooner and also enables the employer to fill the vacant position more quickly. Secondly, the UTP is in the process of building more formal relationships with employers. In essence, future iterations of the programme may feature the UTP as an intermediary (sponsor of record) for multiple employers. The role of the UTP would be to ensure that apprenticeships are completed before participants directly transition to employment with partner employers. This structure is known as the "multiple employers and multiple intermediaries model" (see Figure 7.1).

Through the UTP, partner employers receive employees who have acquired valuable technology competencies as well as less tangible but equally significant "soft" skills. The UTP aims to minimise the "skill gap" between the competences of participants and the requirements of the job opportunities prior to the hiring process. With the current model, the employer's return on investment is high, as minimal money and time is spent training the employees. Additionally, the UTP deals with the bureaucracy and paperwork to manage the registered apprenticeship, and provides the supporting services necessary to help participants prepare for the workforce.

Figure 7.1. **Partnership and programme structures**

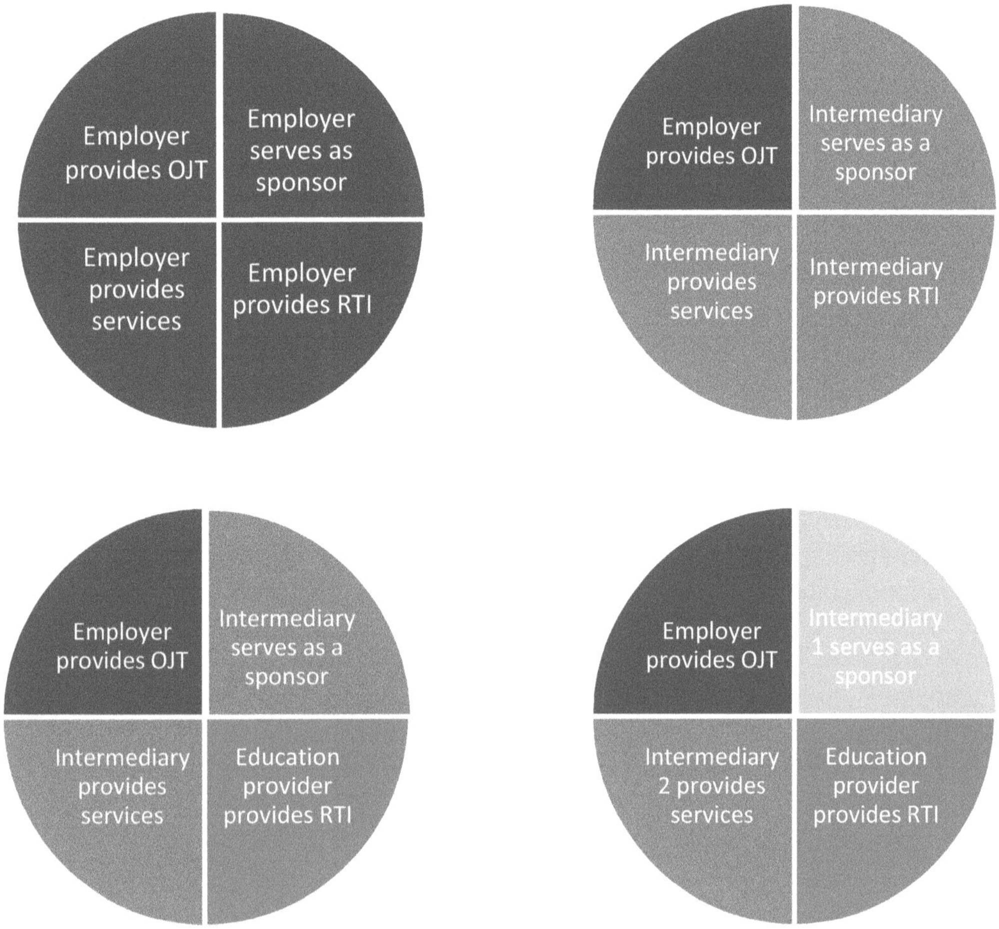

Source: UTP.

Freire explains that over time, employer partners have become more actively involved with the growth of the apprentices and now help to support the training and development of participants who eventually go on to work at the business. In this evolving model, the school district may begin to shift its primary focus towards supporting the pre-apprenticeship programme by incorporating them into Career and Technical Education programmes at the high school level. As these high school students graduate, they would be prepared to directly enter the apprenticeship component of UTP that would take place at an employer partner site.

The school district aims to foster the positive development of Philadelphia's youth, and thus views the movement of pre-apprentices or apprentices to private employment as an acceptable, or even a desirable, outcome. Although the district might not realise a traditional ROI from the apprentice that it has trained and supported, they and the broader community benefit by supporting young people to become productive citizens. Another important benefit of this model is the fact the apprentices receive tailored mentorship in a school environment, which may be a relatively more nurturing environment than a private workplace.

Core components of a registered apprenticeship

The UTP provides participants with what the US Office of Apprenticeship identifies as the five core components of a registered apprenticeship programme:

1. On-the-job training (OJT)

2. Related technical instruction (RI)

3. Reward for skills earned

4. National occupational credentials

5. Direct business involvement

On-the-job training

After an initial orientation, apprentices interview for work site positions and are placed in high schools or administrate offices throughout the school district for 35 hours a week. Each apprentice is assigned a mentor at the work site, usually the technology teacher leader (TTL), and may also themselves serve as a mentor to a pre-apprentice DSF. Apprentices provide support to school-run technology education programmes and assist in providing maintenance services and technology support to school staff, students, and community members.

Related technical instruction (RI)

While completing their apprenticeship, UTP participants are afforded opportunities to earn college credit and industry recognised credentials. They participate in pre-graduate coursework, which can lead to an associate's degree or can be transferred to a four year college. Graduates complete up to 5 000 hours of hands-on training and can earn up to three industry standard certifications.

The UTP's OJT and RI structure is a hybrid of several federal apprenticeship models. In a traditional apprenticeship model, apprentices receive both related instruction and on the job training concurrently throughout the programme. In contrast, a segmented apprenticeship model enables apprentices to alternate between related instruction and on the job training. During the school year, the CSS follow a more traditional model and receive training while working on-site. However, the programme takes advantage of the school district's summer school break by offering apprentices the opportunity to take classes at the Community College of Philadelphia (CCP), a scenario which resembles a segmented apprenticeship model. As the UTP continues to develop, it is planning to offer a front-loaded apprenticeship model in which apprentices receive some related instruction prior to starting on-the-job training. This would enable apprentices to develop initial core technological competences as well as specialised skills while completing the on-the-job training. Currently, all UTP apprentices work on a computer support tech track. However, participants are expressing interest in other technology fields. In transitioning to employment, they often use the skills they've acquired as an entry point to different careers. Shifting to a front-loaded apprenticeship model would enable participants to independently pursue their interests and autonomously engage in training.

Reward for skills earned

The UTP apprentices participate in regular performance evaluations with the Teacher Technology Lead (TTL) and the UTP programme supervisor. They receive progressive wage increases as their skills increase and benchmarks are met.

National occupational credentials

Upon mastery of workplace competencies, apprentices receive a journeyperson certificate. The US Apprenticeship Office promotes three types of programme design for credential attainment. The UTP currently employs a time-based model, in which apprentices receive certification after completing a certain number of hours of on-the-job training and related instruction. However, the programme is moving toward a more flexible hybrid model, which requires a specific allocation of time for training and instruction, in combination with the successful demonstration of competences.

A third programme design is purely competency based. Participants progress at their own pace, and complete proficiency tests without a time requirement. UTP may consider this model for the future. Programmes that are flexible with hourly requirements are particularly well suited for the technology field, where skills and competencies are in constant flux. The UTP's experience is that employer partners are inclined to hire apprentices as soon as they demonstrate certain competencies, even if they have not completed all of the required programme hours. Eliminating strict hourly completion requirements will support apprentices in obtaining journeyperson certification prior to transitioning to employment.

Direct business involvement

As discussed, the UTP partners with employers to support apprentices as they transition to employment. As the UTP's relationship with employer partners evolves, it is moving towards a more complex apprenticeship model. The traditional apprenticeship model features a single employer that provides all components of the apprenticeship by sponsoring the apprentices, providing services and offering both on-the-job training and related technical instruction. In contrast, the UTP strives to offer a multi-stakeholder model that includes multiple employers, an intermediary, and a community college. The intermediary, CISP, sponsors the apprentices and provides services to them. Employers, including the SDP and other business partners provide on-the-job training. As funding permits, the Community College of Philadelphia acts as the education provider for UTP and provides related instruction. By embedding multiple employers into the programme, the UTP is providing increased opportunities for new experiences and networks for apprentices while also boosting future employment opportunities.

Impact

The UTP has sponsored 106 apprentices since the inception of the apprenticeship programme (pre-apprentices and high school students involved with UTP are not included in this figure). Of this total, 69 apprentices completed apprenticeship requirements, 17 are current apprentices, and 20 did not complete the programme. Approximately 68% of participants have remained in an IT occupation (hired by the school district, non-profits, or private industry), 8% are employed in other occupations, and 4% are enrolled full-time in a higher education institution (see Table 7.1).

In terms of demographic data of participants, Tables 7.2 and 7.3 provide an overview of those served by the programme. Approximately 80% of participants are youth of colour, which contrasts heavily with both the typical US apprentice (of whom only 10% are African American) and the local Philadelphia IT workforce (80% white and male). While the programme still features relatively few women (20%), the overall female participation in the UTP is more than double the national average female apprenticeship participation rate (6%).

Table 7.1. **UTP youth apprenticeship outcomes, 2004-16**

Apprenticeship Participant Status	Totals	Employed in IT Field	Employed in other fields	Attending College full-time	No available data
Completed apprenticeship	69	47	6	4	12
Current apprentices (FY16)	17	17	0	0	0
Did not complete apprenticeship	20	8	2	0	10
TOTAL	106	72	8	4	22
Percentage	100%	67.92%	7.55%	3.77%	20.75%

Source: UTP.

Table 7.2. **CSS historical racial/ethnic demographics, 2004-16**

	Totals	Percentage
American Indian/Alaska Native	2	1.9
Asian	7	6.6
Black	56	52.8
Hispanic	20	18.9
White	21	19.8
TOTAL	**106**	**100.0**

Source: UTP

Table 7.3. **UTP youth apprenticeship gender participation, 2004-16**

	Totals	Percentage
Male	85	80.2
Female	21	19.8

Source: UTP.

A recent survey of current and former UTP participants and alumni captured a snapshot of the earning potential of apprentices over time. At the start of the apprenticeship, 79% of participants were classified as "opportunity youth". At present, apprentices who successfully complete the programme earn starting salaries between USD 35 000-50 000. Alumni of the programme report an annual salary range of USD 45 000-100 000 three to eight years after apprenticeship completion. In addition, over 70% of those surveyed report that they continue to pursue further higher education and/or technical training.

The survey also revealed, in their own words, what the apprentices are gaining from the programme. Respondents reflected on how the training and service components of the programme have helped them learn and grow, and how the UTP has supported the transition into professional careers:

"I am learning and doing what I love to do, and the best part is that I am getting paid to do it."

"An incredible alternative to traditional education. Not only do you get to learn new skills on the job, network with established professionals in the community, but it also is ripe with opportunities to give back."

"A great place to learn more about information technology, to grow as an individual, and gain professional experience."

"Provided me a skill set that was transferable to any job, as well as management experience through projects, school settings, and non-profit organisation management."

One participant, when asked how she would describe the programme to others, explained:

"I'd tell them they have the chance to meet amazing people, be part of something bigger than themselves and tell them how they're going to impact youth and their communities."

Many UTP alumni have moved beyond entry-level technical support IT positions and currently hold higher IT positions at a variety of business and government entities, including:

- Network/systems administrator for an architecture company;
- Webmaster at a large public institution;
- Software engineer at a web development company;
- Cyber Security Specialists for private and Governmental entities;
- Vice President of Operations for an IT Solutions Firm;
- Director of Operations at a web development company;
- Investment consultant for one of the top financial firms in the world;
- Owner of retail technology products company;
- Owner of IT Solutions Firm.

Box 7.1. **UTP Alumni spotlight – Jessie**

Director of Operations, Jarvus

Jessie attended college for two years prior to joining UTP. At the time, she struggled financially with the cost of school while also feeling that college wasn't the best learning environment for her at that particular point in her life. The opportunity to learn by serving appealed to her. She describes her time at UTP as a whirlwind of opportunity. While working at her assigned school, Jesse and some of her fellow DSFs connected with Devnuts, a venture of the web software engineering firm Jarvus. Devnuts is described as a tech oriented community centre in Philadelphia. After working at Devnuts and with Jarvus on a variety of projects, Jessie was eventually hired and is currently the Director of Operations for the company.

Jessie believes the many different paths of entry into and exit out of the UTP is a unique and exciting component of the programme. After three years of working at Jarvus, she emphasises that she is still learning, both technology skills as well as how to run a business. She reflects positively on her professional growth at UTP, as well as the variety of life experiences acquired. She values the importance of apprenticeships, and feels all industries should offer this opportunity.

Box 7.2. **UTP Alumni spotlight – Shanelle**

Teacher, School District of Philadelphia

Shanelle was recruited by UTP while attending an alternative high school, YouthBuild. While initially uncertain about her interest in technology, she became enamored with the programme. She has been involved with UTP in varying capacities for almost ten years, and UTP has become a second family to her. After completing the DSF and CSS programmes, she continued to work with UTP as a senior CSS, providing technology support in schools and

---

Box 7.2. **UTP Alumni spotlight – Shanelle** *(cont.)*

mentoring new DSF. Most recently, she accepted a teaching position with the SDP to teach computer support technology in a high school CTE programme.

Shanelle talks to her students often about UTP, and how the programme benefited her. She helps her students work toward many of the same certifications she completed with UTP. She connects with her students by explaining she is from the same challenged neighborhood that they are, and they see her as a role model. She would like to stay with teaching for several years, to work with at least two groups of students as they go through the high school CTE cycle. At the same time, she will continue to pursue her own education, working on a degree in cyber security with an interest in applying this skill in a government job, like of her fellow UTP alumni.

Box 7.3. **Apprentice spotlight – Derek**

Derek is a current Computer Support Specialist, working in a high school where he receives rave reviews from the principal, mentor teacher technology leader (TTL), and the other staff and students he encounters. His principal marvels at Derek's polished people skills, which the administrator stresses are essential for working in a school. The TTL speaks highly of Derek's technological prowess and ability to solve the wide range of problems that crop up during the school day. In addition to supporting the technology in the school, Derek mentors a DSF working at the same school and sponsors a programmeming club for students. Prior to his work at his current school, Derek had been placed as a DSF at the high school that he himself had attended. He was amazed to discover that he felt like a colleague among his former teachers and possessed skills that he could use to assist them in teaching and supporting students.

Derek was referred to the DSF programme by a friend who was a CSS at the time. He credits the programme with developing his thoughts about his identity and direction, and feels he has been able to develop time management and people skills through the programme. He also credits the programme with providing him a sense of professionalism and an understanding of how the real world works. He valued the opportunity to interview for his current school-based work site and he received guidance from the programme about his resume and cover letter.

Like Shanelle, Derek also identifies UTP as a kind of family, one in which everyone is supportive of each other. Derek has a hearing impairment, and has felt like he has always been accommodated by the programme while at the same time has been made to feel normal. He has learned from others, and also enjoys the opportunity to mentor a pre-apprentice.

Box 7.4. **Apprentice spotlight: Maalik**

Maalik is a high school graduate who dropped out because of health problems. As his health improved, he got back on track and earned his diploma from an alternative education public school. At this school he met a Computer Support Specialist, who encouraged him to join UTP. After graduation he became a DSF and completed his service time at the same school from which he graduated. After only 6 months of service, he was hired as a CSS and provides technical support to two alternative schools. He has always

---

Box 7.4. **Apprentice spotlight: Maalik** (*cont.*)

been interested in technology, but more importantly, he is interested in making something of his life and being a role model to younger peers. Through his experiences with UTP, he has gained so much confidence while also developing a sincere love for what he does on a daily basis.

As Maalik continues his development in the IT sector, he wants to focus on getting into the security aspect of technology. He would like to make this a career and earn a comfortable living. Technology is constantly moving, and so is he. His mentors and his apprenticeship experiences have taught him to never stop learning. He plans to achieve at least three certifications during his time at UTP, and make his mother, grandmother and two brothers proud.

Maalik recently spoke at a forum organised by The Century Foundation, entitled "Young, Educated, and Employed: Revitalizing Youth Apprenticeships in America." Maalik provided testimony about what it means to an apprentice. In his words, ""*I am learning and doing what I love to do, and the best part is that I am getting paid to do it.*"

Box 7.5. **Employer Spotlight – Chris**

Founder and Chief Technology Officer, Jarvus Innovations

Chris is the founder and Chief Technology Officer of Jarvus Innovations, a web software engineering firm. He feels strongly that UTP is a wonderful model for youth in Philadelphia, and has mentored several apprentices in coding. He sees the strength in UTP's culture of service as a learning tool, and he believes individuals learn technology best by starting with a real need and being given an opportunity to problem solve. Apprentices who work for the community are able to focus on their own development and learning while providing a positive benefit.

Jarvus' experiences with the two apprentices they hired has sold them on the benefits of apprenticeships. Chris shares that the ROI for the company is huge. The apprenticeship model provides the employer the opportunity to train employees with the relevant skills needed on the job while building loyalty and creating a mentoring work culture that is beneficial for all employees. In addition, the fact that the employee does not carry the burden of a college education debt, lessens the pressure on employees to demand higher salaries and creates stability in the workplace. Presently, Jarvus is working with UTP to develop an apprenticeship track tailored to the skills requirements of local tech startups who need employees who can code. Chris believes UTP is an incubating and nurturing programme that offers a wonderful transition from student to professional career.

Strengths

The UTP is more than a stand-alone apprenticeship programme. The UTP recruits opportunity youth who may not otherwise find their way to a registered apprenticeship programme, and engages this population by offering technology experience through a service framework. Through on-the-job training and related instruction, participants prepare for the workforce by gaining both "hard" technology skills as well as "soft" skills (such as problem solving and self-reliance) that can be utilised in workplaces beyond technology companies. The UTP's registered apprenticeship is strengthened by additional programme components that support the urban youth participants prior to entering the apprenticeship (the pre-apprenticeship DSF programme) as well as after they complete it (transition to employment). The UTP offers long-term, holistic support for participants including a pipeline of service-learning, industry training, on the job training, college coursework, and relevant employment. All UTP programmes are interconnected, providing what many participants identify as a family-like, supportive environment that enhances their learning. Participants engage in community building and develop a "pass it on" philosophy in order to take personal responsibility for determining what they need to learn and what they need to do. This philosophy makes UTP participants life-long learners who apply the lessons learned in the programme in subsequent employment and education experiences. The UTP succeeds in great part because of the flexibility it offers to participants, including multiple entry and exit points and opportunity for youth to reflect on their experiences and direct their learning and job preparation.

The UTP's unique partnership with AmeriCorps, the United States' national service programme, enables the UTP to include a strong pre-apprenticeship programme that offers participants a stipend as well as an educational award that can be used to pay for tuition after service. The AmeriCorps programme supports the UTP philosophy of service, and helps the programme recruit from a larger pool of candidates.

The pre-apprentice and apprentice programmes both involve working with mentors, and both participants and staff identify this as a valuable component of their learning experience. At some sites, the apprentice also acts as a mentor to the pre-apprentice. This fosters strong connections between the youth and adults in the programme, particularly as adults balance high expectations of performance with respect for apprentices. Participants who undertake the programme together also form strong bonds as they support each other with their learning as well as their personal growth. Additionally, the interconnected pipeline model of the UTP deepens links between cohorts in different stages of the programme. The older participants pass on their knowledge to the younger participants and serve as role models for their younger counterparts.

The programme was deliberately designed to use a school setting as the core work and learning site. The participants, many of whom graduated from the school district, view schools as both a valued community as well as a business enterprise where they can build skills for their future career. Apprentices in the schools are recognised as skilled workers charged with the important task of maintaining the school's technological services. The school setting also provides crucial support: apprentices are providing services to teachers they may have studied with when they were younger and who understand the specific needs of the local community. Participants also receive support from UTP staff who are familiar with the needs of recent graduates from the system. Incorporating young apprentices into a high school setting also serves the purpose of influencing the school district's methods of preparing K-12 students for life after education. The apprenticeship programme provides the school district with downward pressure to do a better job of preparing high school students, and helping the district identify what must be changed in order to adequately prepare students for post high school experiences.

As a public-private partnership, the UTP has more flexibility in setting the stage for the employment of participants following the successful completion of the apprenticeship. Rather than focusing primarily on a traditional ROI for the school district, the UTP yields a societal ROI by preparing productive citizens. This flexibility has also enabled the programme to build strong connections with local technology companies who are interested in hiring apprentices as they graduate from the programme, and sometimes prior to completing the apprenticeship. Employer partners have been very pleased with how well UTP participants are prepared for the workplace. Several strong employer partners are interested in formalising a relationship in which they would support apprentices in the programme, both as they develop skills at the school work site and also as they continue apprenticeship activities at the private employer's site.

The UTP is an innovative programme that has developed a unique public-private collaboration to deliver apprenticeships to young people in urban Philadelphia. The UTP's focus on both an emerging industry and a non-traditional population is unusual for apprenticeships in the United States. Technology is a unique industry in that it is constantly changing. The UTP does a good job of keeping abreast of these changes, both by offering relevant training and work experience for participants as well as building connections with employers who can further support the apprentices as they learn in this ever-changing environment. By offering these technological skills coupled with general workplace competencies, the UTP prepares young people for employment in technology companies and other, broader workplaces.

Figure 7.2. **UTP Public/Private Partnership "eco-system"**

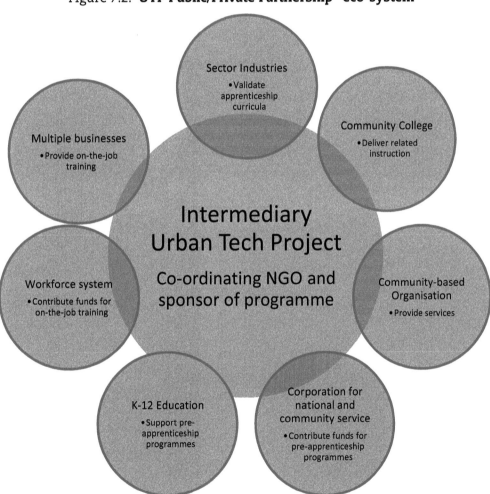

Source: UTP.

Weaknesses

The UTP is limited to some extent by the constraints of the School District of Philadelphia. Ideally, the pre-apprenticeship component of UTP would connect directly with students in high school. However, the district is primarily focused on providing academic experiences for K-12 students and provides limited opportunities to support career and technical education programmes or integrate pre-apprenticeships within the high school environment. Although situated within the district, the UTP lacks a seamless connection between the K-12 experience and the apprenticeship programme. Without this integration it takes longer for youth to complete the programme and move into employment, and it limits the impact that the programme has on the way the district teaches its students.

Today's UTP model prepares all apprentices for entry level positions as computer support specialists. While some alumni have gone on to advance into other aspects of the IT industry, this is not a direct outcome of the programme. In order to serve diverse IT needs, the UTP needs to diversify the occupations that participants are trained for, and offer specialty tracks that apprentices can select based on their interests and career goals.

When reviewing the technical training available for apprentices, it becomes clear that the related instruction offered at Community College of Philadelphia was not developing the necessary IT certifications valued by employers. As a result, the UTP must work with participants to supplement the related instruction and ensure successful attainment of the IT certification. A stronger collaboration with education partners could eliminate duplication between training efforts.

The current model of UTP struggles on a regular basis to secure the funding needed to support and grow the programme. Formalising agreements with partner employers, and developing a plan for long-term stable training funds is a first step, but larger scale efforts are necessary. In order to ensure a secure and sustainable future for the UTP, as well as for other programmes who may wish to pursue the same model, the federal government must make stronger commitments to support apprenticeship programmes with both financial and logistical resources.

Recent data gathering from the programme reveals that females participate in UTP at a much lower rate (19.8%) than males. A participant interviewee also stressed this as a weakness of the programme. While this rate is markedly better than the US apprenticeship rate as a whole (only 6% of US registered apprentices are female), there is much work to be done.

Transferability

The UTP is an example of how to develop and operate a sustainable long-term apprenticeship model. Private employers typically don't have continuous apprenticeship programmes; rather, the existence of programmes ebbs and flows depending on employer need. The UTP is able to sustain an apprenticeship programme in part because the initiative is a strong intermediary for an apprenticeship network that includes private employers and educational institutions. While employers are often primarily concerned with the ROI that an apprenticeship programme brings, the UTP is able to focus on the personal development of participants. As a public entity grounded in a local school district, the UTP is able to focus on social outcomes alongside building skills through on-the-job training, mentoring and other forms of education. In this way, the UTP is able to focus on "disconnected youth" by meeting their specific needs, valuing diversity, and supporting their cultural mores. The result is a societal ROI of preparing youth to be good citizens.

The UTP is a system in which the public sector and private sector connect in a mutually beneficial way. The UTP's mission involves engaging participants and providing the support this population needs to prepare for the workforce. The UTP meets the needs of private employers by offering a skilled workforce for the business community, and employers support the mission of UTP by providing more specialised workplace training and ensuring that apprentices successfully enter the workforce. The fact that UTP includes a consortium of employer partners enables programme participants to find workplace experiences that align with their skills and interests. It also allows the programme to cut across sectors and offer participants experiences in IT companies as well as non-tech companies that need IT (universities, non-profits, etc.)

The UTP's strong pipeline of experiences demonstrates that apprenticeship programmes, and the participants they serve, are strengthened when linked to pre-apprenticeship opportunities and post-apprenticeship networks with private employers. In particular, opportunity youth benefit from this type of continuum as this population is typically removed from apprenticeship opportunities and may need additional support to prepare for this experience. The programme experience is deepened by connecting the pre-apprenticeship with an existing model of national service. The youth are engaged by the opportunity to provide service, and are put in a position to be productive adult, civically engaged, successfully employed citizens that remain life-long learners.

Note

1. GED is an acronym for "General Education Development". It represents a certification that is based on a series of subject tests and certifies that an individual has academic skills at the secondary level.

References

Interview with Eric Anderson, School District of Philadelphia and Urban Technology Project Alumnus, 25 February 2016.

Central High School group interview with Steve Innamarato, TTL and CSS supervisor, Tim McKenna, Principal, CSS, 25 February 2016.

Chang, C. (2016), "The Case for Expanding Youth Apprenticeships", The Century Foundation, 11 January 2016.

Chang, C. (2015), "Apprenticeship Explainer: Why Politicians are Pitching Them", The Century Foundation, 20 July 2015.

Chang, C. (2015), "Can Apprenticeships Help Reduce Youth Unemployment", The Century Foundation, 16 November 2015.

Diavua, S. (2016), "Building Opportunities and Skills for a Growing Digital Workforce", Federal Reserve Bank of Philadelphia, Cascade No. 90, Winter 2016.

Education Week (2014), 11 December 2014, "Apprenticeship Programmes in High-Tech Fields Gets $110 Mil Boost from Dept of Labor" retrieved at: *http://blogs.edweek.org/edweek/DigitalEducation/2014/12/ apprentice_programmes_in_high-te.html.*

Eizenstat, S. and R.I. Lerman (2013), "Apprenticeships Could Help U.S. Workers Gain a Competitive Edge", Urban Institute.

Interview with Jim Foti, *Policy Team Leader, U.S. Department of Labor*, 12 February 2016 and 19 February 2016.

Interview with Edison Freire, School District of Philadelphia, Director and Founder of the Urban Technology Project, 11 February 2016 and 17 March 2016.

Goldstein, F. (2005), "Philadelphia's Urban Technology Project: Embracing the Intellect, the Heart, and the Soul of Youth", *Masters Thesis for the University of Pennsylvania Graduate School of Education*, May 2005.

Greater Philadelphia Chamber of Commerce (2015), Roadmap for Growth: A Vision for the City of Philadelphia, p.18, retrieved at: *www.greaterphilachamber.com/download/public/roadmapreport15-16-lowres%282%29.pdf*.

Harvard Graduate School of Education (2014), "Creating Pathways to Prosperity: A Blueprint for Action", *The Pathways to Prosperity Project and The Achievement Gap Initiative at Harvard University*, June 2014.

Harvard Graduate School of Education (2011), "Pathways to Prosperity: Meeting the Challenge of Preparing Young Americans for the 21st Century", *Pathways to Prosperity Project*, February 2011.

Jacoby, T. (2014), "Why is Germany So Much Better at Training Its Workers", *The Atlantic*, 16 October 2014.

Interview with Jarvus Innovations Group, Chris Alfano Chief Technology Officer, Jessie Cunningham, Director of Operations and Nafis Bey, engineer and former apprentice.

Interview with Everett Katzen, *Owner, Springboard Media*, 29 February 2016.

Knowles, G. (2015), "Revisiting Youth Apprenticeships", *American Youth Policy Forum*, 30 November 2015.

Interview with Meg Shope Koppel, Philadelphia Works, 22 February 2016.

Interview with Ron Leonard, Office of Apprenticeship, US Department of Labor, 19 February 2016.

Lerman, R.I. and A. Packer (2015), "Youth Apprenticeship: A Hopeful Approach for Improving Outcomes for Baltimore Youth: *The Abell Report*, April 2015, Volume 28, Number 2.

Lerman, R.I. (2014), "Expanding Apprenticeship Training in Canada: Perspectives from International Experience", *Taking Action for Canada Jobs and Skills for the 21st Century*, April 2014.

Lerman, R.I. (2014), "Proposal 7: Expanding Apprenticeship Opportunities in the United States", *The Hamilton Project*, American University and Urban Institute, 2014.

Lerman, R.I. (2012), "Can the United States Expand Apprenticeship? Lessons from Experience", American University, Urban Institute, and IZA.

Lerman, R.I. (2010), "Expanding Apprenticeship – A Way to Enhance Skills and Careers", Urban Institute.

Lerman, R.I. (2009), "A Better Way to Get Educated, Employed", Urban Institute, 3 August 2009.

Lerman, R.I. (2009), "Training Tomorrow's Workforce: Community College and Apprenticeship as Collaborative Routes to Rewarding Careers", *Center for American Progress*, December 2009.

Interview with Shanelle Lockhart, Teacher, School District of Philadelphia and Urban Technology Project Alumnus, 24 February 2016.

OECD (2016), Harmonised unemployment rate (HUR) (indicator), *http://dx.doi.org/10.1787/52570002-en* (accessed on 18 March 2016).

Olinsky, B. and S. Ayres (2013), "Training for Success: A Policy to Expand Apprenticeships in the United States", *Center for American Progress*, December 2013.

Philadelphia Works (2015), "Philadelphians with Barriers to Employment | Philadelphia ..." 2015. 15 Mar. 2016, *www.philaworks.org/workforce-trends-data/philadelphians-barriers-employment*.

Roland, K.L. (2016), "Apprenticeships and Their Potential in the U.S.", *Federal Reserve Bank of Philadelphia*, Cascade No. 90 Winter 2016.

The School District of Philadelphia (2015), Action Plan 3.0., retrieved at: *http://webgui.phila.k12.pa.us/offices/a/action-plan*.

United States Census Bureau (2012), American Community Survey, 2012 1-year estimates.

U.S. Department of Labor (2016a), Bureau of Labor Statistics, Unemployment Rate, retrieved at: *http://data.bls.gov/timeseries/LNS14000000*.

U.S. Department of Labor (2016b), Apprenticeship USA Data and Statistics, retrieved at *www.doleta.gov/oa/data_statistics.cfm*.

U.S. Department of Labor (2016c), "Pre-Apprenticeship: Pathways for Women into High-Wage Careers: A Guide for Community-Based Organizations and Workforce Providers", retrieved at: *www.doleta.gov/oa/preapp/*.

U.S. Department of Labor (2014), "The first ever White House Summit on American Apprenticeship", retrieved at *https://blog.dol.gov/2014/07/14/the-first-ever-white-house-summit-on-american-apprenticeship/*, Blog, 14 July 2014.

U.S. Department of Labor (n.d.), "An Assessment and Planning Tool for the Public Workforce System", *Apprenticeship USA ToolKit: Advancing Apprenticeship as a Workforce Strategy.*

U.S. Department of Labor Employment and Training Administration (n.d.), Notice of Availability of Funds and Funding Opportunity Announcement for the American Apprenticeship Initiative.

U.S. Department of Labor (n.d.), "Pre-Apprenticeship: Pathways for Women into High-Wage Careers: A Guide for Community-Based Organizations and Workforce Providers", *Apprenticeship USA ToolKit: Advancing Apprenticeship as a Workforce Strategy.*

U.S. Department of Labor (n.d.), "The Workforce Innovation and Opportunity Act", *Apprenticeship USA ToolKit: Advancing Apprenticeship as a Workforce Strategy.*

White House (2016), TechHire website, retrieved at *www.whitehouse.gov/issues/technology/techhire.*

White House (2014), State of the Union Address, Barack Obama. Retrieved on 29/03/2016 at *www.whitehouse.gov/the-press-office/2014/01/28/president-barack-obamas-state-union-address.*

Chapter 8

Boosting employer engagement in apprenticeships at the local level in Turkey

This chapter explores employer engagement in work-based training programmes enacted as part of wider active labour market policies in the Turkish economy. The legislative background and the implementation of work-based programmes are examined, particularly with respect to their ability to meet the needs of employers while providing vocational skills to apprentices.

Key findings

- Turkey is a vibrant and dynamic economy which has experienced significant improvements in economic growth and development in recent years. Vocational education enjoys a long history in the Turkish labour market, but recent efforts from the central Turkish government have aimed to improve the scope and provision of apprenticeship opportunities.

- This chapter highlights the role of collaboration between employer groups and public employment services in helping to deliver active labour market policies and provide work-based training places to jobseekers.

Introduction

This chapter will address apprenticeship and other types of work-based learning in Turkey with a particular emphasis on employer engagement in skills development for the youth. This report presents a general background description of the Turkish labour market, the education system, and the laws and regulations that operate apprenticeship and work-based learning and then examines a collaboration between the Turkish Employment Agency and the Turkish Confederation of Employer Associations. The collaboration is based on the implementation of a work-based programme from the national employment agency by the member companies of the employer association. A general account of social partners, employers and workers organisations and affiliated associations is presented alongside the predecessor programs which aim to engage employers in skills development of the unemployed, especially the youth.

Background

Although declining, youth unemployment is still a challenge for many countries (ILO, 2015). Promoting and strengthening high quality apprenticeship systems is considered a means for making apprenticeships more valuable to both youth and employers (OECD, 2014). The European Alliance for Apprenticeships (EAfA) was launched on 2 July 2013 with the goal of strengthening the quality, provision and status of apprenticeships in Europe. To this end, EAfA brings together governments with other key stakeholders, like businesses, social partners, industry chambers, vocational education and training (VET) providers, regions, youth representatives or think tanks (EU, 2015). As a candidate country, Turkey also agreed in June 2015 to undertake policy measures that would increase the quality, supply and attractiveness of apprenticeships (EAfA website, National Commitments, Turkey).

Apprenticeship and work-based learning in Turkey has a long tradition and dates back to the 13th century with the foundation of a fraternity organisation named *Ahi* Associations (Özyılmaz, 2011). These associations determined the rules, regulation and operation of trades and workshops. An important function of *Ahi* Associations was training the young through work. Education and training in the *Ahi* system integrated vocational training at the workshop with general and social education at dervish lodge (*zaviye*, religious school) (Çağatay, 1989). One would start working in an occupation as an assistant apprentice and through the years would become first an apprentice, then a journeyman, and finally a master. For centuries, *Ahi* Associations had been the major economic, social and cultural power in the Seljuk and Ottoman Empires although their names and ways of functioning changed over time and were abolished altogether in 1912 (Ekinci, 1990; Çağatay, 1989).

When the Turkish Republic was established, all schools, including vocational schools, were brought under the jurisdiction of the Ministry of Education. In late 1940s, vocational courses were initiated as an important means for the training of a skilled labour force. In the 1960s, vocational high schools were established as well as 1-2 year practical trade schools. Technical high schools were included into the system in the 1970s. The system was restructured in 1973 with the National Education Basic Law No. 1739. According to the law, preparing individuals for an occupation, higher education or labour market was the objective of vocational and technical education (Akpınar, 2004). In these initial years, the "work-based" dimension (practice-orientation of students in companies) discontinued until the legal basis of VET and apprenticeship was established later in late 1970s and 1980s.

Policy context

The Turkish education system consists of "formal education" and "non-formal education", and the main responsible body is the Ministry of National Education (*Milli Eğitim Bakanlığı*, MoNE), except for higher education. Compulsory schooling in formal education is twelve years, which consists of four years of primary education, four years of lower secondary education and four years of upper secondary education. Upper secondary education consists of general secondary education, and vocational and technical secondary education. In recent years, enrolment into VET secondary education has increased substantially. In the 2002-03 academic year, there were fewer than one million students enrolled in secondary VET schools (TURKSTAT, 2010). This has increased by 213% to 2.1 million students in the 2014-15 academic year, almost equalling the number of enrolled students in general secondary schools (2.9 million) (TURKSTAT, 2015a).

Apprenticeships in Turkey are considered non-formal, meaning that successful completion results in certification rather than a diploma. General Directorate of Lifelong Learning (*Hayat Boyu Öğrenme Genel Müdürlüğü*, HBÖGM) is the main body that runs apprenticeship training and non-formal VET courses. Various non-formal educational activities including apprenticeship training is provided by the MoNE, General Directorate of Lifelong Learning. Other social partners like Confederation of Turkish Tradesmen and Craftsmen (*Türkiye Esnaf ve Sanatkarlar Konfederasyonu*, TESK), Union of Chambers and Commodity Exchanges of Turkey (*Türkiye Odalar ve Borsalar Birliği*, TOBB), Turkish Confederation of Employer Associations (*Türkiye İşverenler Sendikası Konfederasyonu*, TİSK) and others provide support to VET in Turkey.

The VET and apprenticeship system in Turkey

The VET system in Turkey is dual in nature, with both theoretical (school-based training) and practical (work-based training/practical training in schools) dimensions. The major types of VET provision are:

- VET upper secondary schools providing theoretical education and training at schools and work-based skills training and internships at enterprises;
- Apprenticeship training, which is mainly based on training provided in enterprises where the person is employed, and theoretical training at vocational training centres;

- Non-formal VET courses;
- Post-secondary VET schools that offer two-year programs. Higher Education Council regulates these schools.

The legislation relating to the laws and regulations in VET changed and developed over the years in Turkey as the need for restructuring emerged. The main law in action is the Vocational Education Law No. 3308[1]1 enacted in 1986. There have been amendments to the Law in 2001, with the Law No. 4702, to set up new and strong co-operation with industry and commerce, and to bring flexibility to the system. With the amendments, Law No. 3308 is still the main law that regulates both VET and apprenticeship system in Turkey. Another important law in relation to the improvement of vocational education in Turkey is the Vocational Qualification Authority Law No. 5544 enacted in 2006.

There have been many projects to develop and strengthen the VET in Turkey. Some of the recent nationally funded projects include "The Specialised Vocational Training Centres Skills'10 Project" (*Uzmanlaşmış Meslek Edindirme Merkezleri, Beceri'10 Projesi*, UMEM) (2010-15), and "Improving the Vocational Skills Project" (*Mesleki Becerilerin Geliştirilmesi Projesi*, MESGEP) (2011-13). A recent internationally funded programme includes the project on "Improving the Quality of Vocational Education and Training in Turkey – I and II" (IQVET; *Türkiye'de Mesleki ve Teknik Eğitimin Kalitesinin Geliştirilmesi Projesi- I ve II*, METEK) (2012-2014, EU-IPA-4 funded).

The Turkish apprenticeship system

According to the Law No. 3308, workplaces are required to send their apprentices one day a week (not less than 8 hours) to Vocational Training Centres (*Mesleki Eğitim Merkezi – MEM*), or training units or institutions approved by the MoNE, to complement their work-based training with theoretical courses. During the other workdays, apprentices work at their workplaces where master trainers are responsible for their work-based development. At the end of their training period, which can take two to three years depending on the type of occupation, apprentices take an exam and become journeymen. Journeymen must also take a certification exam after their training, or if they have worked in the relevant occupational field for a certain period of time, or graduated from VET upper secondary school. Those who pass the exam become masters in their occupational fields and receive mastership certificates. Masters can then become master trainers by completing a 40-hour training course.

Currently, apprenticeship training in Turkey is carried out in 31 occupational fields and 153 branches as the latest revisions done by the 24th Vocational Education Council in December 2011. In the 2012-13 academic year, 104 342 apprentices, 46 286 foremen, and 19 107 master trainers attended programs through 369 Vocational Training Centres. In the same year, 68 412 foremanship certificates and 7 287 certificates to establish work were granted (TURKSTAT, 2014).

Out of 153 occupational branches, 13 listed in Table 8.1 comprise the highest enrolment levels (71.5% in total). The vast majority of apprentices are male (81.3%), between the ages of 15-22 (88.3%), and primary school graduates (94.2%).

Enterprises seek apprentices through direct advertisement. In general, small-scale workplaces seek apprentices either by job advertisements posted on their shop windows, or through various job advertisement channels including the related occupational chamber websites. Aspiring apprentices then apply for their desired positions.

Table 8.1. **Apprentices by type of occupation, gender
and level of education (2010-11)**

Type of occupation	Gender		Age		Level of education			
	M	F	15-22	23+	Primary	Gen. High	VET High	Higher ed.
Hairdresser	6 967	13 190	17 430	2 727	18 511	1 396	159	91
Barber	19 210	35	17 458	1 787	18 614	523	85	23
Wiring/Panel Installation	7 337	72	6 784	625	7 028	291	81	9
Auto Electro-Mech.	5 594	12	5 496	110	5 508	68	27	3
Auto Mechanics	4 505	0	4 324	181	4 452	43	9	1
Turnery	4 153	22	4 106	69	4 115	50	7	3
Making Furniture	4 047	8	3 793	262	3 952	86	14	3
Auto. Framework	2 936	4	2 869	71	2 803	29	107	1
Lathe Operator	2 744	2	2 663	83	2 711	22	11	2
Welder's Work	2 555	32	2 389	198	2 502	66	18	1
Auto Electrician	2 353	2	2 276	79	2 324	24	7	0
Cookery	2 058	347	1 718	687	2 135	206	52	12
Model Machine	1 025	3 220	2 819	1 426	3 759	318	145	23
Others	28 338	4 595	27 745	5 188	30 339	2 091	375	128
Total	**93 822**	**21 541**	**101 870**	**13 493**	**108 753**	**5 213**	**1 097**	**300**

Source: TURKSTAT (2012).

Enterprises are not legally allowed to employ an apprentice below the age of 19 without a written apprenticeship contract. There is a period of probation of between 1-3 months before such contracts become binding. The contract offers some financial benefits to the employers: once under contract, social security insurance premiums and insurance contributions for "Occupational Accidents and Diseases" of candidate apprentices and apprentices are paid by the state, which decreases the financial burden of the employers. Similarly, the employers of the apprentices are also exempt from other financial requirements such as revenue stamps, income tax, tax refund, and severance payment. Moreover, the wages paid to apprentices would be shown as expenditures by the employers. Once an apprentice becomes a journeyman, social security insurance premiums and the insurance contributions are no longer paid by the state.

Work-based skills training in upper secondary VET schools

VET upper secondary schools prepare students for the world of work as well as higher education. The graduates of VET upper secondary education may apply to two-year VET higher education programs for placement without sitting the nation-wide higher education entrance exam. There are 61 job families and 228 branches in VET upper secondary schools, as of 2012. Accordingly, students at VET upper secondary schools are directed to job families at the 10th grade and their occupational branches related to specific job families are determined by the 11th grade. Work-based skills training of VET upper secondary students take place at the 12th grade (MoNE, 2012). The structure of the work-based training was prepared in line with Law No. 3308, and the regulations are set by the MoNE Secondary Education Institutions Regulation issued in September 2013.

In the 12th grade, students go to their schools on two days of the week for theoretical training and the remaining three days they go to enterprises for their skills training. The work and skills training undertaken by students at the enterprises is monitored by the VET upper secondary school co-ordinator teachers (Özcan and Tamer, 2013). The co-ordinator field teacher prepares a folder for each student which explains not only the official requirements to be fulfilled but also the tasks to be carried by the student during the skills training. The student regularly fills in the relevant parts of the folder to indicate which tasks have been addressed through the training. The master trainer at the enterprise monitors the progress of the students and evaluates the tasks that are carried by the trainees and reports by filling in the relevant parts of the folder.

During the skills training process, enterprises are responsible for the interns, and the insurance premium costs for "Occupational Accidents and Diseases" are paid by the MoNE like the apprentices. Furthermore, the interns are paid at least 30% of the minimum wage during their enterprise-based training as required by MoNE Secondary Schools Regulation and Vocational Education Law No. 3308.

Secondary Education Institutions Regulation guides the assessment procedure for the enterprise-based skills training. Accordingly, an examination is conducted by a commission comprising the master trainer or the training personnel at the enterprise, the co-ordinator field teachers of the education institution, and representatives of employers association active in the area. This skills examination may cover practical and/or theoretical questions.

Policy context and issues

In 2015, the overall labour force participation rate was 52.1%. The average rate of unemployment in Turkey was 9.6%, but it was higher for workers in the non-agricultural sector (11.7%) and for young people (17.7%), particularly young women (21.8%) (see Table 8.2).

Table 8.2. **Labour force participation and employment, June 2015**

	Total	Male	Female
15 years and above population (000)	57 818	28 555	29 262
Labour force (000)	30 141	20 683	9 458
Employment (000)	27 261	18 900	8 361
Unemployed (000)	2 880	1 782	1 097
Those not included in labour force (000)	27 677	7 873	19 804
Labour force participation rate (%)	52.1	72.4	32.3
Employment rate (%)	47.1	66.2	28.6
Unemployment rate (%)	9.6	8.6	11.6
Non-agricultural unemployment (%)	11.7	10.0	16.4
Youth unemployment rate (15-24 age)	17.7	15.5	21.8

Source: TURKSTAT (2015b).

Technological developments in recent decades have had an impact on the industrial and service sector where low technology use has given way to high-technology production. There has been a corresponding increase in demand for advanced technological skills. However, education institutions have been slow to respond to the skills needs of the industrial and services sectors. This indicated a serious need to include employers in skills development policy and implementation.

The share of the Turkish workforce employed in the agricultural sector has somewhat declined in the period from 2005 to 2015, while the share of employment in construction and services has somewhat increased (see Table 8.3).

The higher rate of unemployment among the youth can be attributed to a lack of vocational experience or work-related skills. This indicates an increased need for employer

Table 8.3. **Labour force participation and employment by sector and years**

	January 2005	January 2010	January 2015
Labour force (000)	21 320	24 449	29 347
Employed (000)	19 349	21 489	26 339
Agricultural employment (000)	5 323	5 116	5 455
Non-agricultural employment – total	14 026	16 373	20 884
Industry (000)	4 030	4 416	5 349
Construction (000)	1 030	1 394	1 920
Services (000)	8 966	10 564	13 615
Unemployed (000)	1 971	2 960	3 008
Labor force participation rate (%)	44.5	46.7	51.1
Employment rate (%)	40.4	41.0	45.8
Agricultural employment (%)	27.5	23.8	20.7
Non-agricultural employment – total	72.5	76.2	79.3
Industry (%)	20.8	20.5	20.3
Construction (%)	5.3	6.5	7.3
Services (%)	46.4	49.2	51.7
Unemployment rate (%)	9.2	12.1	10.2
Non-agricultural unemployment (%)	12.0	14.9	12.4
Youth unemployment rate (15-24 age)	17.4	21.7	18.5

Source: TURKSTAT (2015).

engagement in skills development to improve the employability of the youth (Ünlühisarcıklı et al., 2014).

MoNE is the main body responsible for VET provision. However, employers, workers organisations and affiliated associations also contribute to vocational and technical education in Turkey. Recently, there have been increased efforts to involve the social partners for VET provision and contribution.

Social partners: Employers and workers organisations and affiliated associations

Turkish Confederation of Employer Associations (*Türkiye İşverenler Kurumu*, TİSK) is the main organisation that brings together the employers in Turkey. The umbrella organisation for the tradesmen and craftsmen is the Confederation of Turkish Tradesmen and Craftsmen (*Türkiye Esnaf ve Sanatkarlar Konfederasyonu*, TESK). The Union of Chambers and Commodity Exchanges of Turkey (*Türkiye Odalar ve Borsalar Birliği*, TOBB) is the highest level representative body of the private sector, and the Turkish Employment Agency (*Türkiye İş Kurumu*, İŞKUR) is the biggest organisation that assists the job seekers and employers in Turkey.

The Law No. 3308 also regulates the roles of social partners and enterprises in the vocational education system in Turkey. Social partners participate in the planning, development and evaluation procedures of VET through the vocational education councils that have a tri-partite structure. Vocational Education Council has been established in accordance with the Law No. 3308 and all the related social partners are represented in this council.[2]

Vocational Education Council functions for making decisions and stating opinions to the MoNE on the planning, development and evaluation of education at any level, in which vocational and technical training curricula have been implemented, non-formal and apprenticeship training provided in vocational training centres, and practical training attained at institutions and enterprises. The MoNE and relevant vocational institutions execute the decisions taken by the Council. The chairman of the council is Undersecretary of Ministry of National Education. The members of the council are the representatives of relevant ministries, institutions, organisations and confederations of employers and employees.

Similarly, in accordance with the Law No. 3308, Provincial Vocational Education Councils have also been established in each of the 81 provinces of Turkey. These councils have the same duties as the Vocational Education Council at provincial level, and also have a tri-partite structure (Law No. 3308). Other platforms the social partners participate in are the National Education Symposia, Occupational Standards Committees, and the preparation of Five Year Development Plans.

In the following section, the contribution of some of the social partners to VET and skills development will be summarised. Then, a recent project that is based on engaging the employers for the skills development of the unemployed with the purpose of providing a job after the skills development program will be presented. Finally, the recent implementation of work-based training skills development programmes will be provided and discussed.

Turkish Confederation of Employer Associations

The Turkish Confederation of Employer Associations (*Türkiye İşveren Sendikaları Konfederasyonu*, TİSK) is the umbrella organisation that represents employers in industrial relations nationally and internationally. At the national level, TİSK represents employers in all tripartite platforms as a social partner, and is also involved with engaging international organisations such as the International Labour Organisation (ILO), the Confederation of European Business (BUSINESSEUROPE), Business and Industry Advisory Committee to the OECD (BIAC), the International Organisation of Employers (IOE), the Union of Mediterranean Confederation of Enterprises (UMCE) and the Union of Black Sea and Caspian Confederation of Enterprises (UBCCE).

Although membership is voluntary, the level of affiliation to TİSK is high for large companies and employer associations. As an umbrella organisation, TİSK represents 20 employers' associations that are active in various economic sectors with 9 600 workplaces and 1 200 000 workers. Dues paid by its member associations constitute the budget of the organisation. TİSK actively participates in vocational education projects.

The fundamental principles adopted by TİSK are (TİSK, nd):

- Maintaining good relations between employers and workers;
- Sustaining free enterprise and market economy;
- Improving international competitiveness of enterprises and the economy;
- Increasing production, productivity, investment and exports;
- Protecting and expanding productive employment, and reducing unemployment;
- Developing bipartite and tripartite co-operation;
- Improving vocational training and lifelong learning opportunities for the labour force by establishing training-employment link;
- Assisting Turkey's integration with the modern world as well as with the EU.

Turkish Employment Agency

The Turkish Employment Agency (*Türkiye İş Kurumu*, İŞKUR) is the biggest organisation that assists both job seekers and employers in Turkey. The main responsibilities of İŞKUR are: helping both job seekers and employers; providing job and vocational consulting services and training programs; implementing active and passive labour market programs; and regulating private employment agencies. The General Board of İŞKUR consists of representatives of employer organisations, trade unions, institutions of higher education, chambers of commerce and industry, voluntary organisations, and government appointees.

İŞKUR, offers various training activities to unemployed people, women, youngsters, disabled people and ex-convicts either by itself or in co-operation with public and private institutions and organisations. These training activities range from market-oriented courses that result in the acquisition of specific entrepreneurial skills. Some of these programmes result in a job guarantee upon successful completion of the programme. Accordingly, İŞKUR is expected to place at least 60% of the trainees to suitable jobs. However, all these activities and efforts for providing educational programmes and job opportunities are not effective at reaching high numbers of people.

Confederation of Turkish tradesmen and craftsmen

The highest level of professional representation for the small enterprises in Turkey is the Confederation of Turkish Tradesmen and Craftsmen (*Türkiye Esnaf ve Sanatkarları Konfederasyonu*, TESK). About 90% of all enterprises in Turkey are small enterprises. The roots of TESK go back to the *Ahi* Associations.

TESK has more than two million members and is organised into 3 098 local Chambers that represent different professional activities, 82 Unions of Chambers in each of the provinces, and 13 Sector Federations grouped under TESK as an umbrella organisation.

TESK carry out three major tasks, namely: to protect the interests of the "occupation"; to keep a record of the members and collecting membership subscriptions; and to organise training activities to increase vocational qualifications of members. More than any other organisation under Law No. 3308, TESK has been involved in vocational and technical training for the provision of apprenticeship training for all occupations under the scope of MoNE.

As a non-governmental organisation, TESK undertakes an important role and responsibility in vocational and technical education by: organising training and giving TESK journeyman and TESK master certificates in occupational branches for which apprenticeship training is not provided by MoNE as defined by Vocational Education Law No. 3308; allocating an amount of share from the Confederation's income for training activities; providing the means for financing vocational and technical training in line with the Vocational Education Fund Regulation (Official Gazette No. 27790, 2010); improving the quality of vocational and technical training by workplace investigations and consultancy when needed; maintaining Vocational Training and Technology Centres (Mesleki Eğitim ve Teknoloji Merkezleri, METEM), in which vocational training is provided for occupational improvement and adaptation to new technologies; and providing training for the young to contribute to their practical skill acquisition at workplaces.

The local Chambers are responsible for carrying out the examination for TESK certification and they also conduct preparatory courses for examination. A TESK journeymanship certificate is granted to those who are at least an elementary school graduate, above the age of 16, worked in a related occupation for at least two-years and succeeded the exam organised by the chamber. There are about 350 such occupations under the responsibility of TESK, usually in production or service fields. These occupations include food production, personal hygiene and beauty, or accommodation and entertainment professions, and the training periods would be no more than a few weeks.

In short, TESK has a crucial role for monitoring and inspecting the vocational and technical training that is taking place at the enterprises, as well as its role in examination and certification system. Therefore, TESK make a major contribution to vocational and technical training in Turkey (TESK website).

The Union of Chambers and Commodity Exchanges of Turkey

The Union of Chambers and Commodity Exchanges of Turkey (*Türkiye Odalar ve Borsalar Birliği*, TOBB) is the highest level representative of the private sector. TOBB was established in 1950 and currently has 365 members. TOBB carries out administrative, representative and advisory functions for the chambers and commodity exchanges, and is also an active organisation in terms of vocational education.

According to Law No. 5174 (the Law of the Union of Chambers and Commodity Exchanges of Turkey, and the Chambers and Commodity Exchanges; date of adoption: 18 May 2004), Article 12, additional duties of the chambers are as follows: opening commercial, maritime business and industry courses; assisting courses that have already been opened; training students abroad or within the country for areas needed and providing traineeship under the permission and supervision of the Ministry of National Education; working for the improvement of the vocational and technical education and training; issuing documents for vocational branches that are not covered by the Law No. 3308 to the member organisations; and others. TOBB is therefore actively involved in vocational and technical education.

A joint project conducted by the private sector, the public sector and university sector and facilitated by TOBB is presented in this chapter.

Existing Turkish programmes

The specialised Vocational Training Centres Skills'10 Project

Over the last decade, with the rapid advancement of technology the skills required in the labour market changed as new jobs with new skills sets came into existence while some traditional jobs disappeared. The Specialised Vocational Training Centres (UMEM) Skills'10 Project was developed with the purpose of producing a solution to the unemployment stemming from the mismatch between supply and demand among employee and employers. The initiative was launched to implement vocational training to decrease the unemployment rate after the 2008-09 crisis by equipping the unemployed with new skill sets that are employable. It also aimed to involve employers in the skills development of the unemployed and also featured an assessment of the needs of the labour market. The project was conducted over a five year period from June 2010.

To serve this purpose, a Labour Force Market Needs Analysis was conducted in 2010 for the first time in Turkey. Vocational training programs were designed based on the results of this needs analysis. Union of Chambers and Commodity Exchanges of Turkey (TOBB), Ministry of Labour and Social Security Turkish Employment Agency (ÇSGB-İŞKUR), Ministry of National Education General Directorate of Vocational and Technical Education (MEB-MTEGM) and TOBB Economy and Technology University (TOBB-ETÜ) were key stakeholders of the project. The project was therefore a co-operative effort between the public and private sectors.

Jobseekers that were registered with İŞKUR could apply for any particular vocational courses through UMEM. UMEM trainings consist of two sections: a course in the project schools (theoretical-practical training) and on-the-job training (internship) at the workplace.

The initiative also enabled 140 VET secondary schools to expand their technical infrastructure to meet the increased demand. The theoretical-practical training period over a maximum of three months was provided through these schools. For another three months, on-the-job training (internships) were provided at chosen workplaces to facilitate the transition from unemployment to the workplace (Ünlühisarcıklı et al., 2014).

To benefit from the project, one should first be registered in İŞKUR as unemployed and looking for a job. After being registered to İŞKUR one would apply for the courses they are interested in, and be interviewed for selection. Over 88 000 unemployed people successfully completed these courses from the initiation of the UMEM Skills'10 Project in February 2011 to December 2015, constituting 74% of the demands from the employers (TOBB-ETÜ SPM, 2015). Throughout the training, trainers received some payment to support themselves during the skills improvement and job seeking process. Companies that employed successful trainees were exempted from paying an insurance premium. During the course of the project more than 60% of the trainees were employed by the employers they were matched with for the on-the-job training part of the program (Ünlühisarcıklı et al., 2014).

Overall, UMEM Skills'10 Project has been an important initiative for involving the employers in skills development of the unemployed.

Work-based Training Programmes

İŞKUR is involved in Active Labour Market Policies (ALMPs) and carries a number of programs, namely, vocational training courses, entrepreneurship program, work-based training program, and community services program.

In 2014, about 109 000 people participated in vocational training courses, 31 000 in entrepreneurship programs, and 60 000 in work-based training programmes (see Figure 8.1). The conditions for participating in these programs are defined in Active Labour Market Policies Regulation (Official Gazette No. 28585, 2013) and Active Labour Market Policies Circular (2013).

Figure 8.1. **Participation in active labour market programmes, 2014**

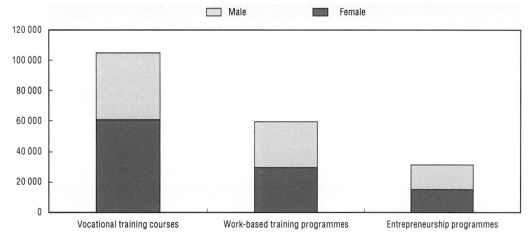

Source: İŞKUR (2014).

Objectives

The aim of the work-based training programme is to increase the employability of those who lack vocational experience of work-related skills. It also provides employers the opportunity to train and provide hands-on experience to trainees before employing them in their enterprise. The broader aim is to improve the match between employers who seek qualified workers and unemployed people with limited or no vocational experience (İŞKUR, 2015).

There have been efforts to increase the involvement of social partners, including employers, in the skills development of young people, particularly those considered vocationally inexperienced. These priorities were emphasised in the Strengthening the Link between Employment and Vocational Training Action Plan (İMEİGEP) (Official Gazette 27642, 2010), and Turkey VET Strategic Paper and Action Plan 2014-2018 (Official Gazette 29024, 2014), which focused on the challenges of the VET system in Turkey. The Employment, Industrial Investment and Production Support Package (*İstihdam, Sanayi Yatırımı ve Üretimi Destekleme Paketi*) announced by the Prime Ministry in April 2015 also stressed the importance of employers to the success of the work-based training programme announced by İŞKUR.

The programme featured collaboration between the Turkish Employment Organisation (İŞKUR) and the Turkish Confederation of Employer Associations (TİSK) on behalf of the Global Apprenticeships Network (GAN). This protocol was signed in 2015 and aimed to enable the members of GAN Turkey to gain priority access to the work-based training programmes implemented by İŞKUR. This access hoped to help broaden access to the programme and engage employers more directly in the provision of vocational skills to the unemployed.

Box 8.1. **Global Apprenticeships Network (GAN) and the Turkish GAN National Network**

As noted in the G20 Declaration on "Key elements of Quality Apprenticeships" (2013), the responsibility for apprenticeships should be shared among employers, governments and trade unions. The curricula of apprenticeships should correspond to the needs of business and remain "work-place centred".

In response, a network of businesses known as the Global Apprenticeships Network (GAN) was founded with the aim of promoting work-based training and improving the status of apprenticeship programmes. It also aims to provide a method of sharing best practices among countries at the local, regional, national and international levels. The GAN is co-ordinated by the International Organisation of Employers (IOE) and the OECD's Business and Industry Advisory Committee (BIAC) with the support of the International Labour Organisation (ILO).

The companies that join the GAN are expected to abide by three core principles:

● strong commitment to integrating apprenticeships and internships in their human capital development strategies and promoting visibility.

● sharing best practices of apprenticeships and on-the-job training.

● encouraging networking between committed organisations at the global and local levels to share experiences and expand international co-operation.

As a GAN member, TİSK then created the Turkish global network in 2014 to promote apprenticeships at the national level. This group then disseminated information, met with representatives from other members and countries and signed a core protocol with the Turkish Employment Agency in 2015. This protocol enabled companies that were members of the Turkish GAN global network to receive young apprentices through the work-based training programme. Since then, 1 058 unemployed youth have benefitted from the programme and 305 of those youth were subsequently hired.

Governance framework and delivery arrangements

The procedure for the work-based training program is described in the Active Labour Market Policies Regulation (items 45-61) and Active Labour Market Policies Circular.

The legislation allows unemployed persons over the age of fifteen who are not immediate family of the employer to participate in a work-based training programme. Those enrolled in formal education programmes can also participate in active labour market programmes if approved by the provincial directorate. These work-based training programmes must be between 5-8 hours per day and cannot exceed 160 work days. The trainees must attend at least 90% of the relevant days.

The employers must be companies that are also registered with İŞKUR, and trainees are placed based on the labour force needs analysis, company visits, vocational consultants, meetings with the unemployed or the demands of the employers or the unemployed. The programme explicitly aims to target the sectors that require additional training or skills and enterprises that employ at least two workers.

The employer is responsible for the planning and the implementation of the work-based training programme in each relevant occupational field. Each company is thus able to organise the training according to their tasks, responsibilities and obligations based on the written agreement between İŞKUR and the company. The enterprise is also obliged to complete Trainee Evaluation Forms on a regular basis and monitor the trainee's attendance. The company is also responsible for occupational health and safety of the trainees as enforced by law (Occupational Health and Safety Law No. 6331) including their training. At the end of the work-based training programme, the trainees receive participation certificates signed both by İŞKUR provincial directorate and the company. The companies involved in the program are required to employ at least 20% of the trainees after the completion of the program.

Budget and financing

The necessary expenses and insurance premium costs of employing a trainee are covered by İŞKUR for the duration of the work-based training programme. The trainees receive around USD12.5 per day from İŞKUR. Any further supplementary wages from employers are partially exempt from expenses (Income-tax Law 193, Article 40/11). If the trainees at the ages of 18-29 are employed within three months' time after the Program, the Social Security Institution (Sosyal Güvenlik Kurumu, SGK) employer premium is covered by the Unemployment Insurance Fund for 42 months in manufacturing industry and for 30 months in others. If trainees over 30 years of age are employed within the same time duration, based on the gender of the trainees, the coverage of the employer premium by the Fund is from 6 months to 30. Those workplaces that have 2-10 employees would be supported with one such trainee for a maximum of 160 work-days, and workplaces with at least 11 or more employees would be allowed to have such apprentices in training up to 10% of their number of employees.

Impacts of the programme

The core aim of the programme was to improve the vocational and occupation skills present among the Turkish labour force. The programme also aimed to increase the involvement of employers and social partners in building skills development among the labour force, particularly as a core issue among the Turkish labour force is a problem of occupational skills mismatch.

As noted above, 59 456 people (30 028 male and 29 428 female) throughout Turkey had successfully completed İŞKUR's "Work-based Training Programme" in 2014. As a result of the collaboration between İŞKUR and GAN Turkey member companies, 1 058 unemployed youth benefitted from the program and 305 were subsequently hired by GAN Turkey member companies. This report focuses on the GAN Turkey member companies and their experiences related to "Work-based Training Program" of İŞKUR.

Experiences of the employers on İŞKUR and GAN Turkey collaboration

Four GAN Turkey member companies were surveyed for their impressions of the experiences of GAN and the work-based training programme. Of these four companies, two were actively involved in the İŞKUR work-based training programme, while the other two were still considered their participation. This sample featured companies in the cosmetics, pharmaceuticals, hospitality and automotive sectors.

Cosmetics company

The company has 90 years of experience in the cosmetics sector, and produces around 600 different types of cosmetics products in their factory.

The company's human resources and training director noted that the VET system no longer provided the skills required in the cosmetics industry, and tended to focus more on theoretical knowledge rather than hands-on experience. He believed that this indicated that the currently high rates of unemployment in Turkey were most likely related to the lack of occupational skills. His own personal experience of vocational education in Turkey in previous decades had a higher focus on practical training and building softer skills, such as social development and character building.

The company has hired three trainees through the GAN-Turkey and İŞKUR work-based training programme. The company has aimed to provide work-based training and also accommodate the occupational aspirations and social development potential of the trainees. The HR director noted that it was necessary for his company to become directly involved in skills development because inexperienced young people did not have the appropriate skills necessary to address the skills shortages in his company. He found that the İŞKUR work-based training programme provided a transitional opportunity both for the employers and the unemployed to provide work-based-training in specific occupational fields.

The cosmetics company training director noted that the financial support of the government, the attitudes of the employers, the competence of the master trainers, and the selection of the trainees were fundamental factors to the programme's success.

Service/Hospitality company

The service/hospitality company is an international company that is experiencing a period of rapid growth in Turkey. As a result, the company has high demand for more staff.

Despite being a GAN member organisation, the company have not yet taken part in İŞKUR's work-based training programme. This is because they require candidates with a good command of English due to the international nature of their business. They noted that they were also interested in feedback from other member companies that benefitted from the programme before considering applying to the work-based training programme again.

The company has other internal workplace development programmes. White collar employees have the opportunity to pursue accelerated training programmes, that also include job rotation and on-the-job training, in order to reach positions such as "finance director". Blue collar workers undergo an initial training period over forty five days.

The company also has strong links with vocational education students pursuing work-based training programmes. Around 100 students complete their internship at the company every year, and approximately 77% of all new hires in their company had previously completed work-based training at the company.

We believe in a 70/30/10 model for learning and development, where 70 percent is learning by doing, 20 percent is learning from others, and 10 percent is learning through courses. – Service/ hospitality company education director

Pharmaceutical company

The company has more than 50 years of experience in the production of medicine and produces approximately 10% of all pharmaceuticals in Turkey. The company aims to become a leading global pharmaceutical producer. As a member of GAN Turkey, the company has engaged in the İŞKUR work-based training programme and has had both positive and challenging experiences.

The company noted that their expectations of the candidates were commensurate with their expectations of standard applicants, and that they expected trainees to undergo medical evaluation before acceptance. This resulted in a shortage of applicants; although the company intended to start with 30 trainees, they were only able to initially recruit 15 applicants, while a further 15 were hired two months later. They remained in constant contact with İŞKUR throughout this process.

The trainees from the İŞKUR work-based training programme complete a custom weekly training program with the pharmaceuticals company. The trainees also have the opportunity to complete the same training offered to all new recruits, which consists of a one-day orientation program and a five-week vocational training program interspersed with work.

- *Orientation program*: The trainees initially attend a one-day orientation to the company program.

- *Five-week program*: Following the orientation, the trainees complete a five-week vocational training program in specific areas. For the first three weeks, the trainees observe trained professionals performing specific job-related tasks. During the fourth week, the trainees complete these tasks under the supervision of more experienced staff. Finally, in the fifth week, the trainee is expected to be able to work independently and are assessed by supervisors and production managers.

- *Weekly training programme*: The trainees are also able to take part in a custom training programme on each Saturday over a period of six months. These sessions are four hours in length and include occupational health and safety training, production and technical training and lessons in self-development, communication, team work and sustainable production.

Throughout the İŞKUR work-based training programme, the company prepared monthly trainee evaluation, and attendance reports for each trainee as required by İŞKUR. They trained 30 trainees through the work-based training programme and expected to hire about 20 of them. They also paid additional stipends to the trainees because the payment from İŞKUR was not enough for them to cover their living expenses.

The company viewed participation in the İŞKUR work-based training program as a core social responsibility. The company representative noted that the experience is beneficial for all recruits, regardless if they are not employed by the company at the end of the process. The programme helps young people build capability and skills, understand their strengths and weaknesses, and determine the best occupation for their future careers.

As a company they also found the program beneficial because they were able to rotate the trainees throughout different sections of the company to ensure the optimal occupational fit. This flexibility is sometimes lacking throughout the standard hiring process because the company often recruits staff for specific positions.

Company from the automotive industry

The automotive company has more than 50 years of experience in the production of automobiles. The company operates internationally and is one of the leading brands in the industry.

The company is not yet involved in the İŞKUR work-based training programme, but has previously participated in the UMEM Skills'10 Project, another active labour market policy programme. Following the completion of the UMEM Skills'10 courses, the company recruited most of the trainees who had acquired the skill sets required at the company. The vocational training manager of the company noted that they perceived the İŞKUR work-based training programme as an incentive for companies to receive trainees but were concerned that the daily allowances would not be sufficient for trainees who had dependants. He also questioned the lack of pre-set programme and noted that each company is responsible for planning and implementation of the work-based training programme based on their expertise. Still, the vocational training manager noted that the programme would be an important experience for the trainees.

The company has a well-developed training unit in a separate building from the factory. Through this unit, the company provides vocational training to different groups, including newly recruited workers, general workers, industrial VET upper secondary school students, VET higher education students, and apprentices.

Vocational training of the newly recruited workers: After the initial recruitment procedure, the newly recruited workers undertake occupational health and safety training for 1.5 days. This is followed by 3 days of orientation training and a further 37-40 days of theoretical and practical vocational training in the related occupational field. Finally, new recruits complete 5-6 days of on-the-job training in the related occupational field.

Apprenticeship training: From time to time the company recruited apprentices who worked 4 days at the company and for one day attended to a Vocational Training Centre for 15 months. They had to give up the apprenticeship training since they could not find new applicants. The company representative reflected that there were apprentices who had family dependents and the apprentices could not earn a living to support them since they received about one-third of the minimum wage.

Strengths of the initiative

The work-based training initiative from İŞKUR was intended to both promote employer engagement in skills development and increase the employability and skills of young jobseekers.

A core strength noted by the surveyed employers was that the initiative allowed workers to develop the competencies and skills required for high value-added production.

The employers noted that they require skills beyond those learned in school, necessitating on-the-job training.

The employers also noted that they valued their ability to work directly with trainees to build positive attitudes and a high sense of personal responsibility to the enterprise. The initial work-based training period gives employers the chance to build softer skills, including motivation, problem solving and social skills, before starting full-time employment.

The programme enables companies to choose the best recruits out of a pool of trainees, and essentially functions as a probation period. At the end of the contract, the trainees receive participation certificates, and references from the company with a number employed after the work-based training program.

The surveyed employers also noted that there were benefits to membership of GAN Turkey. It enabled ease of application and implementation, and also facilitated consistent communication with İŞKUR and vocational consultants. GAN Turkey members were also able to recruit a pool of trainees as large as 20% of their existing workforce, which exceeds the standard limit of 10%. The organisations interviewed noted that they would be hiring most of the trainees following the programme. The companies considered the work-based training programme as both an opportunity to bring new skills into the enterprise and also as a corporate social responsibility initiative.

Weaknesses of the initiative

Overall, those who were interviewed did not mention any specific weaknesses or obstacles to the implementation of the program.

However, some of the companies surveyed had reservations before the implementation of the program. They noted that the administrative procedures associated with application might be more difficult for smaller enterprises. Assistance and vocational consultancy are invaluable for employers, and should be integrated into the programme in order to ensure long-term success. While the application process was streamlined for GAN Turkey members, it may be more difficult for other employers without the assistance of a consultancy or external experts.

During the interviews it was specifically stressed that İŞKUR put certain criteria on the selection of the trainees and numbers of trainees that are allowed during the program to prevent any potential misuse of the work-based training programme. While some employers view participation in such programmes as a matter of social responsibility, others may take the opportunity to exploit recruits and trainees. Including employers and workers associations as partners in the development of programmes can help to deepen the sense of civic responsibility and improve the practices of member companies.

Generally, the companies did not mention any difficulties in the implementation of the work-based training programme. However, it was noted that İŞKUR does not allow trainees to work in shifts as the recruits were in training. This proved to be a challenge for the pharmaceuticals company because the production was run in three shifts throughout the day. Another problem noted by one of the company accountants was that there is a mismatch between the exemption from tax and the Social Security Institution Law No. 5502. Accordingly, the days spent on training would not be counted as days for their retirement although the trainees' insurance and premium costs were paid. The important lesson here is to prepare such procedures and regulations in line with other legislature.

As mentioned above, the work-based training programme lacks a defined programme and the employer is responsible for the organisation of work-based training within the confines of the tasks, responsibilities, and obligations of the occupation. The only regulatory responsibility of the company is to regularly complete Trainee Evaluation Forms and monthly attendance sheets. The company is also responsible for occupational health and safety of the trainees as enforced by law (Occupational Health and Safety Law No. 6331) including their training. Although the employers surveyed had internal skills development programmes of good quality, the lack of standardised criteria for the work-based training of the trainees may lead to bad experiences in other enterprises.

Potential transferability

The overall aim of the Work-based Training Program by İŞKUR is to increase employability of the youth that lack vocational experience or work related skills by matching them with employers who are looking for qualified workers. As noted by one of the representatives of the company, this system is best suited to "countries like [Turkey], where there is [both] unemployment and also skills shortages."

The employers provide the skills training while İŞKUR covers the necessary expenses and insurance premium costs. The funding provided was indispensable although it was mentioned more than once that the allowances were not satisfactory for the trainees. On the other hand, it is understandable that the payment of full wages for the completion of work-based training by the unemployed youth and payment would not be possible. An alternative incentive could be providing some studentship rights to the trainees.

The procedure for the Work-based Training Program is based on a regulation (Active Labour Market Policies Regulation) and circular (Active Labour Market Policies Circular) which provided the conditions and the processes to be followed throughout the program. Therefore, before initiating such a program the legislation would be prepared.

The success of such programmes hinges upon publicity and informing potential trainees. This could be achieved through an official website introducing the program to the potential trainees, social networking websites, and a call centre established for the programme. As in the case of the involvement of GAN Turkey, building a network to promote such a programme to other enterprises, share experiences and provide support for the implementation of the programme can help to build employer engagement.

The success of work-based training programmes depends on funding, the selection and/or matching of the trainees and the willingness of the companies to channel their efforts to train the unemployed for a certain period of time. These are the core considerations for any countries wishing to pursue a similar active labour market policy programme.

Conclusions

To conclude, work-based training is an important method for employers to contribute to the skills development of youth who lack specific work experience or skill sets. Overall, work-based training not only contributes to the unemployed but VET and apprenticeship training in Turkey since companies also provide training opportunities to VET upper secondary school students as interns, and apprentices.

The engagement of employers can also help to ensure that the technology, know-how and skills required for the future workforce are kept up-to-date in vocational education. As noted by one VET school administrator, Turkish VET schools would be outdated quickly even if they were equipped with the best infrastructure and facilities. Work-based training provides a useful bridge between the worlds of school and work in order to equip youth for employment.

Notes

1. The original name was Apprenticeship and Vocational Education Law No. 3308 until the amendment in 2001.

2. Deputy Undersecretary of Ministry of Health, Deputy Undersecretary of Ministry of Labour and Social Affairs, Deputy Undersecretary of Ministry of Industry and Commerce, Deputy Undersecretary of Ministry of Tourism, State Planning Organisation, General Directorates responsible for VET (MoNE), Turkish Tradesmen and Craftsmen Confederation, Turkish Chamber of Commerce, Industry, Maritime Trade and Union of Commercial Exchange, Worker's Confederation with the highest number of members, Turkish Confederation of Employer Association.

References

Akpınar A. (2004), Initial Vocational Education and Training in Turkey, İŞKUR, Ankara.

Çağatay, N. (1989), *Bir Türk Kurumu Olan Ahilik* (The Ahi, a Turkish Organization), Türk Tarih Kurumu Basımevi, Ankara.

Ekinci, Y. (1990), *Ahilik ve Meslek Eğitimi* (Ahi System and Vocational Training), Milli Eğitim Bakanlığı, İstanbul.

EU (2015), Good for Youth Good for Business, European Alliance for Apprenticeships (EAfA), available at *http://ec.europa.eu/social/main.jsp?catId=738&langId=en&pubId=7805&furtherPubs=yes*.

G20 (2013), Key Elements of Quality Apprenticeships: A joint understanding of the B20 and L20, June 2013, available at *http://global-apprenticeships.org/fileadmin/user_upload/GAN/Resource_Centre/EN/Business_20_-_Labour_20_Key_elements_of_quality_apprenticeships_2013.pdf*.

ILO (2015), Global Employment Trends for Youth 2015: Scaling up investments in decent jobs for youth, Geneva: ILO, available at *www.ilo.org/global/research/global-reports/youth/2015/WCMS_412015/lang--en/index.htm*.

MoNE (2012), An overview of Turkish VET system: Summary of a long story, Ankara, 2012.

OECD (2014), *G20-OECD-EC Conference on Quality Apprenticeships for Giving Youth a Better Start in the Labour Market background paper*, Paris: OECD, available at *www.oecd.org/els/emp/G20-OECD-EC%20 Apprenticeship%20Conference_Issues%20Paper.pdf*.

Özcan, M. and M.A. Tamer (2013), *Örgün Mesleki ve Teknik Eğitim Sürecine Genel Bir Bakış* (A general overview of formal vocational and technical education processes), Eğitim Sen Yayınları, Ankara.

Özyılmaz, Ö. (2011), "Ahilik ve Çağdaş Uygulamalar Arasında Mesleki Teknik Eğitim Sistemimiz", in Ahilik (editors: Baki Çakır and İskender Gümüş), Kırklareli Üniversitesi Yayınları, Kırklareli.

TİSK (nd), Turkish Confederation of Employer Associations: Social Partner, 48th Anniversary, available at *https://tisk.org.tr/tr/e-yayinlar/314_tisk_i_tanitici_brosur_/pdf_314_tisk_i_tanitici_brosur_.pdf* .

TOBB-ETÜ SPM (2015), UMEM/Beceri'10 Meslek Kursları İzleme Bülteni, TOBB-ETÜ Sosyal Politikalar Uygulama ve Araştırma Merkezi (16 December), available at *www.spm.etu.edu.tr/tr/publish/2015_12_25-Meslek-Kurslari-izleme-Bulteni.pdf* .

TURKSTAT (2015a), National Education Statistics: Formal Education 2014-2015, TURKSTAT.

TURKSTAT (2015b), Labour Force Statistics, June 2015. Press Release, No. 18641, available at *www.turkstat.gov.tr/PreHaberBultenleri.do?id=18641*.

TURKSTAT (2014), Non-formal Education Statistics 2012/'13, TURKSTAT.

TURKSTAT (2012), National Education Statistics: Non-Formal Education 2010/'11, TURKSTAT.

TURKSTAT (2010), National Education Statistics: Formal Education 2009-2010, TURKSTAT.

İŞKUR (2015), *İşbaşı Eğitim Programı Bilgi Notu* (Work-based training program fact sheet), Turkish Employment Agency, available at *www.iskur.gov.tr/Portals/0/Duyurular/10_soruda_isbasi_egitim_ programi.pdf*.

İŞKUR (2014), 2014 *İstatistik Yıllığı*, Turkish Employment Agency, available at *www.iskur.gov.tr/tr-tr/kurumsalbilgi/istatistikler.aspx#dltop*.

Ünlühisarcıklı, Ö., Ç. Arslan and Y.E. Dinç (2014), "UMEM Skills'10 Project", How the Private Sector Develops Skills: Lessons Learned from Turkey (editor: G. Dikmener), United Nations Development Programme (UNDP) Istanbul International Center for Private Sector in Development (IICPSD).

Chapter 9

Apprenticeships in the formal and informal economy at the local level in Bangladesh

This chapter analyses two case studies of apprenticeship programme design and delivery in the context of the formal and informal economy of Bangladesh. It analyses the methods of improving participation and deepening employer engagement in order to build skills in a context of a labour market with low levels of skill and high levels of informality. Specific challenges and lessons for other emerging economies are also addressed.

Key findings

- Bangladesh has a large and young population, many of whom live below the poverty line and are employed in the informal economy. Bangladesh is also developing rapidly through the growth of high value added export-oriented industries that increasingly demand more skills. Two case studies are presented that engage with formal and informal apprenticeship in this context.

- In the first case study, formal apprenticeships in the context of the high growth and export-oriented leather industry are examined, particularly with respect to the utilisation of employer organisations to align skills supply and demand to meet current and future skills shortages.

- Attempts to improve the standardisation and formalisation of existing relationship between master crafts persons and young people are explored in the second case study. The role of international actors and not-for-profit organisations are also examined.

Introduction

This chapter presents two specific cases of employer engagement in skills training in Bangladesh. The first is a formal apprenticeship model in the Bangladeshi leather sector that has been led and owned by employers with stakeholder support. The other case is an informal apprenticeship model run by an NGO with the support of ILO and UNICEF. This model has been field-tested and adapted to respond to the employment, income and livelihood requirements of young unemployed persons, including women and persons with disabilities (PWDs), through direct engagement with the employers namely Mater Crafts Persons (MCPs).

Though both of these are relatively new initiatives starting about four to six years ago, they illustrate good characteristics of sustainable models of apprenticeship training and employer engagement in both the formal and informal economy. These two examples provide potential alternatives to the traditional apprenticeship system (provided by the labour law) which is currently unable to play any meaningful role in the country's training system. The system has a number of inadequacies, including very insignificant engagement and participation from both employers and apprentices. In 2012, the Government adopted a forward-looking National Skills Development Policy that aims to promote a major reform and revamping of the TVET system. The Policy speaks of, among other things, new employer-led training initiatives and promoting both formal and informal apprenticeships.

Background

In this chapter, the first apprenticeship model (i.e. a formal model) is based on the operations of the *"Centre of Excellence for Leather Sector Skills"* (COEL). The leather sector is one of the most dynamic sectors in Bangladesh with a high export growth rate. As a labour intensive industry, the sector employs a large number of workers, the vast majority of whom are women, and its value addition is very high. The formal apprenticeship model was supported by the TVET reform programme side by side with the funding support of the SDC and USAID.[1]

The other model *"Skill Training for Advancing Resources"* (STAR) focuses on the young people aged between 14 and 20 years. It aims to reach young workers in the informal economy, where the vast majority (approximately 87.5%) of the country's labour force is employed (BBS, 2011). It operates in five administrative locations (i.e. divisions) of the country. Because of the high incidence of poverty and unemployment, one of Bangladesh's main development priorities is to reach out to poor and marginalised groups and increase their access to mainstream national development programmes through improved educational outcomes. Job creation through skills development is one of the major pathways out of deprivation and poverty, particularly for unemployed youth. This apprenticeship model provides an answer to the job creation for the young people. It has been initiated with the support of ILO and UNICEF and is being implemented by BRAC, a reputed NGO. Given its initial success, the STAR model is being scaled up throughout the country.

Policy context

Bangladesh is the eighth largest country in the world in terms of population, with an estimated population is 156.4 million in 2014. The country is one of the most densely populated countries in the world, with about 1 015 persons per square kilometre (UNFPA, 2015). One of the overarching development proprieties is to alleviate poverty among the populace, as approximately 31.5% of the total population in 2013 lived below the poverty line (government estimates). Measures to alleviate poverty are linked to interventions and progress in several important segments of the economy, including skills training. Skills training initiatives are linked to accelerating GDP growth, increasing investment in human development, improving livelihoods, expanding social services, promoting manufacturing growth and increasing infrastructure development.

Labour market trends

Due to steady GDP growth of about 6% on average per year over the past decade or so, the economy of Bangladesh and its labour market have undergone significant changes. The share of the traditional agriculture sector in terms of both GDP and employment has fallen steadily while that of manufacturing, construction and services sectors has grown steadily.

The total labour force increased to 56.7 million in 2010 from 49.5 million in 2005-06. Between these two survey periods, the growth rate of the labour force was estimated to be 3.10% in urban areas and 3.48% in rural areas (BBS, 2011). Approximately 95% of the workforce was employed in 2010 while 2.6 million were looking for jobs (unemployed). In terms of broad sectoral distribution, the share of employment in agriculture, industry, and services stood at 47%, 18% and 35% respectively.

Of the industrial labour force, the manufacturing employment grew from 5.2 million in 2005-06 to 6.7 million in 2010 (or about 12% of the country's labour force). This change in the industrial growth in Bangladesh has opened up opportunities for job creation outside the traditional agriculture sector and has brought more dynamism to the labour market. At the same time, such labour market changes have increased demand for skilled workers to create jobs and improve the competitiveness of the enterprises.

Rapid export growth, albeit from a low base, has also significantly contributed to the transformation of the Bangladesh economy. In particular, growth in the export of readymade garments has been phenomenal and now constitutes almost 80% of the total share of exports. In addition to the readymade garments, export earnings in other sectors, including leather goods, ship building, pharmaceuticals, furniture making, and agro-foods, are also showing promise.

Figure 9.1. **Employment by industry, Bangladesh, 2010**

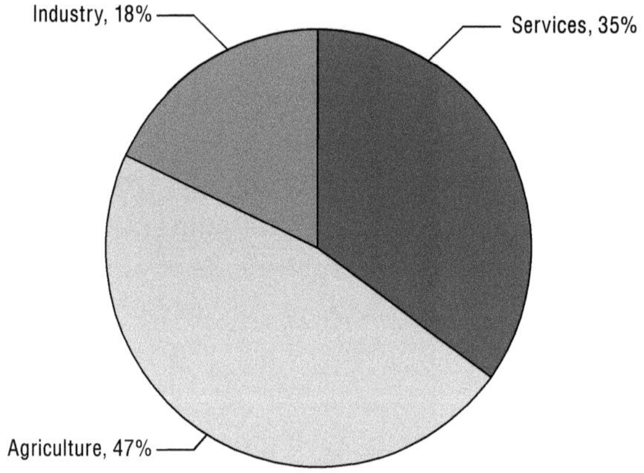

Source: Bangladesh Bureau of Statistics (2010).

Table 9.1. **Change in sectoral composition of the national workforce**

	2002-03		2005-06		2010	
Total size of employed workforce (millions)	44.30		47.40		54.10	
	Total employment (millions)	*Percentage share of total employment*	*Total employment (millions)*	*Percentage share of total employment*	*Total employment (millions)*	*Percentage share of total employment*
Agriculture	22.90	52%	22.80	48%	25.70	48%
Construction	1.5	3.3%	1.5	3.1%	2.6	4.6%
Manufacturing	4.30	10%	5.20	11%	6.70	12%

Source: Bangladesh Bureau of Statistics (2011).

Technical and vocational education and training (TVET)

The importance of technical and vocational education and training (TVET) is important to Bangladesh for a number of reasons.

First, according to the Government estimates, about 1.8 million to 2 million mostly unskilled young persons are entering into the labour market every year (GOB, 2011). Compared to this, the number of jobs available is only a small fraction of the number of job seekers. The majority of the young persons, including disproportionate amounts of women and disadvantaged groups, find low-skilled and poorly-productive jobs in the informal economy, or are self-employed. Upgrading skills is one method of improving the income and livelihoods of these workers and can help to bring them out of poverty.

Second, there has been a significant structural economic shift away from traditional agriculture and towards export-oriented manufacturing and services sectors. This has also increased demand for skilled workers, particularly in export-oriented manufacturing industries like garments, leather, furniture, agro-food, pharmaceuticals, and ceramics. Although reliable demand estimates for skilled workers are not available, employers frequently cite the shortage of skills as a major constraint.

Third, Bangladesh's relatively young population implies a growing workforce for the future, but most remain unskilled. About 63% of the country's total population belongs to the age group of 15 to 49 years and 37% of the labour force in the age group 15-29 years (GOB, 2011). This relatively young population is often cited as the country's "*demographic dividend*". However, the main challenge is to equip this vast young labour force with employable skills and to provide enhanced support services to ensure a better transition from school to work.

Fourth, the Government of Bangladesh has adopted a policy of overseas employment promotion because of the huge unemployment and underemployment pressure in the domestic labour market. However, about 52% and 14% of the migrant workers are low skilled and semi-skilled respectively. As the Government wishes to increase the percentage of skilled workers for employment abroad, the standard and quality of the TVET system needs to be improved. This will require major enhancements to the quality and relevance of training and greater participation from the enterprise and the private sector in skills training.

Finally, Bangladesh has an ambitious plan to reach middle income status by 2021. To do so, the country should increase investment in the socio-economic development, expand the share of manufacturing in GDP and reduce the share of agriculture, increase and diversify exports, and send abroad more and more skilled workers. These require concerted efforts to produce more and more skilled workers, expand access to technical and vocational education and training (TVET), and to design and develop an inclusive skills system that provides opportunities for those excluded from the formal education system. Most important of all, the system needs to be demand-driven with stronger links with employers and the private sector.

Recognising these trends, the country has embarked on a major expansion of its technical and vocational education and training system, including several donor-supported programmes to reform and expand the system. The development partners include the European Union (EU), ILO, ADB, Canadian Government, World Bank, UK Aid and SDC.

One significant development in TVET is the reform of the system which started from 2008 with the launching of the major GOB/EU/ILO TVET reform programme (GOB, 2012). A major achievement of this reform process has been the adoption of the National Skills Development Policy 2011 (NSDP 2011). This policy sets out a broad-based and forward looking skills system framework for Bangladesh and has made a positive impact on the renewed interest in skills development in the country, including apprenticeships.

Addressing skills matches by emphasising apprenticeship

Bangladesh is facing a paradoxical situation with regard to mismatch between the supply and demand for skills. For example, a skills demand survey by National Skills Development Council (NSDC) had revealed the shortage of skilled workers in nine growth sectors of the economy (GOB, 2012).[2] While employers report shortages of skilled workers, huge numbers of unemployed young people are seeking jobs. This is partially due to the fragmented Bangladeshi TVET system, which is comprised of a large number of technical and vocational training centres in both the public and private sectors. These training providers train thousands of graduates, but many remain unemployed. Employers are unaware or sceptical about the quality of the institutionally-trained graduates. In other words, the formal TVET system was highly supply driven.

In response to this situation, the Government of Bangladesh initiated reforms of the system, including through increasing the participation of private sector enterprises in skills training. At the same time, it has undertaken measures to invest in large skills development projects funded by the government from its own and external sources. For example, the National Skills Development Policy 2011 (NSDP 2011) states: *"It is important that the TVET and skills training institutions are aware of the skill needs in industry and understand the latest technology trends. Without this knowledge, the skills produced by institutions will not meet the needs of industry"* (NSDP, 2011).

Current state of apprenticeship in Bangladesh

Existing programmes

The apprenticeship law was adopted by the Government through the enactment of the *Apprenticeship Ordinance (1962)* which constituted part of the country's labour laws. In 2006, the Government of Bangladesh enacted the *Bangladesh Labour Act (2006) (or BLA 2006, 11 October 2006)* which contains Section XVIII on Apprenticeship. This new Labour Act supersedes the 1962 Apprenticeship Ordinance. According to the legal definition, *"Apprenticeship means a system of training in which an employer undertakes to employ a person and to train him or have trained him systematically in an apprenticeable trade or occupation for a period fixed in advance and in the course of which the apprentice is bound to work in the employer's service"*.

Even with the enactment of law as early as in 1962, formal apprenticeship as a mode of training has remained insignificant and unattractive to the employers. Most of the employers are either not aware of the legal requirement for apprenticeship or not willing to participate in the programme. This was pointed out by a survey on apprenticeship carried out by the ILO and the TVET Reform Project in 2009:

> *"With this definition, formal apprenticeship in Bangladesh is extremely limited with a total of 54 formal apprentices within three formal apprenticeship programs in the private sector. Few businesses are even aware that a government mandate for the incorporation of an apprenticeship structure even exists."*

The NSDP-2011 has identified the Bureau of Manpower, Employment and Training (BMET) as the responsible government entity for implementing the apprenticeships in the country[3] to carry out its responsibilities, BMET has three apprenticeship offices in the three regions: Dhaka, Chittagong and Khulna.

With the initiation of the TVET reform programme, the concept of apprenticeship has gained prominence, particularly as a result of the formation of Industrial Skills Councils (ISCs) with support from the TVET Reform Project. These ISCs were established sector wise and initially five such councils (ISCs) were established. Currently there are 12 ISCs representing 12 industrial sub-sectors. They are playing a vital role in bridging the gap between the formal institutional training system and the enterprises. One of the tasks of the ISCs is to establish Centres of Excellence (COE) in each sector to support and promote employer participation in skills training including a strengthened and expanded apprenticeship system. With the closure of the TVET reform project in December 2015, its successor *"Bangladesh Skills for Employment and Productivity Project"* (B-SEP) will continue to support the strengthening of both formal and informal apprenticeship in Bangladesh. The project aims to train 6 200 formal and 6 200 informal apprentices.

Apprenticeships in the informal economy

In the Bangladeshi labour market, the informal economy plays the primary role in terms of employment generation and skills formation. Millions of workers, mostly young people, work in the informal economy and only gain skills through informal employment relationships between a skilled worker and one or more apprentices working under their supervision. Since the formal apprenticeship system plays hardly any role in the overall country context, the huge demand for skills is met through the well-developed informal apprenticeship system.

Consequently, efforts have been made to revamp the informal system by introducing a supervised and well-structured model that will follow a standard methodology and process. Such an approach also seeks to improve informal apprenticeships through skills recognition, content standardisation and certification. This has been highlighted in a recent ILO report as follows:

"Despite the system's strength of providing skills relevant to local markets, informal apprenticeship has a number of weaknesses. Long working hours, unsafe working conditions, low or no allowances or wages, little or no social protection in case of illness or accident, and strong gender imbalances are among the decent work deficits often found in apprenticeships.

On the one hand, upgrading informal apprenticeship is considered important to address these weaknesses. On the other hand, compared to investing in expanding formal technical education and training, it is a cost-effective way to invest in a country's skills base and enhance employability of youth, since training is integrated into the production process. Improved informal apprenticeship systems can also dynamize local economies by contributing to the diversification of products and services and the innovation, productivity and adaptability of micro and small enterprises." (ILO, 2012)

Box 9.1. The importance of the informal economy in Bangladesh

The informal economy plays a very dominant role in the labour market.

- It employs a staggering 87.5% of the labour force (2010) or 47.35 million, in comparison with 6.79 million (or 12.5% of the labour force) in the formal economy.
- Most of the country's working poor live in this sector.
- There is flexibility of entry and exit in the sector.
- Skill formation is done in a traditional, unrecognised and unstructured way.
- The productivity, income and earnings of the workforce are usually low.
- A disproportionate number of women work in this sector: 92.3% compared to the national average of 87.5%.

Thus, notwithstanding the merits and demerits of informal apprenticeship modality, an inclusive TVET system needs to take into account both formal and informal apprentices.

Ongoing apprenticeship initiatives in Bangladesh

A summary of the ongoing apprenticeship initiatives is provided in Table 9.2.

National Skills Development Policy 2011

An important aspect of the NSDP 2011 is the emphasis on the role of the enterprises in the expansion and promotion of apprenticeships in Bangladesh through the encouragement of public-private partnership (PPP). In section 12, the policy describes both

Table 9.2. **Ongoing apprenticeship initiatives**

Name of the programme	No. of trainees	Duration of the courses	Agency responsible	Details
Formal apprenticeships				
Traditional type of apprentices (several enterprises) as per the labour law	359	3 years and 1 year	BMET	The total of number of trainees shown here is for the period 2010-14 from BMET records. The figure changes over time. This type of programme is being delivered as per the country's formal apprenticeship law. The process is managed by BMET which registers the apprentices, monitors the progress with the employers, and issues certificates upon successful completion of the apprenticeship period. Although no record of post-training employment is kept by BMET, the employability of the apprentices is very high since the credibility of training is high.
Leather sector (25 enterprises) Supported by TVET reform project and SDC	11 944	I year	ISC Leather, COEL	This is a programme strongly backed by the employers in the leather sector through the ISC Leather organisation. The number of trainees shown here is the total figure from 2011 to 2015 for a single occupation, namely machine operator. This is widely considered as a successful initiative and supported by several partners and external donors. Employability of the trainees is very high – more than 99%. Training is conducted through a combination of 3-month classroom training at COEL training facility and 9 months workplace training.
Furniture sector Supported by B-SEP project	250	6 months	ISC Furniture Sector	This programme has commenced recently (November 2015) in two factories with the full backing and participation of the Furniture ISC organisation. Though training is still ongoing, the likelihood of employment for most of the trainees upon completion of the training is very high. This programme is a part of B-SEP programme that trains 12 400 apprentices (6 200 formal and 6 200 informal).
Informal apprenticeship				
STAR (13 trades) Implemented by BRAC (supported by ILO, UNICEF and BNFE)	6 000	6 months	BRAC	The training figure is for three years (2012-15). It has been a successful programme with good results. The employment rate for the graduates is almost 99%. More than 50% of the trainees are disadvantaged women (mainly school dropouts) and 8% are PWDs. 3000 MCPs have also been trained which created a large pool for further training.
Construction sector ILO/Japan Way Out of Informality Project	1 602	6 months	ILO and MOLE	This programme is supported by an ongoing ILO programme which plans to eventually train approximately 3 500 persons by 2016. The programme is cost-effective and supported by the government and construction sector trade union. Once the programme is completed, lessons learned and sustainability issues will be addressed.

Source: BMET (2010); ILO (2014).

formal and informal apprenticeship as an effective means of promoting and expanding demand-driven skills in the country. There is reference to introduction of Competency Based Training and Assessment (CBTA), recognition of qualification through a nationally-recognised qualifications framework known as NTVQF, and recognition of prior learning (RPL).

The policy also notes a *"Strengthened Role for the Industry Sectors in Skills Development"* and includes provisions for setting up and supporting the *"Industrial Skills Councils"* (ISCs) as a major vehicle and interface between the training providers and private sector. The ISCs will, among other things, *"Support strengthening of industrial apprenticeship program"*. In order to expand the apprenticeship system, the NSDP 2011, in *"Section 12 Strengthened Apprenticeships"* (p.19), states:

"Through the Ministry of Labour and Employment (MOLE) and the Bureau of Manpower, Employment and Training (BMET), the apprenticeship system will be strengthened and expanded so that employers, master crafts persons and learners, from both formal and informal economies, can participate in the new system."

Formal apprenticeships: Centre of Excellence for Leather Skills in Bangladesh Ltd (COEL)

The leather goods and footwear manufacturing industry is an important sector in Bangladesh in terms of both employment generation and export earnings. The sector is comprised of three sub-sectors: leather; leather goods; and leather footwear. In terms of share of exports, it stands second after the RMG sector and its total earning for 2013-14 stood at USD 1.12 billion or close to 4% of the GDP (Manzur et al., 2014). It is a labour intensive manufacturing with strong forward and backward linkages, high value addition, and high growth potential. About 800 000 workers are directly employed in the sector and there is considerable indirect employment (Manzur et al., 2014). However, according to Centre of Excellence for Leather Skill Bangladesh Ltd (COEL) estimates, there is still demand for 60 000 skilled labourers and additional shortages of managers and entrepreneurs.

The COEL was established in 2009 by the Leather Industry Skills Council (ISC) and was registered as not-for-profit organisation under the Company Act. It is a good example of employer-led initiative that leads to qualifications recognised in the public education and training system. The ISC leather manages this initiative. It is a dual apprenticeship model with classroom training for 3 months and workplace training in the factory for 9 months.

The training centre of COEL is situated outside the capital town at Chandra, Gazipur which serves as the hub of COEL's Leather Skill Training Programs and has the capacity to train 300 trainees at a time. Other than the main training centre, COEL with joint collaboration with the interested factories, are in the process of establishing sub-centres to increase the productivity of the respective factories.

Objectives

The main objective of COEL is to increase and improve the overall skill level of the workforce of the leather sector to meet the sector's immediate and long-term skills needs. To achieve this, it seeks to operate as one-stop solution for enterprise-driven training, research, course curriculum development and other skills development events while building its own capacity through international accreditation, certification and public private partnerships (PPP).[4] It will formulate policy and procedures, perform advocacy, and monitor enterprise skill development practices in the leather sector.

In the long run, creating employment by upgrading the skills of workers in a major manufacturing sector like leather will contribute to increased income and ultimately reduce poverty.

The COEL are targeting unemployed youth from low socio-economic backgrounds, including women from low-income families who are willing to be engaged in work and increase their earnings and livelihoods. The COEL has also made attempts to include disabled persons in its training programme and organisational policies.

Activities

The services provided by the COEL include:

- Training for several categories of workers such as Machine Operator, Supervisor and Machine Maintenance.
- Enterprise specific training, including compliance services such as audit and training in environmental issues, labour law, social compliance, fire and electrical safety, and occupational health and safety;
- Design and product development services like basic and advanced designing training, grading and pattern making;
- Consultancy services such as business planning, training needs analysis, project proposal development, manual development, and tracer studies; and
- Research and statistical and data services.

Activities relating to the above services include:

- Advocacy and promotion of skills development programme in the country;
- Development of public-private partnerships as well as developing partnerships with the donors;
- Fostering relations between governments, workers, chambers of commerce and industrial associations.

Governance framework and delivery arrangements

The COEL is managed by the Leather Industry Skills Council as a not-for-profit organisation registered under article 29 of the Companies Act. Demand for training is done through an initial assessment and consultation with the enterprises in the sector, which lead to arrangements for the placement of trainees in those factories. Training is delivered through a combination of classroom training in COEL training centre (3 months) followed by training in the enterprise for 9 months. A performance monitoring mechanism is in place. A mentor from each batch of the respective enterprise supervises every trainee. A log-book of each trainee is routinely checked by the supervisor.

Partnership development

The COEL has developed strong links with a large number of partners. These include:

- Development partners
  - ❖ Government of the People's Republic of Bangladesh
  - ❖ Swiss Agency for Development & Co-Operation (SDC)
  - ❖ International Labor Organisation
  - ❖ European Union
  - ❖ USAID-PRICE
- Skill development partner organisations
  - ❖ Leather Technologists Small and Medium Enterprises Co-Operative Society
  - ❖ Bangladesh Paduka Prostutkarak Shamity (Bangladesh Shoemakers Association)
  - ❖ *Gana Unnonoyon Kendra* (People's development centre)
  - ❖ BRAC

❖ Centre for Rehabilitation of the Paralysed (CRP) – Bangladesh

❖ Action on Disability and Development Bangladesh

❖ Leathergoods and Footwear Manufacturers and Exporters Association of Bangladesh

❖ Social Development Foundation

● International training partners

❖ KAIZEN Institute (Japan)

❖ CORE Knowledge

❖ Footwear Design and Development Institute (India)

❖ Intertek

❖ Worldwide Responsible Accredited Production

❖ I-Train International Training Consultants

Budget and financing

The COEL was supported by several international agencies including US AID, the ILO and EU through the TVET Reform Project and SDC. The enterprises provided the building and other infrastructure while the equipment and other costs are being provided through the donor support like USAID (through PRICE), ILO-EU project and SDC.

Impacts

Tables 9.3 and 9.4 outline the results of the COEL training. The figures show the positive impact of the training through comparing statistics of pre-training and post-training situation of the trainees. The relatively high participation of women in training, at 64%, also contributes to women's empowerment.

Table 9.3. **Skills training for machine operators**

Year	Male	% of total	Female	% of total	Total
2011	151	23	494	77	645
2012	714	33	1 434	67	2 148
2013	1 274	38	2 104	62	3 378
2014	1 665	36	2 911	64	4 576
2015	513	43	684	57	1 197
Total	**4 317**	**36**	**7 627**	**64**	**11 944**

Source: COEL.

Table 9.4. **Soft skills training for mid-level management**

Year	Participants
2012	181
2013	262
2014	365
2015	798
Total	**1 606**

Source: COEL.

The COEL is a model which has proved its strength because of high levels of employer participation, demand-driven skills delivery and post-training job creation. Training is provided after signing an MOU with the factory concerned and assessment of skills is carried out in consultation with enterprises. This facilitates successful placement of trainees after training.

Strengths and key factors underlying success

The COEL model has several strong points.

First and foremost, most of the persons interviewed noted that success of COEL can be squarely attributed to a dynamic and committed enterprise leader in the Leather ISC. This has resulted in smooth co-operation between the ISC and COEL and represents a good practice example of employer involvement in skills development. This also underlines the importance of local leadership in driving increased apprenticeship engagement.

Second, the design and delivery of training have been carried out through close collaboration between the training provider (i.e. COEL) and the participating factories. Such mutual interactions have contributed to effective training and highly satisfactory training outcomes as illustrated by subsequent employment of more than 99% and high percentages of females in training and employment.

Also, despite being a relatively newly-established institute, the COEL has been able to develop partnerships with a number of different organisations as a result of strong advocacy and mobilisation by the COEL team and the ISC leadership.

COEL has ensured that its programs deliver credentials through the national qualifications framework that are accredited with BTEB at NTVQF Level – 1. This gives the trainees greater labour market mobility and improved career paths.

Innovative aspects of the initiative

There are several points that could be considered as innovative in the COEL model.

First, the "dual system" used by the COEL model features a combination of classroom training and factory-based training. While these models are relatively common in countries with developed apprenticeship systems, they have rarely been successfully implemented in non-OECD countries.

Second, training was based on competency standards and the trainers drawn from the enterprises were trained, thus building capacity at the enterprise level. Supervisors and management personnel were also trained to further enhance the capacity of the enterprise.

Third, there has been continuous development of training modules to match the needs of the enterprise including in emerging occupations. Because of strong employer and institute collaboration, training materials are regularly updated and both the Institute and employers are involved in the selection of trainees.

Fourth, strong post-training monitoring and follow up as well as the focus on registering as a registered training organisation (RTO) under BTEB as a part of the formal TVET system and having trainees registered with BMET as apprentices.

Finally, strong female empowerment and promotion of gender equity in skills training also contributes to the broader agenda of inclusion.

Weaknesses of the initiative

It was initially difficult to convince the enterprises in the private sector that skills development was necessary for long-term benefit. The private sector is often reluctant to allocate time and resources for development where there is less scope for immediate and direct benefit. This was addressed by strong advocacy by organisations like the ILO through the TVET reform project to generate interest and pro-active support from private sector business leaders. Despite these efforts, the number of participating factories in the COEL programme has remained limited, and more efforts in liaison and dialogue with the private sector should be pursued.

The capacity of the relevant government institutions to deliver services is also relatively limited. This can hinder the expansion and delivery of the apprenticeship programme. ISCs are also generally weak, and do not necessarily have broad industry support. These issues are somewhat mitigated by strong support from key international stakeholders and donors, which can help to create a long-term self-supporting model in future years. There has also been a broader effort to include stakeholders including the private sector and workers organisations into the formulation of skills policy, such as the National Skills Development Policy 2011.

Informal apprenticeships: Skills Training for Advancing Resources (STAR)

This case study examines the Skill Training for Advancing Resources (STAR) programme which was developed and supported by GOB, EU and ILO through the TVET reform project and UNICEF. The Bureau of Non-formal Education (BNFE) of the Government of Bangladesh was involved as the government counterpart of the UNICEF BEHTRUC (Basic Education for the Hard to Reach Underprivileged Children) programme which supported this apprenticeship model.

STAR is managed and implemented by BRAC, a reputed and well-known NGO which has worked towards the alleviation of poverty and empowerment of the poor for the past 40 years. BRAC has offices in 18 countries. Through the provision of microfinance, it has created opportunities for self-employment, skills development and livelihood improvements for many of its 8.35 million microfinance members. As of now, in partnership with the Ministry of Youth, BRAC has facilitated training for a total of 64 839 youth, 36 044 of whom are young women.

The STAR model, which evolved from collaboration between BRAC, ILO, and UNICEF, is a "dual system" of training delivery that features a combination of theoretical training from a technical trainer, and practical on-the-job training from a master crafts person (MCP). Over the six-month duration of the apprenticeship, the theoretical training component comprises one day per week and the remaining working days are spent on the job. This "dual" system is preferable to open-ended on-the-job training because it provides structured learning opportunities for young apprentices. Similarly, the time-bound nature of the off-the-job training is ideal for young people at lower income levels that cannot afford prolonged periods "without work" to sustain themselves.

Training is provided through structured curricula and standard list of competencies to be gained over the training period, which is recorded through a Competency Skills Log Book (CSLB). This provides a uniform standard and system of measurement even though the training is conducted at different workplaces. Their competencies and skills can be recognised nationally through a system of prior learning and national certification to allow occupational mobility and benefit young people in the long run.

The STAR beneficiaries include disadvantaged and marginalised groups: 50% of the learners are women and about 8% are persons with disabilities. Trainees and the MCPs are trained on workplace safety and health issues and required to observe a "Code of Practice" at the workplace.

Another feature of the programme is the decentralised and flexible approach to programme design and delivery. BRAC selects and clusters the learners by trade and MCPs based on local employment demand and the choice of the learners and their parents. Distance from the learner's home to the workplace (i.e. MCP's shops) is taken into account while selecting these clusters. This is particularly important for the young women and persons with disabilities (PWDs) who find it difficult to travel long distances every day from their homes.

Box 9.2. **Development of Master Crafts Persons**

Master Crafts Persons (MCPs) have a central role in informal apprenticeships as they supervise the apprentice and deliver training based on the Competency Skills Log Book (CSLB). They are selected based on following criteria: experience, location of the workplace, workforce capacity, job prospects for the learners. Once selected, the MCPs receive a 3-day basic orientation. This orientation includes material on: Competency Based Training and Assessment (CBTA), child rights, decent employment, the code of conduct, and Occupational Safety and Health (OSH). The MCPs will sign a contract that obliges them to abide by the code of conduct. During the training period, the MCPs receive financial support to compensate for the costs related to the training and complying with the above criteria. BRAC Technical trainers and the MCPs are trained to use the Competency Skill Log Books for the specific trade and prepare the six-month work plan for the learners together using a CBTA approach. This ensures consistency in learning across trades as well as regions.

During the initial implementation phase, BRAC and ILO collaborated to develop skills and knowledge of MCPs. This was "a win-win" situation for both MCPs and the implementing partners and had sustained long-term impacts on the overall project outcome.

Under the STAR programme, the first batch covered training of 500 Master Crafts persons (MCP) and 1000 learners (each MCP to train 2 learners on average). In subsequent batches, about 6 000 apprenticeships under this programme have been trained and about 3 000 MCPs are involved in the program.

After completion of training, BRAC supports the graduates to undertake assessment examinations under NTVQF. Currently, the practical trainers (i.e. MCPs) assess the competencies achieved by the trainees but the assessment from the government's part is facing bottlenecks due to lack of assessors from the responsible government agency (i.e. Bangladesh Technical Education Board). However, 2 000 trainees have been registered as apprentices under BMET and given certificates.

Source: ILO and BRAC – compilation from selected documents and questionnaires.

Objectives

The objective of the STAR programme is to develop a model that utilises informal apprenticeships to act as a structured and effective means of creating skilled workers. The initiative also aimed to equip master crafts persons in multiple trades with skills to minimise hazardous work, improve occupational safety and health and link formal and non-formal organisations for large-scale national upskilling and formal qualifications across the country. It was also expected that learning centres/technical institutes and technical trainers for in-house learning would be identified and supported to be actively engaged in the pilot activities and training.

The groups targeted were both male and female disadvantaged youth, youth from low socio-economic backgrounds and those who had dropped out of school.

Activities

The training process of STAR programme is described here.

- **Initial selection of the potential trainees and master crafts persons (MCPs) is based on the selected criteria.**
- **Specific trade based onsite technical training** is delivered to the learners by master crafts people (MCP) and technical trainers. Trades offered are decided according to area-specific demand.
- **The learners are placed into an apprenticeship** under an MCP who provides hands-on training for five days a week. Side by side, the technical trainers provide classroom or **theoretical training** on basic concepts, introducing tools and equipment, measurement, and works process. **Basic English lessons** are provided to the learners to minimise their chances of falling behind due to poor communication skills.
- Learners receive **life skills training** on occupational safety, health issues, child rights and the pitfalls of early marriage. They are taught to take on a realistic and patient approach in order to **adapt to the demands of the market,** improving their quality through training and development, and helping them seek employment in markets where there is demand.
- Learners are also taught the importance of **basic money management and financial security.** They are enabled to open bank accounts to save their allowances (from BRAC), their salaries (earned from their apprenticeship), and sometimes family savings as well. Once the training is completed, **BRAC links up the learners with employers** for wage employment. For those who are keen on self-employment, BRAC offers information, guidance and technical assistance.
- Regular monthly monitoring is carried out by BRAC to check performance and progress of learning. Post-training support is provided to the completed graduates.

Governance framework and delivery arrangements

BRAC is an entity with multiple programmes and funding support and does not have separate management arrangements for STAR, which is located with BRAC's education programme. As is the case with other programmes, the wider governance framework of BRAC applies to STAR. The Research and Evaluation Division, Monitoring Division, Finance Division and Training Division provide support to all BRAC programmes including STAR.

Budget and financing

UNICEF, ILO, UKAid and AusAid have been the main donors of the programme since its inception in 2012. BRAC has already plans to continue and expand the STAR programme.

Impacts of the initiative

The programme is now operational in five divisional cities, including Dhaka, Chittagong, Khulna, Rajshahi and Sylhet. About 6 000 graduates (50% girls, 8% PWDs) have completed the training at the time of preparing this report. Of these, 99% have been employed within one month of completing their training, according to the BRAC report. About 3 000 MCPs, many of them owners of SMEs, have received training and support in order to enable them to provide apprenticeship places.

The STAR programme is a highly result-oriented initiative in terms of employment generation, income, and female empowerment. It not only provides enterprise-based on-site technical training to the learners, but also grooms them through soft skill development training to prepare them for the world of work.

A strength of the initiative is its focus on young disadvantaged youth, including men, women and people with disabilities, who are seeking employment. Target groups include school drop outs and young people in the age bracket of 14 to 20 years. Of them, more than 50% are females and 8% are persons with disabilities (PWDs). Particularly for the young females, this programme potentially prevents early marriage which is a major problem in Bangladesh. Following the training, there has been an increase in the income level of the trainees, which helps them to further their careers and improve their quality of life.

Strengths of the initiative

A core strength of the programme was its combination of practical learning with theoretical training to help the learner become more skilled in a certain trade. This facilitates a better transition to the labour market as on-the-job training, following CBTA, has worked very well to ensure learners learn the skills that are in line with the market requirement. This type of training has opened up opportunities for the young learners to transition from lower to higher paid work opportunities.

A further strength has been a focus on soft-skills training, including knowledge awareness, financial literacy and negotiation skills. These skills have been crucial to the holistic development of learners.

Third, in comparison to institution-based TVET model, the apprenticeship model has much more flexibility in responding to the changes in the labour market demand since no institutional set-up is required. Hence, the need for new capital investment for training purposes is modest. The STAR programme also enables a decentralised and flexible approach to meeting the needs of the labour market in each of the five cities. It has a strong focus on furthering development through the ability to adapt to local circumstances. BRAC's access to local community groups at the grassroots level has allowed the programme to successfully reach out to the girls and learners with disabilities.

The STAR apprenticeship model naturally incorporates market trend to some extent since only those shops, whose services are in demand, survive in the market. Hence, being an apprentice in such a shop has an added advantage. It is thus highly probable that the learner would be a skilled graduate in a trade that is already in demand in the market, which is supported by the 99% employment rate of recent STAR graduates.

A final strength of the initiative is the joint expertise and lessons learnt from the UNICEF, ILO and BRAC. A cross-organisational approach to this programme enabled horizontality that maximised the chances of a successful implementation. The strong management and monitoring capacity of BRAC was also fundamental to the success of the programme by enabling a regular system of monitoring and following-up of training. The training provider's overall capacity for outreach, access to grassroots levels, and track record of long experience in development work for the poorer groups is a strong success factor.

What was innovative?

The core innovations of the STAR programme is in relation to formalising the tradition of informal apprenticeship and ensuring quality training for the most disadvantaged learners. This provides young people with a definite career path through the recognition of prior learning and potential portability and transferability of qualifications.

The STAR programme was also unique in that it leveraged the knowledge of the market and motivated SME owners to provide training for disadvantaged youth in their own community. This enabled SMEs to directly engage with MCPs and enlist them as partners in programme implementation and delivery.

The initiative also explicitly aimed to create good quality of work for apprentices. This was achieved through a focus on practical hands-on training, particularly for workplace welfare and protection issues such as occupational health and safety and a code of conduct at the workplace.

The programme's strong local focus that enables flexible implementation at the local level was also a key innovation.

Weaknesses of the initiative

A challenge was in relation to maintaining minimum standards in the workplace. Master Crafts Persons (MCPs) were generally not familiar with formal training arrangements and there was a need for time consuming and intense monitoring to develop their capacity to deliver training in a structured and time-bound training manner. There was also a need for capacity building with regard to respecting the workplace code of conduct and occupational health and safety issues. This was addressed by providing MCP with training in BRAC learning centres and offering them close monitoring and support throughout the training process.

The second challenge was in relation to the traditional social attitudes toward gender roles and production. Because of prevailing socio-economic factors, the labour markets in local Bangladeshi cities are male-dominated and female apprentices are uncommon. Improving women participation in the programme to parity was particularly challenging. Similarly, the inclusion of persons with disabilities (PWDs) proved quite difficult due to the fact they are highly marginalised in terms of education, barriers to mobility, and lack of awareness at community and family levels about special needs. This was overcome by BRAC's grassroots links, who conducted workshops and meetings to advocate for the inclusion of women and learner's with disabilities.

Finally, a major bottleneck is encountered in the assessment and certification of the trainees and the cost of assessments. Availability of competency based learning materials in the local language was another constraint because of inadequate translation services. This was resolved by liaison with the Bangladesh Technical Education Board (BTEB), the designated authority to provide these services.

Transferable lessons for other non-OECD countries

The programme highlighted that employer ownership, participation and feedback are essential to successful programmes that target informal enterprise. It was also important to utilise a strong and dedicated training provider with a good outreach and strong advocacy capacity, due to the predominantly unorganised nature of the informal economy.

Second, the dual apprenticeship model with a delivery method of combining actual workplace experience and theoretical (or classroom) lessons delivered benefits to both learners and enterprises. This approach is particularly important for the apprentices in the informal economy (usually early school leavers, male and female, and disadvantaged groups) which allows them to pursue potential career progression through the system of recognition of prior learning and issuance of nationally recognised certification. This raises the prospects of increased income and livelihoods.

Third, high level policy support and reform of the TVET system should include pro-active measures and institutional arrangements for the delivery of effective training. Government involvement and backing by providing access for the informal system to the formal system is important to facilitate smooth transition of young people from school to work.

Fourth, there is great potential to deliver programs in the informal economy through a structured training system that feature elements of skills training with workplace improvement and workplace health and safety issues. Engaging with both of these issues can help to create quality employment conditions for young people and MCP alike.

Fifth and final, the apprenticeship system, whether formal or informal, should have a strong focus on inclusion to gain maximum results. This is particularly important from the perspective of poverty alleviation, job creation, gender-mainstreaming and disability inclusion.

Considerations for successful adoption in other non-OECD countries

First of all, strong policy support and the backing of the government at the highest level is important to scale up interventions and link the formal and informal training systems. It is important that the apprenticeship system is linked to national qualifications and certification frameworks, including making provision for the Recognition of Prior Learning (RPL). This is particularly important in areas where informal apprenticeships in SMEs are the primary method of skills development. It is also important to have strong management, supervision capacity and outreach to design and deliver good quality and effective training.

Second, strong advocacy, mobilisation efforts and incentives are needed to generate enterprise and private sector interest and to ensure their spontaneous involvement and investment in various modes of skills training, including apprenticeships. In other words, employer engagement in skills training is vital as we have seen in the case of the two examples here. While legislative reform is important to create an enabling environment, the interest and commitment of the employers to participate in skills training is fundamental to broadening access to apprenticeship.

Finally, gender mainstreaming and inclusive approaches in skills development is a viable option if designed consciously and pro-actively from the start. Results from the two examples are ample proofs of that.

Conclusion

The two case studies of formal and informal apprenticeship training of Bangladesh presented here are relatively new – one started in 2009 and the other in 2012. However, the experience and lessons learnt provide important insights into skills training through apprenticeship.

In case of the formal model (i.e. COEL), it is clear that strong employer engagement in the form of dynamic and committed leadership was key to the programme's overall success. Institutional mechanisms like the formation of Industrial Skills Councils (ISCs) are effective means of ensuring that employers remain engaged in the vocational education system. Strong participation and engagement of employers in the formulation of policy as well as participation in the TVET system reform process can help to design a demand-driven and inclusive training system that also has a decent work dimension.

In case of the informal apprenticeship example presented here, the main lessons learnt are that it has a strong equity and poverty focus and promotion of decent work principles at the workplace. This approach has an expressed aim on reaching out to the poorer and marginalised groups at the local levels and promoting their access to the formal system from which most of them remain excluded. The involvement of credible, high-quality local partners are key to success.

Lastly, both these examples show that low rate of female participation in the technical and vocational training system (which currently stands at about 24% taking into account both public and private sector institutions combined) can be successfully addressed through pro-active design and delivery of training.

Notes

1. The TVET reform programme is a programme of the Ministry of Education (MOE) which is being implemented by ILO with the funding support of the European Union (the project operated over the period of 2008-15).

2. Government of Bangladesh, National Skills Development Council: *Bangladesh Skills Snapshot 2012*, funded by the Swiss Agency for Development Co-operation (SDC) and managed by the ILO TVET Reform Project. Nine sectors covered by the survey include: agro-food, construction, informal skills, information technology, leather and leather goods, light engineering, ready-made garments, tourism and hospitality and water transport/ship building.

3. There is a bit of anomaly between the Apprenticeship Ordinance 1962 and the BLA 2006 and the Amendment of the Labour Act (in 2013) regarding the competent authority to oversee the apprenticeship programme. The 2013 amendment of BLA designates the Chief Inspector of Factories and Establishments as the *"Competent"* authority to inspect and supervise the apprenticeships. However, BMET is still keeping its previous responsibility for registration, monitoring and certification of the apprentices (both formal and informal). It is understood from the BMET sources that this provision of the labour act will be amended.

4. COEL received equipment and funding support from the externally-funded government development projects. It is registered as a "Registered Training Organisation" with the Bangladesh Technical Education Board (BTEB). In that sense, it can be termed as a PPP initiative.

References

Bangladesh Labour Act (2006), Section XVIII, Dhaka, 11 October 2006.

Bangladesh Bureau of Statistics (BBS), *Report of the Labour Force Survey, 2010-11*, Dhaka, Aug. 2011.

UNFPA Country Office for Bangladesh, *The Impact of the Demographic Transition on Socioeconomic Development in Bangladesh: Future prospects and Implications for Public Policy*, Dhaka, Jan. 2015.

Government of Bangladesh (GOB) (2012), National Skills Development Council (NSDC): Bangladesh Skills Snapshot 2012.

Government of Bangladesh (GOB) (2011), Five Year Plan Document (2011-15), Dhaka.

ILO (2012), *Overview of Apprenticeship Systems and Issues, ILO contribution to the G20 Task Force on Employment*, Geneva, Nov. 2012Manzur, Syed Nasim Manzur: Crouching Tiger, Paper presented at the 5th World Footwear Congress, Leon, Mexico, 25 Nov. 2014.

ILO (2009), *Survey and Assessment of Formal and Informal Apprenticeships in Bangladesh*, Dhaka, March 2009.

Islam, Md. Amirul et al. (2014), COEL Industry-led Apprenticeship Project for Leather Industry (2012-14): Tracer Study of the Trainees under the Industry-led Apprenticeship Project, Dhaka, October 2014.

Chapter 10

Reforming the Indian apprenticeship system to boost local engagement

India faces what has been called a stupendous challenge in increasing the portion of its workforce with VET qualifications. Most of the Indian workforce does not even have secondary education (70% in 2009-10), and only 2% had VET qualifications at that time. The apprenticeship system in India suffers from the same problems as the Indian VET system more broadly; namely that there are insufficient participants. Young people do not tend to see apprenticeship as a valued career path, and employers have been reluctant to employ apprentices. In 2012, the Indian government embarked upon a significant reform effort of the apprenticeship system in particular and the VET system more generally. This chapter describes and evaluates the elements of that reform.

Key findings

- The Indian VET system was implemented in the 1960s but has remained relatively static and unresponsive to changes in the broader industrial structure and development of India's economy.

- Apprenticeship has very poor reach in India, despite a large workforce and an economy with current and forecast skills shortages.

- Building employer engagement in the Indian system involves removing punitive punishments and existing legislative burdens. The legacy system disincentivised participation from both small and large employers due to a combination of high reporting requirements and systemic fragmentation.

- Legislative reforms have aimed to improve the ease and function of the apprenticeship system for both apprentices and employers. Increased efforts to raise awareness about apprenticeships will continue to improve the scope and penetration of apprenticeship in India.

Introduction

India is the world's second-most populous country with over 1.3 billion people. Its population grew at 1.76% per annum between 2001 and 2011, a somewhat slower rate than 2.13% per annum in the previous decade (1991-2001). If population growth continues at the current rate, India will overtake China's population by 2022, according to UN estimates. The labour force is estimated at 487 million of which 256 million are in the non-farm sector (Ministry of Skill Development and Entrepreneurship, 2015).

India is also one of the world's fastest-growing economies, with an annual GDP growth rate of 5.8% over the past two decades. The growth rate peaked at 6.1% during 2011-12 and then slowed in 2012-14 (Mohan and Kopur, 2015). The Indian economy is worth USD 1.676 trillion and is the eleventh-largest economy by market exchange rates. Economic growth in recent years has been driven by the expansion of services (communication, business, financial and community sectors), which have consistently grown faster than other sectors. The public sector is the leading investor in infrastructure (Mohan and Kapur, 2015).

It has been argued that the pattern of Indian development has been unique and that the country may be able to skip the intermediate industrialisation-led phase in the transformation of its economic structure. But concerns have been raised about what has been depicted as the jobless nature of the economic growth (Virmani, 2004). It is argued that there are impediments (such as overly restrictive regulatory frameworks) to the growth of manufacturing in India in comparison to other competitor countries (Mohan and Kapur, 2015).

Policy Context

The Indian labour force is the world's second largest (Economist, 2011) with 487.6 million workers in 2011. The agricultural sector employs most of the national workforce and produces the second largest national farm output worldwide. For the economy to continue to grow and expand, it is assumed that a large portion of the workforce will migrate from the primary sector (agriculture) to the secondary and tertiary sectors. The service sector provides 55.6% of GDP, the industrial sector 26.3% and agricultural sector 18.1% (IMF, 2011).However, the skills that are required in the secondary and tertiary sectors are quite different from those required in the agricultural sector (Federation of Indian Chambers of Commerce and Industry [FICCI], 2010), implying that there will inevitably be a large skill gap when such a migration occurs. India has set an ambitious policy aspiration of developing a skilled workforce of 500 million by 2022 (Ministry of Labour and Employment [MOLE], 2010).

The Indian Government's Twelfth Five Year Plan for 2102-17 (Planning Commission, 2013) includes workforce development matters in its third volume (Social Sectors) which includes a section on Education and one on Employment and Skill Development. According to the plan, the mission of TVET in India is to help the country's economic and social development, and specifically transform its increasing manpower to a skilled and competent workforce.

A useful summary by UNESCO-UNEVOC (2015) provides an overview of the TVET provisions of this Plan. These include aspirations to:

- Link secondary, and specifically vocational and technical programmes, to the needs of the labour market in collaboration with industry and the Ministry of Labour;

- Improve residual access and equity gaps to TVET programmes by for example targeting out-of-school children;

- Expand the number of TVET programmes;

- Encourage and facilitate students to take pre-vocational programmes in the secondary education level;

- Develop a mechanism for convergence of vocational programmes offered by various ministries, private institutions, and vocational educational institutions;

- Improve TVET teacher training programmes to ensure a high quality of education; and

- Integrate and closely align vocational programmes with the academic curriculum. TVET programmes should contain modules on various generic and specific vocational skills with the involvement of industry.

The Indian education and training system

Figure 10.1 (UNESCO-UNEVOC, 2015) indicates the relationship between TVET and the wider Indian education system.

The numbers enrolled in VET are very small compared with secondary and higher education systems. For example, in 2010, 227 million students were enrolled in schools, 14 million in higher education (including 690 000 in Polytechnics) and only just over 1 million students in the Industrial Training Institutes (ITIs) and Industrial Training Centres (ITCs) in the VET system (MOLE, Annual Report 2009-10). ITIs are state-owned and ITCs are privately-owned.

Many students do not complete primary education, mainly in the state-regulated schools. Approximate 12-13 million school leavers, either those completing education or leaving early, move to the education and job market yearly (FICCI, 2010). India has 241 million young people aged 14-25 (UNESCO-UNEVOC, 2015). The Twelfth Five Year Plan noted that young people did not consider VET as an aspirational pathway. Consequently, the perceived

Figure 10.1. **TVET and the Indian Education System**

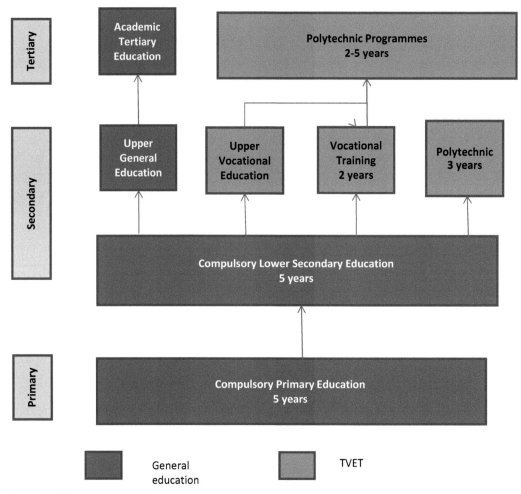

Source: UNESCO-UNEVOC (2015).

quality and status of VET needed to be enhanced in order to increase the proportion of young people pursuing VET.

Apart from the Five Year Plan, the most important regulatory and policy provisions that have relevance for apprenticeship are:

- Apprentices Act (1961) (discussed further below);
- Institutes of Technology Act (1961);
- National Policy for Skill Development (2009 and 2015); and the
- National Youth Policy (2012).

Figure 10.2 shows the basic structure and the responsibilities of the various components of the Indian educational and training systems in 2010. There has since been a realignment of responsibilities, which is explained in further depth below.

Education, including all aspects of higher and college education, is overseen by the Ministry of Human Resource Development (MHRD) The University and Higher Education arm of MHRD is responsible for college education (Arts, Science, Commerce etc.), while engineering education and polytechnics are categorised as Technical Education.

Figure 10.2. **Current Indian Education and Skill Development structure**

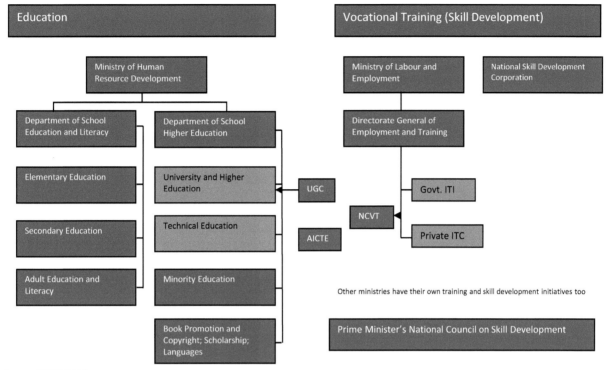

Source: FICCI (2010).

The technical education bureau is responsible for TVET in each State and also the quality of TVET teachers and the curriculum. The All India Council for Technical Education (AICTE) is the regulatory body for Technical Education in India. Its objectives are:

● The promotion of quality in technical education though accreditation of programmes;

● The planning and co-ordinated development of technical education system through establishment of new ITIs and ITC; and

● Overall administration of TVET programme.

The National Council on Vocational Training (NCVT) plays a key role in the formation of training curricula and policy standards, as well as the certification of apprentices by means of the "trade test". TVET teachers and trainers are trained at a variety of teacher-training institutes. There are also Central Training Institutes which are responsible for the professional development of TVET teachers and trainers.

The nature of the Indian apprenticeship system before the current reforms

As in most countries, apprenticeship in India means a system of training in which an employer engages a person as an apprentice and agrees to train him/her systematically in the designated trade for a prescribed period. The Indian National Apprenticeship Scheme began in 1959 on a voluntary basis. However the Scheme did not achieve the expected results, so the Apprenticeship Scheme was brought under the ambit of the Apprentices Act (1961). It had two primary objectives:

● To regulate the programme of training of apprentices in the industry so as to conform to the prescribed syllabi, period of training and other requirements laid down by the Central Apprenticeship Council; and

● To fully utilise the facilities available in industry for imparting practical training with a view to meeting the requirements of skilled manpower for industry.

While apprentice opportunities are available at higher levels (Graduate and Technician apprentices) this paper only addresses apprentices under two specific schemes: the "Craftsman Training Scheme" and the "Apprenticeship Training Scheme". These schemes do not require entry qualifications beyond school-leaving certificates and are similar to apprenticeship schemes in other countries.

The Apprenticeship Act (1961) has been amended multiple times over the years to address the concerns of employers, industry, candidates and Government. But it is generally agreed that these changes have hitherto not had the desired effect of increasing the participation of employers and school leavers. The number of apprentices in the country remained stagnant and has not increased in numbers over the years. Only 215 000 persons were undergoing apprenticeship training in 2008-09, despite a total seating capacity of 320 000 (Directorate General of Employment and Training [DGET], 2009).

Figure 10.3 shows the numbers of participants and the coverage by numbers of occupations, of trade apprentices in 2009, including those in the Craftsman Training Scheme (which is at lower secondary level) and the Apprenticeship Training Scheme.

Figure 10.3. **India's apprenticeship regime**

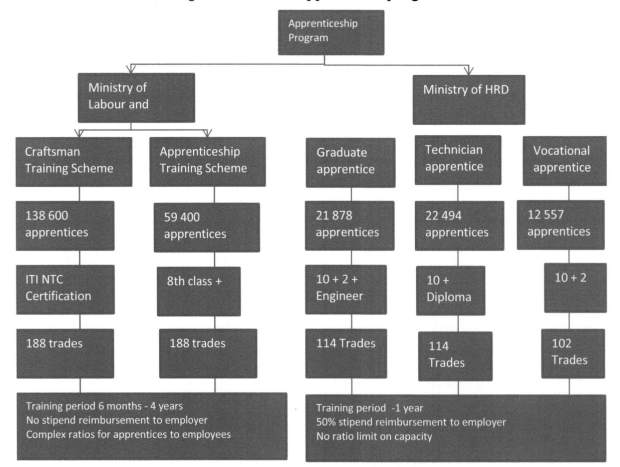

Source: Planning Commission Sub-committee on re-modelling India's apprenticeship regime (2009).

The Directorate General of Employment and Training (DGET) in the Ministry of Labour was, until 2015, responsible for implementation of the Act in respect of Trade Apprentices in the Central Government Undertakings and Departments. This was (and still is) operationalised through six Regional Directorates. The Department of Secondary and Higher Education in the Ministry of Human Resource Development was responsible for implementation of the Act in respect of Graduate, Technician and Technician (Vocational) Apprentices. A Central Apprenticeship Council acts as a peak statutory body with responsibility for apprenticeship policies and standards.

Employers in both the public and private sectors are obliged to have a training infrastructure, as laid down in the Act, before they can engage apprentices.

According to the annual report (2008-09) of Ministry of Labour and Employment (*http://dget.nic.in/*), 254 groups of industries are covered under the Act, and about 23 900 establishments engage apprentices.

Apprenticeships are time-based, with the duration specified at six months, one year, 18 months, two years, three years or four years. The assessment of apprentices at the end of their training is undertaken using the All India Trade Test, administrated by the National Council for Vocational Training. The number of apprenticeship places available in each occupation and region is officially set. "Seats" for trade apprentices are determined by the Apprenticeship Adviser on the basis of the prescribed ratio of Apprentices to workers, and the availability of training facilities. Every apprentice and employer needs to enter into a contract of apprentice training which is registered by the Apprenticeship Advisers.

Educational prerequisites apply to entry into each of the apprenticeship categories. Trade apprentices may enter by two routes, depending on their prior qualifications. If they have completed only basic education, they enter the "Apprentice Training Scheme"; these apprentices are known as "full-term apprentices". If they have completed training and certification at an ITI or ITC, they enter the "Craftsman Training Scheme", which considerably shortens the term of training. The training terms, and the trades covered by apprenticeships (188 in 2009) are contained in the Schedule to the Act. Regardless of route, successful completers receive the "National Apprenticeship Certificate". (Directorate General of Training, 2015a).

Apprentices are paid a stipend, which is specified in government regulations and revised every two years based on the consumer price index (DGET, 2007). The arrangements vary with the category of apprenticeship. The stipend of trade apprentices is paid by the employer and increases over the period of the training programme. The monthly rates prior to the reforms were IND 1 490 in the first year, IND 1 700 in the second year, IND 1 970 in the third year and IND 2 220 in the fourth year (taking effect from 18 October 2010). The stipend of graduate, technician and technician (vocational) apprentices is shared equally between the employer and the Government. In 2008 it was IND 2 600 per month for graduate apprentices, IND 1 850 for technician apprentices and IND 1 440 for technician (vocational) apprentices (MOLE Annual Report, 2009). Stipends are partly refunded to employers of graduate, technician and vocational apprentices, but not to employers of trade apprentices. As will be explained later, stipend rate and distribution have changed.

Legislation

Legislation, and the ways in which the legislation is enacted, has a powerful influence on the environment in which apprenticeships are conducted. Legislation can enable or constrain the expansion of apprenticeships by facilitating or inhibiting the involvement of all stakeholders. The level of legislative responsiveness to changes in the economy, the demography and the "voices" of industry is a crucial factor in the continuing success of apprenticeships as a way of providing skilled labour for a country.

In India, the Apprentice Act (1961) governs the employment, conditions, training and wage structures that apprentices and employers operate within in India.

The goals of the Act are:

1. To regulate the training programme of apprentices in industry, according to the prescribed curriculum, period of training and other requirements, as set down by the Central Apprenticeship Council;

2. To utilise the facilities available in industry for practical training.

The Act covers the four categories of apprenticeship mentioned earlier, and also outlines a number of apprenticeship requirements, as follows:

- The number of apprentices for a designated trade
  - ❖ The central government determines the ratio of trade apprentices to workers in that trade.
  - ❖ The central government determines the appropriateness of the facilities for apprentice training inside the particular industries.
  - ❖ The Apprenticeship Adviser may require employers to engage trade apprentices within the ratio determined by the government.
  - ❖ Several employers may join together for the purpose of providing practical training to the apprentice.
  - ❖ The government may require employers to train additional numbers of apprentices.
- The practical and basic training of apprentices
  - ❖ Employers must make arrangements for practical training in the workplace.
  - ❖ Central Apprenticeship Advisers have the right of inspection.
  - ❖ If employers have more than 500 workers, a separate area must be set up for apprentice training and some government loans are available for this.
  - ❖ Basic training for the apprentices is provided in training institutes set up by the government.
  - ❖ Complex arrangements for various categories of apprentices for the provision of basic training and the funding of this.
  - ❖ The costs of training are to be carried by the employer.
- Related instruction of apprentices
  - ❖ An apprentice is to receive theoretical training approved by the Central Government.
  - ❖ This related instruction is to be financed by the appropriate government but the employer must provide the facilities.
  - ❖ Training is included in the calculation of work time for the apprentice.

Apprenticeship contract

The Apprenticeship Contract is registered with the Apprenticeship Adviser whose decision is final in the event of a dispute. If a business closes, the Apprenticeship Adviser can move the apprentice to another employer. The apprentice is required to undergo an All

India Trade Test conducted by the National Council for Vocational Training and a practical test at the end of the apprenticeship.

Offences and penalties

These occur when an employer:

1. Engages an ineligible apprentice;

2. Does not carry out the terms and conditions of the contract of apprenticeship;

3. Contravenes the Act in terms of the number of apprentices which he is required to engage; he will be punished with a term of imprisonment which may extend to 6 months and accompany a fine; or

4. Does not complete the mandatory documentation, or provides incorrect information or refuses to answer certain questions or employs an apprentice to undertake work that is not connected with his training, or pays according to a piece rate, or requires the apprentice to be part of a bonus scheme; the employer will be punished by imprisonment.

The Act has been amended many times to meet criticisms and suggestions from employers, businesses, Chambers of Commerce and other stakeholders.

Coverage of the Act

The Act specifies the groups of industries to which the Act applies. Currently there are 254 groups of industries covered under the Act and 24 815 establishments engage trade apprentices (*http://dget.nic.in/schemes/ats/ATSOverview.htm*, accessed 7/8/2012).

In 1997, the groups of industries were clustered into the following industry groupings:

1. Primary production and agricultural production	17. Electricity generation and gas and steam generation
2. Forestry and logging	18. Construction
3. Fishing	19. Wholesale trade
4. Mining	20. Retail trade in textiles
5. Manufacture of food products	21. Restaurants and hotels
6. Manufacture of beverages	22. Land, air and water transport
7. Manufacture of cotton and other textiles and textile products	23. Warehousing
8. Manufacture of wood products such as furniture	24. Communication services
9. Manufacture of paper and paper products	25. Banking and insurance
10. Manufacture of leather and leader products	26. Real estate
11. Chemical production	27. Business services
12. Plastics production	28. Public administration and defence
13. Manufacture of non-metallic mineral products	29. Sanitary services
14. Manufacture of machinery and parts	30. Community services
15. Transport equipment and parts	31. Recreational and cultural services
16. Repair of capital goods	32. Personal services

Source: DGET.

Implementation of the Act

There are six Regional Directorates of Apprenticeship Training located throughout India. These are responsible for the implementation for the Act. State Apprenticeship Advisers have legislated powers and they are responsible for the implementation of the Act in relation to Trade apprentices in State government departments and private establishments.

The Central Apprenticeship Council is a statutory body and advises the government on policies relating to the Apprenticeship Training Scheme. The Central Apprenticeship Council has representatives from both central and state governments, employers and trade unions.

Problems with the Indian apprenticeship system prior to the current reforms

In recent years, a number of assessments of the apprenticeship system in India have been conducted by national and international stakeholders to examine the issues that confront India in its attempts to solve the dual problem of high youth unemployment and skill shortages in critical industries through the expansion of the apprenticeship system. Five of these documents were analysed in greater detail in order to inform the analysis of the issues faced by the Indian apprenticeship system.

The first document was the National Policy on Skill Development (MOLE, 2009) which looks at national skill development as a whole, of which apprenticeship forms one, currently minor, part. The second document, the Planning Commission Sub-Committee on Remodelling India's Apprenticeship Regime (2009) was the most recent high level government endorsed effort to propose change. The third document was an analysis of Indian apprenticeship law commissioned by the ILO and the Kamataka Employers' Association (Akhilesh, 2010). The fourth document consisted of input from the Confederation of Indian Industry (CII) into a consultation process convened by the Ministry of Labour and Employment (2011a); the CII document gives an industry perspective, including some issues raised elsewhere. The fifth was the Ministry of Labour and Employment's report "Trade Apprenticeship Training in India under Apprenticeship Training Scheme" (October 2011). This publication was the 13th in its series and reflected an attempt to create a reliable database for planning and taking corrective action in apprenticeship training under the Apprentices Act, 1961. This publication "presented statistics on establishments engaged in apprenticeship training, intake capacity, output and their employability in the labour market along with a brief analysis of the current status of the scheme" (Preface).

It is notable that many identified problem areas, and many recommendations, were common among the documents. Underpinning all of the discussions and reports were the issues of disparities among regions and groups of people, high unemployment, the rapidly growing economy, and the large informal economy. Apprenticeships were regarded as a part of a much broader policy thrust to improve the skill levels of the population while simultaneously addressing some of the social, economic and educational problems that confront India.

Thirteen issues were identified from telephone interviews with major stakeholders, analysis of the reports mentioned above, and other literature (see Box 10.1). The current case study directly engages with many of these issues.

These identified problems were set against the background of contextual matters relating to the TVET system and the economy more generally. The broader economic context in India indicates an imperative for an expanded apprenticeship system, including: Requirements for large numbers of skilled workers; limited capacity of institutional training to provide larger numbers of qualified and skilled workers; high unemployment and high youth unemployment in particular; and oversupply of graduate-qualified people versus trade-qualified people.

Some contextual factors that made expansion of apprenticeships difficult were also identified, including: Low status of VET; low social status of apprenticeships in particular; the large informal economy; large proportion of population in rural areas; and the limited capacity of government to administer a larger system of the current level of complexity.

Box 10.1. **Issues identified by stakeholders as needing reform**

1. **Lack of enterprise engagement in the system:** Considering the size of the Indian economy, the number of enterprises taking on apprentices was extremely low – around 24 000 establishments. In comparison, there are 120 000 sites in the United Kingdom that employ apprentices.

2. **Inappropriate requirements for in-company training:** Indian employers were required to provide trade apprentices with basic training and "related instruction training" as outlined by the Apprentices Rules, in addition to practical training gained through working. It is unusual among national apprentice systems for employers to be required to provide formal classroom-based training. The in-house classroom training could not be outsourced except in exceptional circumstances. The qualifications of the training staff and the facilities for the in-company training were mandated, with stringent requirements oriented to manufacturing companies with large workforces, and limited relevance to the growing service skills sector.

3. **Concerns about quality of workplace curriculum:** Indian companies, under the Act, needed to take apprentices where directed; but there was no guarantee that the training was relevant or of high quality. One of the major reasons for the lack of uniform quality was the absence of a workplace curriculum that was current, accessible and able to be implemented in the workplace. The training curriculum was recognised as outdated and there were concerns that there was an insufficient theoretical component.

4. **Lack of external off-the-job training:** Once people commenced an apprenticeship, having completed either ITI/ITC vocational qualifications or basic training, they did not undergo any further external training. This contrasts with the 'dual system' in many countries.

5. **Limited occupational coverage:** The Indian formal apprenticeship system had a limited, and sometimes outdated, list of designated trades in which apprenticeships could be offered. Numbers in most trades were small; in 2009 only nine occupations had an intake of more than 1 000 apprentices. Many trades had just a handful, or nil, entrants, and there was under-representation of the service and business sectors in the lists of trades in which apprenticeships could be offered. While it was possible for new occupations to be added by the government on request from enterprises, the system for doing this was cumbersome and slow.

6. **Limited employer and industry involvement:** The complexity of the apprenticeship system, the absence of public knowledge about its operation and the lack of branding all contributed to a lack of industry involvement in the formulation of apprenticeship policies and practices. Under the National Policy on Skills Development, Sector Skills Councils were being slowly established; however, industry still did not feel that it had a "voice" in the formulation of policy or in the practical day to day implementation of the apprenticeship system. Individual employers also faced obstacles; for example, companies that employed apprentices in more than four Indian states had to negotiate state and central government instrumentalities.

7. **Overly strict and burdensome regulation and compliance:** Compliance was onerous for employers, involving extensive and expensive reporting requirements, and penal consequences and fines for breaches of the legislation and the accompanying Schedule of Rules. Enforcement of the rules was said to be lax, but this was unlikely to comfort employers who were afraid to participate in the formal system because of strict penalties associated with any legal breach, including imprisonment. Apprentices received more favourable employment conditions (apart from a low stipend) and employment protection than other employees.

8. **Low status of apprenticeship training:** India has had a very long tradition of informal training and workplace learning. This tradition is preserved in the "informal apprenticeship system" that exists alongside the formal system. However the formal system appeared to have been beset by a range of problems that have resulted in a low level of esteem and status. The perceived low status of vocational education meant that the better graduates of secondary schools were unlikely to choose to undertake apprenticeships.

Box 10.1. **Issues identified by stakeholders as needing reform** *(cont.)*

9. **Responsibilities of parties unclear:** The overly complex administrative systems meant that it was difficult for apprentices, employers and other stakeholders to understand the system and their roles in it. There was a relative lack of easily accessible information. At a higher level, there was a willingness among stakeholders such as industry bodies to help to grow the apprenticeship system but the points of intervention were difficult to pinpoint. In most if not all other countries, apprenticeship systems are regarded as complex; so in itself complexity is not necessarily an issue. However there were few identifiable 'nodes' of expertise in the system where people can receive advice, information and support.

10. **Need to involve more diverse participants:** Apprentices were predominantly young people, with no system for mature-aged people to access apprenticeships. In India, a large proportion of the adult population is unskilled, and apprenticeship could offer these people the possibility of upskilling. Gender was identified as an issue, with women being under-represented. This is a common feature of countries with relatively small apprenticeship systems, and was partially due to the fact that most apprenticeships are in male-dominated industries and occupations. An under-representation of rural areas in apprenticeships could also be related to the type of occupations involved, rather than any specific urban bias. There were physical fitness requirements of the Apprenticeship Rules, which limited the opportunity for some people to participate; but there was provision for people with specific disabilities.

11. **Inadequate stipend:** The stipend paid to apprentices was very low and was insufficient to live on, thus discouraging participation by potential apprentices. While employers might choose to pay more to their apprentices, there was no obligation to do so. Unlike in other countries, low wages were not compensated for by the certainty of post-apprenticeship employment.

12. **Lack of progression into higher qualifications:** In the continuing absence of a well-developed national qualifications framework, it was difficult for apprenticeships to offer progression into higher level qualifications. Apprentices who passed their trade tests (All India Trades tests) obtained a National Apprenticeship Certificate, which, however, stood outside the formal educational system.

13. **Limited progression into permanent employment:** Apprenticeships tended not to lead to permanent employment. Apprentices were not often retained by the employer who provided them with the apprenticeship, nor were they greatly in demand in the labour market among other employers. There was also no provision for finding alternative places for apprentices who lost their jobs through no fault of their own.

Source: Smith and Brennan Kemmis (2013b).

Options for development of the system were developed as part of the project, and presented to a group of 81 senior stakeholders in New Delhi in late 2012. The options were grouped under four major headings:

1. Simplification of access

2. Improvement of training quality

3. Harmonisation of the system

4. Increased participation in the system.

Table 10.1 shows the options under these headings. Some proposed methods were suggested for each option, involving major changes and/or minor changes to the system. The stakeholders supported the methods proposed for the shaded options below. Their views are important as the major players in the system attended the meeting and any major changes would need their support.

Table 10.1. **Proposed options for changes to the Indian apprenticeship system**

The shaded items were supported by stakeholders

Themes	Proposed options
1. Increase access	i. Replace compulsory participation requirements with voluntary registration. ii. Reduce the regulatory burden on employers. iii. Introduce new third parties to the system to help manage economic ebbs and flows, and to provide support for some groups and employers.
2. Improve training quality	i. Introduce off-the-job training throughout the period of an apprenticeship ii. Upgrade quality and recognition of apprentice certification iii. Improve workplace curriculum iv. Improve skills and expertise of those delivering training
3. Harmonise the system	i. Greater involvement of stakeholders in system ii. Simplify and harmonise the system iii. Increase "market currency" of apprentice qualifications
4. Increase participation	i. Cover more of the economy. ii. Provide financial incentives to participants, enterprises and training providers iii. Introduce non-financial strategies to increase participation among more people.

Source: Adapted from Smith and Brennan Kemmis (2013b).

Many of the proposed options and associated methods were supported at a system level, but stakeholders seemed not to support potential changes that involved the introduction of new bodies at the local level or an increased flow of government money to employers and especially to training providers.

Changes in the apprenticeship system from 2013

Several separate but related changes have taken place in the Indian apprenticeship system since the project in 2012. The momentum for change has been maintained and there have been changes to the apprenticeship system itself, to the VET system more generally, and in the government's overall economic development program.

Context

The reforms to the apprenticeship systems need to be seen in the context of two related initiatives. One is the "Make in India" initiative which is about boosting manufacturing; and the other is "Skill India" which aims for a rapid increase in skill levels in the population.

In September 2014, Prime Minister Modi and the Department of Industrial Policy and Promotion (DIPP, 2015) launched the "Make in India" initiative to transform India into a global design and manufacturing hub. The programme involved significant consultation with trade unions (DIPP, 2015) and collaboration between a number of stakeholders, including Union Officials, Ministers and Secretaries, state government, industry leaders and knowledge partners. A National Workshop in December 2014 brought together leaders to create an action plan with the aim of increasing manufacturing to 25% of GDP by 2020 (DIPP, 2015).

The "Skill India" initiative was launched in July 2015 and contained four major initiatives:

1. *National Skill Development Mission.* This is the institutional framework for the proposed rapid development of the Indian VET system. There are 13 key objectives with seven foci: i) Institutional Training, ii) Infrastructure, iii) Convergence, iv) Trainers, v) Overseas Employment, vi) Sustainable Livelihoods, vii) Leveraging Public Infrastructure. The Mission Directorate will work with the National Skill Development Agency, the National Skill Development Corporation, and the Directorate General of Training.

2. *National Policy for Skill Development and Entrepreneurship,* discussed in more detail below.

3. *The "PMKVY" scheme* which provides financial rewards to young people who complete training programmes, including Recognition of Prior Learning.

4. *The Skill Loan scheme*, providing loans for young people to attend training.

The "Skill India" initiative was launched on World Youth Skills Day and the last two initiatives were confined to young people. The programme is intended to focus on both vocational and general education.

Governance and administrative arrangements for VET

In April 2015, a Ministry of Skill Development and Entrepreneurship (MSDE) was established which absorbed the Training and Apprenticeship responsibilities from the Directorate General of Employment and Training (DGET) and the Ministry of Labour and Employment (MoLE). They are known as the Directorate of Training and the Directorate of Apprenticeship Training. Through these Directorates, MSDE is responsible for a range of activities and bodies in the vocational education and training (MSDE, 2015). These include the National Vocational Qualifications Framework and the Sector Skills Councils.

The National Skill Development Corporation (NSDC) is a public-private partnership which aims to promote skill development through equity and grant funding to enterprises, companies and organisations that provide skill training. It also administers quality assurance and information systems for the training programs that it funds. It has also helped to establish a number of new training institutions, including some that train the training academies. The NSDC has also overseen the development of the Sector Skills Councils and has commissioned "Skills Gap" studies for a number of States.

The majority of the state governments have created State Skill Development Missions (SSDMs) that prioritise skill development based on local industry needs, allowing sectors to create employment opportunities and promote skills required with industry, government bodies and training organisations. There has also been an attempt to integrate the activities of the State Missions with the National Skill Development Mission. Apprenticeships feature among the activities of these missions; for example, Uttar Pradesh has an explicit objective of "Strengthening Apprenticeship Programme" with two activities:

- The Department of Technical and Vocational Training, in consultation with the UPSSDM, will formulate and plan schemes to increase the current number of apprentices in the State

- Collaborations will be made with industries and large companies of the State for increasing the number of trainees under the scheme.

The web site includes information about the number of students enrolled in VET, the number of Training Centres and so on.

New National Policy for Skill Development and Entrepreneurship

The "National Policy for Skill Development and Entrepreneurship" (Ministry of Skill Development and Entrepreneurship [MSDE], 2015) is the second National Policy on Skill Development. The inclusion of "Entrepreneurship" in the title of the policy, as with the Ministry, indicates a drive towards the creation of new businesses.

The National Policy for Skill Development and Entrepreneurship (MSDE, 2015) set out to increase apprenticeship by ten-fold within five years through the following initiatives:

- Work with industry including the Micro, Small and Medium-sized Enterprises (MSME) sector to increase apprenticeship places;

- Include the service sector into the apprenticeship system;
- Raise awareness of VET, including apprenticeship, among young people (MSDE, 2015).

More specific plans in relation to apprenticeship include the establishment of new Training Institutes (Multi-Skill Institutes) which were to be designated as Skill Hubs. Links between all training providers and industry were to be encouraged. A quality Assurance Framework for the VET sector was to be developed, to which all Institutes would be required to align. The National Skills Qualifications Framework would be further rolled out, and Sector Skills Council would be strengthened in their work.

To increase the formal qualifications of those in the informal sector, MSDE proposed using Recognition of Prior Learning (RPL) to assist those with skills in unorganised sectors by incorporating the informal sector into the formal realm of skilling. This was aimed at providing an opportunity to allow those with skills to obtain relevant certification of competency.

The policy set out ambitious plans to improve the quality and supply of trainers and assessors. These included setting up a national trainer/assessor portal; registration for trainers and assessors; upskilling programs for people moving from industry or the Defence Sector, and benchmarking pay scales with secondary school teachers. There was also a proposal for setting up specialised Institutes for VET teacher-training (at least one per State).

Apprentice Protasahan Yojana Scheme

The National Policy for Skill Development and Entrepreneurship proposed sharing the cost of the apprentice stipend between employers and the government in the MSME sector. The Apprentice Protsahan Yojana (APY) scheme, which began in October 2014, enacted this policy, and was implemented through the Regional Directorates of Apprenticeship Training (Directorate General of Training, 2015b). The scheme aimed to increase the number of employers, particularly MSME employers, involved in apprenticeships, and hoped to create 100 000 extra apprenticeship places. The scheme covers all apprentices (those in trades and also in "optional trades") and any company with six or more employees, but only two apprentices per employer can be covered at any one time. In assessing applications, manufacturing is given preference above other sectors, and within sectors, registered MSMEs are given preference above non-MSMEs.

The government pays 50% of the stipend following registration of the apprentice on the web-based portal and details of payment made by the employer to the apprentice and of attendance by the apprentice. The government's payment is made directly into the apprentice's bank account, although for the first six months of the scheme the government payment was made via the employer. The scheme covers the first two years of apprentice training.

Changes in the legislative framework for apprenticeships

Long-awaited changes to the Apprentices Act 1961 were enacted in 2014. An Inter-Ministerial Group was convened in late 2013 by the then DGET to work on all the schemes managed by the DGET. It made recommendations on 17 issues. These recommendations were informed by submission from relevant stakeholder groups.

The 17 issues, with associated recommendations, were as follows (CII, 2014). In some instances, the eventual provisions of the Act were not the same as those recommended by the Inter-Ministerial Group but were "toned down".

The most significant changes to the amended Act and associated Rules, from both the employer and apprentice's point of view, include:

- *To assist apprentices:* The minimum age of apprenticeships undertaken in hazardous industries is 18 years of age. For other industries not considered hazardous, the minimum age to undertake an apprenticeship remains 14 years of age. The minimum stipend is increased. The stipend is increased. Employers are required to formulate policies about recruiting completed apprentices. Apprenticeships extended to new "optional trades".

- *Better data collection:* Amendments to section 4 include the development of a portal site by the government to register and verify apprenticeships, to be sent by the employer within 30 days to the Apprenticeship Adviser.

Promotion of apprenticeships

The National Policy for Skill Development and Entrepreneurship contains several proposals to increase the status of VET in general, including apprenticeships.

- *Promotion to young people:* The National Policy states that the network of Post Offices and Citizen Service will be leveraged with industry support to promote career counselling and awareness of training opportunities. The network of 285 000 Youth Clubs/Mahila Mandals of Nehru Yuva Kendras which has wide coverage (in 623 districts) will also be utilised as will the National Service Scheme, a public service scheme under the Ministry of Youth Affairs and Sports. The Policy also proposes a Skill Development Fellow scheme to use talented young people who work in government to raise awareness in local areas and help to build training opportunities in their areas.

- *Promotion to small and medium-sized employers:* Small and medium-sized enterprises will be eligible for incentives to make space in their facility available for the training of apprenticeships. Industry will also be encouraged to actively contribute to the training of youth, enabling young people to access real industry experience (MSDE, 2015). Recent ILO research notes that the benefits of hiring an apprentice exceed the costs for Indian employers within the first year of retention as a full-time employee. Such findings assist in challenging the idea that investing in apprenticeships offers little financial incentive to SME (Rothboeck, 2014).

Summary of changes affecting employer engagement

In the Apprenticeship Act changes and rules

Employers can choose, within certain parameters, how many apprentices they employ. Employers now have the "opportunity of being heard" in relation to breaches of the law that involve the engagement of an apprentice who is not qualified to be engaged, or the failure to meet the terms and conditions of the contract of apprenticeship. The relevant penalty has also been reduced from imprisonment to a fine. Employers are allowed to outsource basic training. Apprenticeships are extended to new "optional trades", meaning that apprenticeships can be implemented in the service sector. The central registration portal allows registration to be conducted online and does not require individual registration processes for each region. Employers are now required to formulate policies about recruiting completed apprentices, although there is no specific obligation to do so.

In other provisions and developments

The APY program that allows 50% of the apprentice stipend to be paid by the government is an important development for employers. The State Skill Development Missions and the provisions in the National Policy for Skill Development and Entrepreneurship for promotion and marketing of apprenticeships will help to raise awareness of apprenticeships and attract good candidates. The establishment of over thirty Sector Skills Councils will also provide another opportunity for employers to engage with apprenticeships and to seek information.

Strengths and weaknesses of the reform of the apprenticeship system

It is as yet too early to evaluate the impact of the reforms to the apprenticeship system, as the changes have been too recent. However, in a country the size of India it should be seen as a major achievement to implement governance, legislative and regulatory reform as well as to co-ordinate national and State activities in the area of VET.

The changes in the Act and Rules, and more general changes in VET proposed in the National Policy for Skill Development and Entrepreneurship can be mapped against the options proposed in the 2012 "Possible Futures for the Indian Apprenticeship" project.

Table 10.2. **Potential changes to the Indian VET system**

Themes	Proposed options (shaded options supported by stakeholders at the time)	Addressed since 2010 in Apprenticeship Act changes and the new National Policy?
1. Simplify access	Replace compulsory participation requirements with voluntary registration	-
	Reduce the regulatory burden on employers	Yes (remove imprisonment threat; allow larger employers to deal centrally with government)
	Introduce new third parties to the system to help manage economic ebbs and flows, and to provide support for some groups of apprentices and employers	-
2. Improve training quality	Introduce off-the-job training throughout the period of an apprenticeship	-
	Upgrade quality and recognition of apprentice certification	-
	Improve workplace curriculum	Yes (allow outsourcing of "Basic Training")
	Improve skills and expertise of those delivering training	Yes (plans for improving VET teacher-training and the status of VET teaching)
3. Harmonise the system	Greater involvement of stakeholders in system	-
	Simplify and harmonise the system	Yes (closer links across States)
	Increase "market currency" of apprentice qualifications	-
4. Increase participation	Cover more of the economy	Yes (allow "optional trades" i.e. apprenticeships in the service sector)
	Provide financial incentives to participants, enterprises and training providers	Yes (financial incentives for apprentices and other VET learners; sharing of stipend for trade apprentices under the APY scheme)
	Introduce non-financial strategies to increase participation among more people	Yes (utilisation of local outlets such as Post Offices to market VET, including apprenticeships; apprentice portal)

Source: Author's own elaboration.

While this may seem to indicate that changes are incremental only, the changes to the Apprenticeship Act and Rules and to VET more generally reflect the need to compromise due to the conflicting wishes and needs of stakeholders. However, the changes to the Apprenticeship Act have been fairly minor, indicating only conservative reform. Much greater attention has been paid to methods of attracting young people into vocational training, of which apprenticeship is only one form.

Some concerns were raised during the finalisation of the changes to the Apprenticeship Act and the Rules. These included concerns about the apparent lower status of the "Optional Trades" and provisions attached to them. There were concerns about the omission of references to the National Skill Qualification Framework in relation to apprentice certification, and the lack of requirement for recoding training and assessment delivered in the workplace. There are also concerns about the trade-off between what are still seen as overly-punitive attitudes towards employers in the Act (i.e. that participation is not voluntary), and the fact that apprentices can still be used as cheap labour.

More generally, the provisions for public-private funding in some of the proposals in the National Policy have raised concerns, along with the flow of funds to the private training sector. It is reported that the National Skills Development Council has had some of its autonomy removed as a result of its incorporation within the Ministry of Skills.

Das (2015) reviewed several Indian skills development initiatives from 2007 to 2013 in terms of their benefits for SMEs. He noted that, while some had succeeded, many failed because they did not reach the targeted enterprises. He also points to lack of monitoring mechanisms. It is not clear from the published documents on the current reforms whether these previous shortcomings have been adequately addressed.

Finally, the refashioning of the apprenticeship system also provided an opportunity to consider the incorporation of the informal economy and informal apprenticeships into the broader VET system. There have been attempts to be more inclusive of the informal economy (for example via Recognition of Prior Learning provisions) in the broader VET policy direction of the new National Policy, but this does not specifically address apprenticeships. It could be argued that there was a need to regularise and harmonise the formal apprenticeship system before moving onto the more difficult questions of incorporating the informal system. The favourable provisions for MSMEs under the APY scheme indicates a favourable attitude towards the informal sector but the documentation that is required from employers favours formal and structured enterprises.

Strengths and weaknesses relating to employer engagement

The Confederation of Indian Industry (CII) was pleased with the outcome of the changes to the system. The CII Director – Skills and Affirmative Action, Mr Sougata Choudhury, noted in an interview that there was nothing major that the CII, on behalf of employers, had advocated that had been missed. He cited as the three major achievements:

- The removal of requirements for percentage of apprentices, allowing for flexibility and business forecasting;
- The removal of the threat of imprisonment for breaches of the legislation;
- The central registration portal.

While there are no publicly available figures on the success of the Apprentice Protsahan Yojana scheme, a newspaper article reported that there were almost 300 apprentices were engaged through the scheme in the first three months of operation (The Hindu, 2015). This indicates that the systems for the scheme were functional.

The changes to legislation to enable better administration of the system are certainly favourable to employer engagement. However, more needs to be done to promote the system to employers in order to prepare for the radical expansion of the apprenticeship system to meet the economic and social demands placed upon it. The International Labour

Organisation has been active in making suggestions in this area; the Organisation has proposed a tripartite Apprenticeship Network and also pilot programmes to test the elements of the new system in a range of industry areas and locations (ILO, 2013). These proposals were supported by industry but have not yet been adopted by the Government.

Finally, an important issue is whether individual employers are aware of the considerable changes that have been made. In late 2015, the Confederation of Indian Industry (CII) launched a number of industry workshops around India to improve awareness of the changes. The workshops featured speakers from the DGT as well as HR and production managers from industry, and provided employers with the chance to ask questions. There were 150-200 people at each of these eight workshops, and it was reported that employers were excited by the opportunities available. The reforms were also promulgated through CII magazines, online and in hard copy. As Mr Choudhury put it, "it is up to industry now".

Potential transferability and lessons for other non-OECD countries

India has had a well-established and regulated apprenticeship system. However, while the modern-day Indian apprenticeship system was laid down in the mid-twentieth century, there have been few subsequent reforms. Other Anglophone countries, including the UK and Australia, have been moving towards a mass apprenticeship system with coverage (in non-graduate jobs) across all sectors in the economy. These countries have allowed mature-aged workers and those already employed by a company to undertake apprenticeships. In the UK, for example, apprenticeships have increased ten-fold in less than a decade. On the other hand, countries like Canada have continued to restrict their apprenticeship system to manufacturing and construction jobs, and although their systems are successful, they are narrow in reach. The German system has been struggling with declining numbers which partly result from an increased demand for higher education rather than vocational training among young people (Deissinger and Gonon, 2015).

India has faced a choice about whether to move into mass apprenticeships or to remain with a relatively limited apprenticeship system. In 2012, India only had approximately 300 000 apprentices out of a labour force of nearly 500 million people. This proportion of less than 0.01% of the workforce compares unfavourably with "large system countries" such as Germany and Australia, which both have around 3.7% of their workforces participating in apprenticeships. The achievement of the government's policy aim of a tenfold expansion will leave India with a comparatively smaller apprenticeship workforce than those in other countries. The contextual issues and economic barriers in India are immense, however, and would make any immediate expansion beyond this problematic. There are inherent risks in over-hasty expansion of apprentice system, as Smith and Brennan Kemmis (2013b) point out.

The most recent policy reforms have aimed to build on the current system rather than refashion it. It has definitely been made easier for employers to participate in the system and it would be expected that as more employers participate, they will bring other employers with them and also play a more active role in the system.

The Indian system reforms that have transferability for other countries are as follows:

● Move towards harmonisation across jurisdictions (Federal and State);

● Involvement of all stakeholders in consultations around reforms to the system (this was done extensively, including via the Inter-Ministerial Group);

- Easily-accessible web portals: for data collection from employers and also for information for would-be employers and would-be apprentices;

- A stipend that is affordable for employers but also liveable for apprentices;

- Sharing of the stipend between employers and the government in specified cases (APY scheme) and payment of the government share directly to the apprentice rather than through the employer;

- The requirement for employers to develop policies for employing ex-apprentices (ensuring that the possibility was at least considered, but not mandating retention);

- Consideration of medium and small enterprises in redesigning apprentice systems;

- Provision of apprentice opportunities outside traditional engineering and manufacturing trade areas.

  For non-OECD countries there are additional lessons:

- The use of pre-existing local networks such as Post Offices and Youth Clubs to disseminate and promote information about vocational training;

- The provision for out-sourcing 'in-house training' in the absence of good facilities in-house;

- Balancing protection of apprentice rights against the availability of opportunities.

References

Akhilesh, K.B. (2010), *A study on the Apprenticeship law in India*. Bangalore, India: International Labour Organisation (ILO) and Karnataka Employers' Association (KEA).

Confederation of Indian Industry (CII) (2014), Proposed amendments to the Apprentices Act 1961, unpublished paper.

Das, A.K. (2015), "Skills Development for SMEs: Mapping of Key Initiatives in India", *Institutions and Economies*, 7(2), 120-143.

Deissinger, T. and P. Gonon (2015), Stakeholders in the German and the Swiss VET system and their role in innovating apprenticeship. *Architectures for apprenticeship: Achieving economic and social goals*, 6th INAP Conference, Federation University Australia, Ballarat, 1-2 September.

Department of Industrial Policy and Promotion (DIPP) (2015), *Make India: About us*, retrieved 17 December 2015, from *www.makeinindia.com/about*.

Directorate General of Employment and Training (2009), *Annual Report 2008-2009*, Ministry of Labour and Employment (MOLE).

Directorate General of Training (2015a), *An overview of Apprenticeship Training Scheme*, *www.dget.nic.in/content/innerpage/overview-ats.php*.

Directorate General of Training (2015b), *Apprentice Protsahan Yojana Scheme*, *www.dget.nic.in/upload/files/5453f082befc7APY.pdf*.

Economist (2011), *India's economy: The half-finished revolution*, (2011), retrieved from *www.economist.com/node/18986387*.

FICCI (2010), *The skill development landscape in India and implementing quality skills training*, ICRA Management Consulting Services, retrieved from *www.ficci.com/SPdocument/20073/IMaCS.pdf*.

International Labour Organization (2013), ILO Apprenticeship Pilots Concept Note, New Delhi, ILO.

International Monetary Fund (2011), *India: IMF Report 2011*, Washington, IMF.

Ministry of Labour and Employment (2010), ILO/MOLE programme on Operationalisation of Skills Development, *Policy Paper*.

Ministry of Labour and Employment (MOLE) (2011a), *Trade Apprenticeship Training in India under Apprenticeship Training Scheme*. New Delhi, Government of India, Ministry of Labour and Employment, Survey and Study Division.

Ministry of Labour and Employment (MOLE) (2011b), *Second annual report to the people on employment 2011*, Ministry of Labour and Employment. New Delhi, Government of India, Ministry of Labour and Employment, Survey and Study Division.

Ministry of Labour and Employment (MOLE) (2009), *Annual Report 2008-2009*, retrieved from *http://labour.nic.in/annrep/annrep2008.htm*.

Ministry of Skill Development and Entrepreneurship (2015), *National Policy for Skill Development and Entrepreneurship 2015, www.skilldevelopment.gov.in/National-Policy-2015.html*.

Mohan, R. and M. Kapur (2015), *Pressing the Indian growth accelerator: Policy imperatives*, International Monetary Fund (IMF), *Working Paper* WP/15/53, IMF.

Planning Commission Sub-Committee on Re-modelling India's Apprenticeship Regime (2009), *Report and Recommendations*, New Delhi, *www.planningcommission.nic.in/reports/genrep/skilldev/sbcom_app.pdf*.

Rothboeck, S. (2014), "Using Benefit Cost Calculations to Asses Returns from Apprenticeship Investment in India: Selected SME Case Studies", *International Labour Organisation AsiaPacific Working Paper Series*.

Smith, E. and R. Brennan Kemmis (2013a), *Towards a model apprenticeship framework: A comparative analysis of national apprenticeship systems*, Geneva, Switzerland, ILO Publications.

Smith, E. and R. Brennan Kemmis (2013b), "Possible Futures for the Indian Apprenticeship System", *Options Paper for India*, New Delhi, India, ILO Publications.

The Hindu (2015), 288 apprentices engaged in Apprentices Protsahan Yojana, *The Hindu*, 18 January 2015.

UNESCO-UNEVOC (2015), *World VET Database: India*, Bonn: UNESCO-UNEVOC.

Virmani, A. (2004), *India's Economic Growth: From Socialist Rate of Growth to Bharatiya Rate of Growth*. Dehli, India, Indian Council on International Economic Relations.

Telephone interview with Mr Sougata Choudhury, Director – Skills and Affirmative Action, Confederation of Indian Industry.

WITHDRAWAL

OECD PUBLISHING, 2, rue André-Pascal, 75775 PARIS CEDEX 16
(84 2016 10 1 P) ISBN 978-92-64-26658-2 – 2017